MW00848764

MANETHO

LCL 350

MANETHO

WITH AN ENGLISH TRANSLATION BY

W. G. WADDELL

HARVARD UNIVERSITY PRESS
CAMBRIDGE, MASSACHUSETTS
LONDON, ENGLAND

First published 1940

LOEB CLASSICAL LIBRARY® is a registered trademark
of the President and Fellows of Harvard College

ISBN 978-0-674-99385-3

*Printed on acid-free paper and bound by
The Maple-Vail Book Manufacturing Group*

CONTENTS

Hermes Trismegistus speaks:

O Aegypte, Aegypte, religionum tuarum solae supererunt fabulae, eaeque incredibiles posteris tuis; solaque supererunt verba lapidibus incisa, tua pia facta narrantibus. ["O Egypt, Egypt, of thy religious rites nought will survive but idle tales which thy children's children will not believe; nought will survive but words graven upon stones that tell of thy piety."]

> The Latin Asclepius III. 25, in W. Scott, *Hermetica*, i. 1924, p. 342.

*　　*　　*　　*　　*　　*　　*

"Never has there arisen a more complicated problem than that of Manetho."

> —BOECKH, *Manetho und die Hundssternperiode,* 1845, p. 10.

INTRODUCTION

Among the Egyptians who wrote in Greek, Manetho the priest holds a unique place because of his comparatively early date (the third century B.C.) and the interest of his subject-matter—the history and religion of Ancient Egypt. His works in their original form would possess the highest importance and value for us now, if only we could recover them ; but until the fortunate discovery of a papyrus,[1] which will transmit the authentic Manetho, we can know his writings only from fragmentary and often distorted quotations preserved chiefly by Josephus and by the Christian chronographers, Africanus and Eusebius, with isolated passages in Plutarch, Theophilus, Aelian, Porphyrius, Diogenes Laertius, Theodoretus, Lydus, Malalas, the Scholia to Plato, and the *Etymologicum Magnum*.

Like Bêrôssos, who is of slightly earlier date, Manetho testifies to the growth of an international

---

[1] F. Bilabel (in P. Baden 4. 1924, No. 59 : see also *Die Kleine Historiker*, Fragm. 11) published a papyrus of the fifth century after Christ containing a list of Persian kings with the years of their reigns (see further Fr. 70, note 1), and holds it to be, not part of the original *Epitome*, but a version made from it before the time of Africanus. It certainly proves that Egyptians were interested in Greek versions of the Kings' Lists, and much more so, presumably, in the unabridged Manetho. See Fr. 2 for Panodôrus and Annianus, who were monks in Egypt about the date of this papyrus. *Cf.* also P. Hibeh, i. 27, the Calendar of Saïs, translated into Greek in the reign of Ptolemy Sôter, *i.e.* early in the lifetime of Manetho.

spirit in the Alexandrine age : each of these
" barbarians " wrote in Greek an account of his
native country ; and it stirs the imagination to
think of their endeavour to bridge the gulf and
instruct all Greek-speaking people (that is to say
the whole civilized world of their time) in the history
of Egypt and Chaldaea. But these two writers
stand alone : [1] the Greeks indeed wrote from time to
time of the wonders of Egypt (works no longer
extant), but it was long before an Egyptian successor
of Manetho appeared—Ptolemy of Mendês,[2] probably under Augustus.

The writings of Manetho, however, continued to

---

[1] *Cf.* W. W. Tarn on Ptolemy II. in the *Journal of
Egyptian Archaeology*, 1928, xiv. p. 254 : (Activity at
Alexandria had no effect at all on Egyptians) " Ptolemy
Sôter had thought for a moment that Egyptians might
participate in the intellectual activities of Alexandria :
. . . but, though Manetho dedicated his work to Ptolemy
II., in this reign all interest in native Egypt was dropped,
and a little later Alexandria appears as merely an object
of hatred to many Egyptians. (Its destruction is prophesied in the Potter's Oracle.) " (See p. 123 n. 1.)

The complete isolation of Manetho and Bêrôssos is the
chief argument of Ernest Havet against the authenticity
of these writers (*Mémoire sur les écrits qui portent les
noms de Bérose et de Manéthon*, Paris, 1873). He regards
the double tradition as curious and extraordinary—
there is no other name to set beside these two Oriental
priests ; and he suspects the symmetry of the tradition
—each wrote three books for a king. *Cf.* Croiset, *Histoire de la Littérature Grecque*, v. p. 99 ; *Abridged History
of Greek Literature*, English translation, p. 429 (Manetho's
works were probably written by a Hellenized Oriental
at the end of the second century B.C.) ; and F. A. Wright,
Later Greek Literature, p. 60.

[2] See p. x.

be read with interest ; and his *Egyptian History* was
used for special purposes, *e.g.* by the Jews when they
engaged in polemic against Egyptians in order to
prove their extreme antiquity. (See further pp.
xvi ff.) Manetho's religious writings are known to
us mainly through references in Plutarch's treatise
On Isis and Osiris.

The Life of Manetho : Traditions and Conjectures.

Our knowledge of Manetho is for the most part
meagre and uncertain ; but three statements of
great probability may be made. They concern his
native place, his priesthood at Hêliopolis, and his
activity in the introduction of the cult of Serapis.

The name Manetho ($M\alpha\nu\epsilon\theta\acute{\omega}s$, often written
$M\alpha\nu\acute{\epsilon}\theta\omega\nu$) has been explained as meaning " Truth
of Thôth ", and a certain priest under Dynasty XIX.
is described as " First Priest of the Truth of Thôth ".[1]
According to Dr. Černý[2] " Manetho " is from the
Coptic ⲩⲁⲛⲉϩⲧⲟ " groom " (ⲩⲁⲛⲉ " herdsman ",
and ϩⲧⲟ " horse ") ; but the word does not seem to
occur elsewhere as a proper name. In regard to the
date of Manetho, Syncellus in one passage[3] gives us
the information that he lived later than Bêrôssos :
elsewhere[4] he puts Manetho as " almost contemporary with Bêrôssos, or a little later ". Bêrôssos, who

---

[1] W. Spiegelberg, *Orient. Literaturz.* xxxi. 1928, col.
145 ff., xxxii. 1929, col. 321 f. Older explanations of the
name Manetho were " Gift of Thôth," " Beloved of
Thôth," and " Beloved of Neith ".

[2] In the centenary volume of the Vatican Museum : I owe
this reference to the kindness of Dr. Alan H. Gardiner.

[3] Manetho, Fr. 3.   [4] Syncellus, p. 26.

was priest of Marduk at Babylon, lived under, and wrote for, Antiochus I. whose reign lasted from 285 to 261 B.C. ; and Bêrôssos dedicated his Χαλδαϊκά to this king after he became sole monarch in 281 B.C. The works of Manetho and Bêrôssos may be interpreted as an expression of the rivalry of the two kings, Ptolemy and Antiochus, each seeking to proclaim the great antiquity of his land.

Under the name of Manetho, Suidas seems to distinguish two writers : (1) Manetho of Mendês in Egypt, a chief priest who wrote on the making of *kyphi* (*i.e.* Fr. 87) : (2) Manetho of Diospolis or Sebennytus. (Works) : *A Treatise on Physical Doctrines* (*i.e.* Fr. 82, 83). *Apotelesmatica* (or *Astrological Influences*), in hexameter verses, and other astrological works. (See p. xiv, note 3.) Nowhere else is Manetho connected with Mendês ; but as Mendês was distant only about 17 miles from Sebennytus across the Damietta arm of the Nile, the attribution is not impossible. Müller suspects confusion with Ptolemy of Mendês, an Egyptian priest (probably in the time of Augustus), who, like Manetho, wrote a work on Egyptian Chronology in three books. In the second note of Suidas Diospolis may be identified, not with Diospolis Magna (the famous Thebes) nor with Diospolis Parva, but with Diospolis Inferior, in the Delta (now Tell el-Balamûn), the capital of the Diospolite or 17th nome [1] to the north of the Sebennyte nome and contiguous with

---

[1] The Greek word νομός means a division of Egypt, called in Ancient Egyptian *sp.t*,—a district corresponding roughly to a county in England. Pliny (*Hist. Nat.* 5, 9) refers to nomes as *praefecturae oppidorum.*

it. Diospolis Inferior lay near Damietta, some 30 miles from Sebennytus. (See Strabo, 17. 1, 19, and Baedeker, *Egypt and the Sûdân*, 8th ed. (1929), p. 185.) We may therefore accept the usual description of Manetho (Fr. 3, 77, 80 : Syncellus, 72, 16), and hold that he was a native of Sebennytus (now Samannûd)[1] in the Delta, on the west bank of the Damietta branch of the Nile. Manetho was a priest, and doubtless held office at one time in the temple at Sebennytus ; but in the letter (App. I.) which he is said to have written to Ptolemy II. Philadelphus, he describes himself as " high-priest and scribe of the sacred shrines of Egypt, born at Sebennytus and dwelling at Hêliopolis ". Although the letter, as we have it, is not genuine in all its details, this description may have been borrowed from a good source ; and while his precise rank as a priest remains in doubt, it is reasonable to believe that Manetho rose to be high-priest in the temple at Hêliopolis.[2] This eminent position agrees with the important part he played in the introduction of the cult of Serapis. As a Heliopolitan priest, Manetho (to quote from Laqueur, Pauly-Wissowa-Kroll, *R.-E.* xiv. 1, 1061) " was, without doubt, acquainted with

---

[1] See Baedeker[8], p. 185. Sebennytus was the seat of Dynasty XXX., and therefore a place of great importance shortly before the time of Manetho. In Ancient Egyptian, Sebennytus is *Tjeb-nûter*, " city of the sacred calf " : it is tempting to connect with Sebennytus the worship of the Golden Calf in *O.T. Exodus* xxxii., *1 Kings* xii. 28 ff. (P. E. Newberry).

[2] See Strabo, 17. 1, 29 for the " large houses in which the priests had lived ". According to Herodotus (ii. 3, 1), " the Heliopolitans are said to be the most learned of the Egyptians ".

the sacred tree in the great Hall of Hêliopolis,—the tree on which the goddess Seshat, the Lady of Letters, the Mistress of the Library, wrote down with her own hand the names and deeds of the rulers.[1] He did nothing more than communicate to the Greek world what the goddess had noted down.[2] But he did so with a full sense of the superiority which relied on the sacred records of the Egyptians in opposition to Herodotus whom he was contradicting " (Fr. 43, § 73 : Fr. 88). His native town, Sebennytus, was visited as a place of learning by Solon when Ethêmôn was a priest in residence there (see Proclus *in Plat. Tim.* i. 101, 22, Diehl) ; and the Greek culture of the place must have been a formative influence upon Manetho at an early age.

In the introduction of the statue of Serapis to Alexandria as described by Plutarch (Manetho, Fr. 80), Manetho the Egyptian was associated with the Greek Timotheus as a priestly adviser of King Ptolemy Sôter. It is natural to suppose that the cult of Serapis itself, which was a conflation of

---

[1] See Erman-Ranke, *Ägypten*, 1923, pp. 396 f. ; or Erman, *Die Religion der Ägypter*, 1934, pp. 56 f. ; or the original drawing in Lepsius, *Denkmäler*, iii. 169. This illustration shows the goddess, along with Thôth and Atûm, making inscriptions upon the leaves (or fruit) of the venerable tree.

[2] It may be added that the Egyptians are surpassed by no nation in their strong and ever-present desire to leave upon stone or papyrus permanent records of their history, their motive being to glorify the ruling king. *Cf.* Herodotus, ii. 77, 1 (of the Egyptians who live in the cultivated country), " the most diligent of all men in preserving the memory of the past, and far better skilled in chronicles than any others whom I have questioned ".

Egyptian and Greek ideas intended to be acceptable to both nationalities, had already been organized [1] with the help of the two priests, and the magnificent temple in Rhakôtis, the Egyptian quarter in the west of Alexandria, had doubtless been built. The date is not certain : according to Jerome (Fotheringham, p. 211, Helm, p. 129) " Sarapis entered Alexandria " in 286 B.C., while the Armenian Version of the *Chronicle* of Eusebius says that in 278 B.C. " Sarapis came to Alexandria, and became resident there " (Karst, 200). Perhaps the two statements refer to different stages in the development of the cult : if the former describes the entry of the statue by Bryaxis, the latter may possibly refer to the final establishment of the whole theology. As a proof that the work of Manetho in building up the cult of Serapis must not be belittled, it may suffice to refer to the inscription of the name $Μανέθων$ on the base of a marble bust found in the ruins of the Temple of Serapis at Carthage (*Corpus Inscr. Lat.* viii. 1007). The name is so uncommon that the probability is that the bust which originally stood on this base represented the Egyptian Manetho, and was erected in his honour because of his effective contribution to the organization of the cult of

---

[1] The earliest date for Serapis is given by Macrobius, *Sat.* i. 20, 16, a questioning of Serapis by Nicocreon of Cyprus, c. 311-310 B.C. For Dittenberger, *O.G.I.S.* 16 (an inscription from Halicarnassus on the founding of a temple to Serapis-Isis under (the satrap) Ptolemy Sôter), the date is uncertain, probably c. 308-306 B.C. Already in Menander's drama, $Ἐγχειρίδιον$ (before 291 B.C. when Menander died), Serapis is a " holy god " (P. Oxy. XV. 1803).

Serapis.[1] Hence it is not impossible also that the
following reference in a papyrus of 241 B.C. may be
to Manetho of Sebennytus. It occurs in a document
containing correspondence about a Temple Seal
(P. Hibeh, i. 72, vv. 6, 7, γράφειν Μανεθῶι). The
person named was evidently a well-known man in
priestly circles : he was probably our Manetho, the
writer on Egyptian history and religion, if he lived
to a considerable age.[2]

Manetho's Works.

Eight works [3] have been attributed to Manetho :
(1) Αἰγυπτιακά, or *The History of Egypt*, (2) *The Book
of Sôthis*, (3) *The Sacred Book*, (4) *An Epitome of
Physical Doctrines*, (5) *On Festivals*, (6) *On Ancient
Ritual and Religion*, (7) *On the Making of Kyphi*
[a kind of incense], (8) *Criticisms of Herodotus*.

Of these, (2) *The Book of Sôthis* (App. IV. and

---

[1] *Cf.* Lafaye, *Histoire du Culte des Divinités d'Alexandrie*
(1884), p. 16 n. 1 : " At all events, there is no doubt
that the adepts of the Alexandrine cult had great venera-
tion for Manetho, and considered him in some measure
as their patriarch ".

[2] Bouché-Leclercq (*Histoire des Lagides*, iv. p. 269 n. 4)
holds a different opinion : " the reference is not necessarily
to the celebrated Manetho, whose very existence is prob-
lematical ".

[3] A work wrongly attributed in antiquity (*e.g.* by Suidas,
see p. x) to Manetho of Sebennytus is Ἀποτελεσματικά, in
6 books, an astrological poem in hexameters on the
influence of the stars. See W. Kroll (*R.-E. s.v.* Manethon
(2)), who with Köchly recognizes in the 6 books 4 sections
of different dates from about A.D. 120 to the fourth century
after Christ. Books I. and V. open with dedications to
King Ptolemy : *cf.* Pseudo-Manetho, Appendix I.

pp. xxvii. ff.) is certainly not by Manetho ; and there is no reason to believe that (8) *Criticisms of Herodotus* formed a separate work, although we know from Josephus, *C. Apion.* i. 73 (Fr. 42), that Manetho did convict Herodotus of error. Six titles remain, but it has long been thought that some of these are "ghost" titles. Fruin (*Manetho*, p. lxxvii) supposed that Manetho wrote only two works—one on Egyptian history, the other on Egyptian mythology and antiquities. Susemihl (*Alex. Lit.-Gesch.* i. 609, n. 431) and W. Otto (*Priester und Tempel in Hellenistischen Ägypten*, ii. 215, n. 4) modified this extreme view : they recognized three distinct works of Manetho (*The History of Egypt, The Sacred Book*, and *An Epitome of Physical Doctrines*), and assumed that the titles *On Festivals, On Ancient Ritual and Religion*, and *On the Making of Kyphi* referred to passages in *The Sacred Book*. In the paucity of our data, no definite judgement seems possible as to whether Manetho wrote six works or only three ; but in support of the former theory we may refer to Eusebius (Man. Fr. 76).

The History of Egypt.

The *Egyptian History* [1] of Manetho is preserved in extracts of two kinds. (1) Excerpts from the original work are preserved by Josephus, along with other passages which can only be pseudo-

---

[1] Or *Notes about Egypt.* There are two variants of the Greek title : Αἰγυπτιακά (Josephus in Fr. 42), and Αἰγυπτιακὰ ὑπομνήματα (*Aegyptiaca monumenta*, Eus. in Fr. 1), with a possible third form Αἰγυπτίων ὑπομνήματα (*Aegyptiorum monumenta*, Eus., p. 359).

Manethonian. The Jews of the three centuries
following the time of Manetho were naturally
keenly interested in his *History* because of the
connexion of their ancestors with Egypt—Abraham,
Joseph, and Moses the leader of the Exodus ; and
they sought to base their theories of the origin and
antiquity of the Jews securely upon the authentic
traditions of Egypt. In Manetho indeed they found
an unwelcome statement of the descent of the Jews
from lepers ; but they were able to identify their
ancestors with the Hyksôs, and the Exodus with
the expulsion of these invaders. The efforts of
Jewish apologists account for much re-handling,
enlargement, and corruption of Manetho's text, and
the result may be seen in the treatise of Josephus,
Contra Apionem, i.

(2) An *Epitome* of Manetho's history had been
made at an early date,—not by Manetho himself,
there is reason to believe,—in the form of Lists of
Dynasties with short notes on outstanding kings or
important events. The remains of this *Epitome* are
preserved by Christian chronographers, especially by
Africanus and Eusebius. Their aim was to compare
the chronologies of the Oriental nations with the
Bible, and for this purpose the *Epitome* gave an
ideal conspectus of the whole *History*, omitting, as
it does, narratives such as the account of the Hyksôs
preserved by Josephus. Of the two chronographers,
the founder of Christian chronography, Sextus
Julius Africanus, whose *Chronicle* [1] came down to

---

[1] For a later miscellaneous work, the Κεστοί, see P. Oxy.
iii. 412 (between A.D. 225 and 265) ; and Jules Africain,
Fragments des Cestes, ed. J.-R. Vieillefond, Paris, 1932.

A.D. 217 or A.D. 221, transmits the *Epitome* in a more accurate form ; while Eusebius, whose work extends to A.D. 326, is responsible for unwarranted alterations of the original text of Manetho. About A.D. 800 George the Monk, who is known as Syncellus from his religious office (as " attendant " of Tarasius, Patriarch of Constantinople), made use of Manetho's work in various forms in his Ἐκλογὴ Χρονογραφίας, a history of the world from Adam to Diocletian. Syncellus sought to prove that the incarnation took place in Anno Mundi 5500 ; and in his survey of the thirty-one Egyptian dynasties which reigned from the Flood to Darius, he relied on the authoritative work of Manetho as transmitted by Africanus and Eusebius, and as handed down in a corrupt form in the *Old Chronicle* (App. III.) and the *Book of Sôthis* (App. IV.) which had been used by the chronographer Panodôrus (*c.* A.D. 400).

Even from the above brief statement of the transmission of Manetho's text, it will be seen that many problems are involved, and that it is extremely difficult to reach certainty in regard to what is authentic Manetho and what is spurious or corrupt. The problems are discussed in detail by Richard Laqueur in his valuable and exhaustive article in Pauly-Wissowa-Kroll, *R.-E. s.v.* Manethon ; and it may be sufficient here to quote his summary of the results of his researches in regard to Manetho (1) in Josephus, and (2) in the Christian Chronographers.

(1) Manetho in Josephus, *Contra Apionem*, i. (see Fr. 42, 50, 54.)

" (*a*) Extracts from the genuine Manetho appear in §§ 75-82, 84-90, 94-102*a*, 232-249, 251. Of these passages, §§ 75-82, 94-102a, 237-249 are quoted *verbatim*, the others are given in Indirect Speech.

" (b) A rationalistic critique of the genuine Manetho was written by a Hellenist, and was used by Josephus for his work. The remains of this critique appear in §§ 254-261, 267-269, 271-274, 276-277. Perhaps §§ 102b-103 is connected with these.

" (c) The authoritative work of Manetho was further exploited by Jews and Egyptians in their mutual polemic, in the course of which additions to Manetho's works were made : these additions were partly favourable to the Jews (§§ 83, 91), partly hostile to the Jews (§ 250). These passages, like those mentioned in (b), were collected before the time of Josephus into a single treatise, so that one could no longer clearly recognize what had belonged to Manetho and what was based upon additions.

" (d) Josephus originally knew only the genuine Manetho (*cf.* (a)), and used him throughout as a witness against the aggressors of Judaism. In this it was of importance for Josephus to show that the Hyksôs had come to Egypt from abroad, that their expulsion took place long before the beginning of Greek history, and that they, in their expedition to aid the Lepers, remained untainted by them.

" (e) After Josephus had completed this elaboration, he came later to know the material mentioned in (b) and (c) : so far as it was favourable to the Jews or helpful in interpretation, it led only to short expansions of the older presentation ; so far, however, as it was hostile to the Jews, Josephus found himself induced to make a radical change in his attitude towards Manetho. He attacked Manetho sharply for his alleged statement (§ 250), and at the same time used the polemic mentioned in (*b*) in order to overthrow Manetho's authority in general.

" (*f*) From the facts adduced it follows that Manetho's work was already before the time of Josephus the object of numerous literary analyses." [1]

Cf. the following summary.

(2) Manetho in the Christian Chronographers.

" (*a*) Not long after the appearance of Manetho's work, an *Epitome* was made, giving excerpts from the Dynasty-Lists and increasing these from 30 to 31. The possibility that other additions were made is not excluded.

" (*b*) The *Epitome* was remodelled by a Hellenistic Jew in such a way that the Jewish chronology became compatible with that of Manetho.

" (*c*) A descendant of version (*a*) is extant in Julius Africanus : a descendant of version (*b*), in Eusebius."

The *Chronicle* of Africanus in five books is lost except for what is preserved in the extracts made by Eusebius, and the many fragments contained in the works of Syncellus and Cedrenus, and in the *Paschale Chronicon.* For Eusebius we have several lines of transmission. The Greek text of Eusebius has come down to us in part, as quoted by Syncellus ; but the whole work is known through (1) the Armenian Version, which was composed in v./A.D.[2]

---

[1] A further study of the transmission of Manetho in Josephus is made by A. Momigliano, " Intorno al Contro Apione," in *Rivista di Filologia*, 59 (1931), pp. 485-503.

[2] The Armenian MS. G (Codex Hierosolymitanus) printed by Aucher (1818) is dated by him between A.D.

from a revision of the first Greek text,[1] and is, of
course, quite independent of Syncellus ; and (2) the
Latin Version made by Jerome towards the end of
the fourth century.

Possible Sources of the Αἰγυπτιακά.

An Egyptian high priest, learned in Greek literature, had an unrivalled opportunity, in early
Ptolemaic times, of writing an excellent and accurate
history of Egypt. He had open access to records of
all kinds—papyri [2] in the temple archives (annals,
sacred books containing liturgies and poems), hieroglyphic tablets, wall sculptures, and innumerable
inscriptions.[3] These records no one but an Egyptian
priest could consult and read ; and only a scholar
who had assimilated the works of Greek historians
could make a judicious and scientific use of the
abundant material. It is hardly to be expected,

1065 and 1306. Karst quotes readings from this and two
other Armenian MSS., but the variations are comparatively unimportant.

[1] See A. Puech, *Hist. de la Litt. grecque chrétienne*, iii.
p. 177.

[2] Herodotus (ii. 100 : *cf.* 142) mentions a papyrus roll
(βύβλος) containing a list of 331 kings. Diodorus (i. 44, 4)
tells of " records (ἀναγραφαί) handed down in the sacred
books " (ἐν ταῖς ἱεραῖς βίβλοις), giving each king's stature,
character, and deeds, as well as the length of his reign.

[3] *Cf.* the Annals of the Reign of Tuthmôsis III. (Breasted,
Ancient Records, ii. §§ 391-540) : this important historical
document of 223 lines is inscribed on the walls of a corridor in the Temple of Amon at Karnak, and " demon-
strates the injustice of the criticism that the Egyptians
were incapable of giving a clear and succinct account of
a military campaign ".

INTRODUCTION

however, that Manetho's *History* should possess more
worth than that of his sources ; and the material at
his disposal included a certain proportion of un-
historical traditions and popular legends.[1]

There is no possibility of identifying the particular
records from which Manetho compiled his *History* :
the following are the kinds of monuments which he
may have consulted and from which we derive a
means of controlling his statements.

(1) *The Royal List of Abydos*, on the wall of a
corridor of the Temple of Sethôs I. at Abydos, gives
in chronological order a series of seventy-six kings
from Mênês to Sethôs I.   Dynasties XIII. to XVII.
are lacking.   A mutilated duplicate of this list was
found in the Temple of Ramessês II. at Abydos
(now in the British Museum: see *Guide*, p. 245):
it arranges the kings in three rows, while the more
complete list has them in two rows.

(2) *The Royal List of Karnak* (now in the Louvre)
has a list of kings, originally sixty-one, from Mênês
down to Tuthmôsis III., Dynasty XVIII., with
many names belonging to the Second Intermediate
Period (Dynasties XIII.-XVII.).

The Royal Lists of Abydos and Karnak give the
tradition of Upper Egypt.

(3) *The Royal List of Sakkâra* (found in a tomb at
Sakkâra, and now in the Cairo Museum) preserves the
cartouches of forty-seven (originally fifty-eight) kings
previous to, and including, Ramessês II.   It begins
with Miebis, the sixth king of Dynasty I. ; and like

---

[1] The popular tales introduced kings as their heroes,
without regard to chronological order : see G. Maspero,
Bibliothèque Egyptologique, vol. vii. (1898), pp. 419 ff.

the *Royal List of Abydos*, it omits Dynasties XIII.-XVII. Like (4) the *Turin Papyrus*, the *Royal List of Sakkâra* gives the tradition of Lower Egypt.

(4) More important than any of the preceding is the *Turin Papyrus*, written in hieratic on the *verso* of the papyrus, with accounts of the time of Ramessês II. on the *recto* (which gives the approximate date, *c.* 1200 B.C.). In its original state the papyrus must have been an artistically beautiful exemplar, as the script is an exceptionally fine one. It contains the names of kings in order, over 300 when complete, with the length of each reign in years, months, and days ; and as the definitive edition of the papyrus has not yet been issued, further study is expected to yield additional results.[1] The papyrus begins, like Manetho, with the dynasties of gods, followed by mortal kings also in dynasties. The change of dynasty is noted, and the sum of the reigns is given : also, as in Manetho, several dynasties are added together, *e.g.* " Sum of the Kings from Mênês to [Unas] " at the end of Dynasty V. The arrangement in the papyrus is very similar to that in the *Epitome* of Manetho.

(5) *The Palermo Stone* [2] takes us back to a much greater antiquity : it dates from the Fifth Dynasty, *c.* 2600 B.C., and therefore contains Old Egyptian annals of the kings. The Stone or Stele was origin-

[1] See Sir J. G. Wilkinson, *Fragments of the Hieratic Papyrus at Turin*, London, 1851 : E. Meyer, *Aeg. Chron.* pp. 105 ff., and *Die Ältere Chronologie Babyloniens, Assyriens, und Ägyptens*, revised by Stier (1931), pp. 55 ff.

[2] Plate II. See H. Schäfer, *Abhandl. Akad. Berl.* 1902 : Breasted, *Ancient Records*, i. §§ 76-167 : Sethe, *Urkunden des Alten Reichs*, pp. 235-249 ; and *cf.* Petrie, *The Making of Egypt*, 1939, pp. 98 f.

ally a large slab [1] of black diorite, about 7 feet long and over 2 feet high ; but only a fragment of the middle of the slab is preserved in the Museum of Palermo, while smaller pieces of this, or of a similar monument, have been identified in the Cairo Museum and in University College, London. Although the text is unfortunately fragmentary, this early document is clearly seen to be more closely related to the genuine Manetho than are the Kings' Lists of later date (1, 2, 3, 4 above).[2] In a space marked off on each side by a year-sign and therefore denoting one year, notable events are given in an upper section of the space and records of the Nile-levels in a lower. A change of reign is denoted by a vertical line prolonging the year-sign above, on each side of which a certain number of months and days is recorded—on one side those belonging to the deceased king, and on the other to his successor. In the earliest Dynasties the years were not numbered, but were named after some important event or events, *e.g.* " the year of the smiting of the '*Inw*," " the year of the sixth time of numbering ". Religious and military events were particularly common, just as they are in Manetho. A year-name of King Snefru (Dynasty IV.) states that he conquered the Nehesi, and captured 7000 prisoners and 200,000 head of cattle : *cf.* Manetho, Fr. 7, on the foreign expedition of Mênês. So, too, under

[1] More plausibly, according to Petrie (*The Making of Egypt*, 1939, p. 98), the text of the annals was divided among six slabs each 16 inches wide, both sides being equally visible.

[2] Borchardt, in *Die Annalen* (1917), quoted in *Ancient Egypt*, 1920, p. 124, says, " Manetho had really good sources, and his copyists have not altogether spoiled him ".

Shepseskaf, the last king of Dynasty IV., the
building of a pyramid is recorded, and under
Dynasties I., IV., and VI. Manetho makes mention
of pyramid-building. It is especially noteworthy
that the first line of the Palermo Stone gives a list
of kings before Mênês : *cf.* the *Turin Papyrus*, as
quoted on Fr. 1. (For the Cairo fragments see
Sethe, *op. cit.*)

* * * * * * *

In regard to Manetho's relation to his Greek
predecessors in the field of Egyptian history, we
know that he criticized Herodotus, not, as far as
we can tell, in a separate work, but merely in
passages of his *History*. In none of the extant
fragments does Manetho mention by name Hecataeus
of Abdera, but it is interesting to speculate upon
Manetho's relation to this Greek historian. The
floruit of Hecataeus fell in the time of Alexander and
Ptolemy son of Lagus (Gutschmid gives 320 B.C. as
an approximate estimate) ; and it is very doubtful
whether he lived to see the reign of Philadelphus,
who came to the throne in 285 B.C. (Jacoby in
R.-E. vii. 2, 2750). His *Aegyptiaca* was " a philosophical romance," describing " an ethnographical
Utopia " : it was no history of Egypt, but a work
with a philosophical tendency. Manetho and
Hecataeus are quoted together, *e.g.* by Plutarch,
Isis and Osiris, chap. 9, perhaps from an inter-
mediary writer who used the works of both Manetho
and Hecataeus. If we assume that Hecataeus wrote
his " romance " before Manetho composed his
History, perhaps one of the purposes of Manetho
was to correct the errors of his predecessor. No

criticism of Hecataeus, however, has been attributed to Manetho ; and it is natural that similarities are found in their accounts (*cf.* p. 131, n. 2). Be that as it may, Hecataeus enjoyed greater popularity among the Greeks than Manetho : they preferred his " romance " to Manetho's more reliable annals. Yet Manetho's *Aegyptiaca* has no claim to be regarded as a critical history : its value lies in the dynastic skeletons which serve as a framework for the evidence of the monuments, and it has provided in its essentials the accepted scheme of Egyptian chronology.[1] But there were many errors in Manetho's work from the very beginning : all are not due to the perversions of scribes and revisers. Many of the lengths of reigns have been found impossible : in some cases the names and the sequence of kings as given by Manetho have proved untenable in the light of monumental evidence. If one may depend upon the extracts preserved in Josephus, Manetho's work was not an authentic history of Egypt, exact in its details, as the *Chaldaïca* of Bêrôssos was, at least for later times. Manetho introduced into an already corrupted series of dynastic lists a number of popular traditions written

[1] *Cf.* H. R. Hall, *Cambridge Ancient History*, i. p. 260 : " So far as we are able to check Manetho from the contemporary monuments, his division into dynasties is entirely justified. His authorities evidently were good. But unhappily his work has come down to us only in copies of copies ; and, although the framework of the dynasties remains, most of his royal names, originally Graecized, have been so mutilated by non-Egyptian scribes, who did not understand their form, as often to be unrecognizable, and the regnal years given by him have been so corrupted as to be of little value unless confirmed by the Turin Papyrus or the monuments."

in the characteristic Egyptian style. No genuine historical sense had been developed among the Egyptians, although Manetho's work does illustrate the influence of Greek culture upon an Egyptian priest. He wrote to correct the errors of Greek historians, especially of Herodotus (see Fr. 88); but from the paucity of information about certain periods, it seems clear that in ancient times, as for us at the present day, there were obscure eras in Egyptian history.[1] Before the Saïte Dynasty (XXVI.) there were three outstanding periods—in Dynasties IV.-VI., XI.-XII., and XVIII.-XX., or roughly the Old Kingdom, the Middle Kingdom, and the New Kingdom (sometimes called the Empire); and these are the periods upon which the light falls in all histories.

The significance of Manetho's writings is that for the first time an Egyptian was seeking to instruct foreigners in the history and religion of his native land.

Other Works attributed to Manetho.

To judge by the frequency of quotation, the religious treatises of Manetho were much more popular in Greek circles than the *History of Egypt* was; yet the fragments surviving from these works (Fr. 76-88) are so meagre that no distinct impression of their nature can be gained. The *Sacred Book* (Fr. 76-81)

---

[1] *Cf.* H. R. Hall, *Ancient History of the Near East* [8], p. 14: "In fact, Manetho did what he could: where the native annals were good and complete, his abstract is good: where they were broken and incomplete, his record is incomplete also and confused. . . ."

xxvi

was doubtless a valuable exposition of the details
of Egyptian religion, as well as of the mythological
elements of Egyptian theology. It testifies to the
importance of the part played by Manetho in support
of Ptolemy Sôter's vigorous policy of religious
syncretism. It seems probable that the *Sacred Book*
was Manetho's main contribution in aid of this
policy : it may have been the result of a definite
commission by the king, in order to spread a knowledge of Egyptian religion among the Greeks. That
an Egyptian priest should seek to instruct the
Greek-speaking world of his time in the history of
Egypt and in the religious beliefs of the Egyptians,
including festivals, ancient rites and piety in general,
and the preparation of *kyphi*, is not at all surprising ;
but it seems strange that Manetho should feel called
upon, in the third century B.C., to compose an
Epitome of Physical Doctrines (Fr. 82, 83) with the
apparent object of familiarizing the Greeks with
Egyptian science. One may conjecture that his
special purpose was to give instruction to students
of his own.

The Book of Sôthis (Appendix IV.).

The Book of Sôthis [1] or *The Sôthic Cycle* is transmitted through Syncellus alone. In the opinion of
Syncellus, this *Sôthis-Book* was dedicated by Manetho

---

[1] Sôthis is the Greek form of *Sopdet*, the Egyptian
name for the Dog-star, Sirius, the heliacal rising of which
was noted at an early date : on the great importance of
the Sôthic period in Egyptian chronology, see Breasted,
Ancient Records, i. §§ 40 ff., and H. R. Hall, *Encyclopaedia
Britannica* [14], *s.v.* Chronology. *Cf. infra*, Appendix III.,
p. 226, and Appendix IV., p. 234.

to Ptolemy Philadelphus (see App. I.). The king wished to learn the future of the universe, and Manetho accordingly sent to him " sacred books " based upon inscriptions which had been written down by Thôth, the first Hermês, in hieratic script, had been interpreted after the Flood by Agathodaemôn, son of the second Hermês and father of Tat, and had been deposited in the sanctuaries of the temples of Egypt. The letter which purports to have accompanied the " sacred books " is undoubtedly a forgery ; but the *Sôthis-Book* is significant for the textual transmission of Manetho. According to the LXX the Flood took place in Anno Mundi 2242 (see Frags. 2, 6 : App. III., p. 232). This date must close the prehistoric period in Egypt and in Chaldea : the 11,985 years of the Egyptian gods are therefore regarded as months and reduced to 969 years. Similarly, the 858 years of the demigods are treated as quarter-years or periods of three months, thus becoming $214\frac{1}{2}$ years : total, $969 + 214\frac{1}{2} = 1183\frac{1}{2}$ years (Fr. 2). In Chaldean prehistory, by fixing the saros at 3600 days, 120 saroi become 1183 years $6\frac{5}{8}$ months. Accordingly, the beginning of Egyptian and Babylonian history is placed at $2242 - 1184$, or 1058 Anno Mundi : in that year (or in 1000, Fr. 2) falls the coming of the Egregori, who finally by their sins brought on the Flood. The *Book of Sôthis* begins with the reign of Mestraïm, Anno Mundi 2776 (App. IV., p. 234 : App. III., p. 232), *i.e.* 534 years after the Flood, and continues to the year 4986, which gives 2210 years of Egyptian rule—almost the same number as Manetho has in either Book I. or Book II. of his *History of Egypt.*

BIBLIOGRAPHY

Greek text of Manetho in

1. C. Müller, *Fragmenta Historicorum Graecorum*, ii. (1848), pp. 512-616.
2. *Manethonis Sebennytae Reliquiae*, R. Fruin, 1847.

Greek text of the *Epitome* in

3. G. F. Unger, *Chronologie des Manetho*, Berlin, 1867.

Greek text of Kings' Lists summarized in parallel columns:

4. R. Lepsius, *Königsbuch der alten Ägypter*, Berlin, 1858.

Greek text of religious writings in

5. *Fontes Historiae Religionis Aegyptiacae*, Th. Hopfner, 1922-25.

Accounts of Manetho and his work.

1. Richard Laqueur in Pauly-Wissowa-Kroll, *R.-E.* xiv. 1 (1928), *s.v.* Manethon (1).
2. F. Susemihl, *Alex. Lit.-Geschichte*, i., 1891, pp. 608-616.
3. W. Otto, *Priester und Tempel im hellenist. Aegypten* (1908), ii. pp. 215 f., 228 f.

Subsidiary Works.

Josephus
   ed. Niese, Vol. v., 1889.
   ed. Thackeray (L.C.L., Vol. i., 1926).
   ed. Reinach and Blum (Budé, 1930).

Arnaldo Momigliano, *Rivista di Filologia*, 59 (1931), pp. 485-503.

Syncellus or George the Monk, in *Corpus Scriptorum Historicorum Byzantinorum*, W. Dindorf, 1829.

Heinrich Gelzer, *Sextus Julius Africanus*, 1880-89.

Eusebius, *Praeparatio Evangelica*, E. H. Gifford, 1903.

Eusebii chronicorum lib. I., A. Schöne, 1875.

Eusebius, *Chronica* (in Armenian Version):

   (*a*) Latin translation by Zohrab-Mai, 1818 (in Müller's *F.H.G.* ii.).

BIBLIOGRAPHY

(b) Latin translation by Aucher, 1818 (partly quoted in R. Lepsius, *Königsbuch*—see above).

(c) Latin translation by H. Petermann, in Schöne (above).

(d) German translation by Josef Karst in *Eusebius, Werke V. Die Chronik*, 1911.

Ed. Meyer, *Aegyptische Chronologie*, 1904 (Nachträge, 1907 : Neue Nachträge, 1907). French translation by Alexandre Moret, 1912.

Ed. Meyer, *Geschichte des Altertums* [5], I. ii., II. i., ii.

James H. Breasted, *Ancient Records*, 1906.

T. E. Peet, H. R. Hall, J. H. Breasted, in the *Cambridge Ancient History*, Vols. i.-vi.

A. von Gutschmid, *Kleine Schriften*, iv., 1893.

For further works and articles relating to Manetho, see the article by Laqueur, Pauly-Wissowa-Kroll, *R.-E.*

MSS.

Syncellus

A = 1711 of Paris (dated A.D. 1021), used by Scaliger and Goar, the first two editors. Editions : Paris, 1652 ; Venice, 1729.

B = 1764 of Paris—a much better MS. than A.

G signifies readings of Goar.

m signifies conjectures and notes in the margin of Goar's edition.

Eusebius, *Chronica* (Armenian Version)

G = Codex Hierosolymitanus (see Intro., p. xix n. 2).

Josephus, *Contra Apionem*, i.

L = Codex Laurentianus plut. lxix. 22 of eleventh century.

Hafniensis, No. 1570, at Copenhagen, fifteenth century.

Bigotianus, known from readings transmitted by Emericus Bigotius.

Quotations by Eusebius (A.D. 264-340), sometimes best preserved in the Armenian version.

Lat. = Latin version made by order of Cassiodorus, the minister of Theodoric, c. A.D. 540.

Editio princeps of Greek text (Basel, 1544).

LIST OF ABBREVIATED TITLES USED IN REFERENCE

Ann. Serv. Antiq. = *Annales du Service des Antiquités de l'Égypte*, Le Caire, 1900–

Baedeker [8] = *Egypt and the Súdán*, by Karl Baedeker (English translation, 8th edition, 1929).

Karst = Joseph Karst's German translation *Die Chronik*, in *Eusebius, Werke*, v., 1911.

P. Baden = F. Bilabel, *Griechische Papyri* (*Veröffentlichungen aus den badischen Papyrus-Sammlungen*), Heidelberg, 1923-24.

P. Hibeh = Grenfell and Hunt, *The Hibeh Papyri*, I., 1906.

P. Mich. Zen. = C. C. Edgar, *Zenon Papyri in the University of Michigan Collection*, 1931.

P. Oxy. = Grenfell, Hunt, and Bell, *The Oxyrhynchus Papyri*, 1898-1927.

Petermann = H. Petermann's Latin translation in Schöne (below).

Schöne = *Eusebii Chronicorum lib. I.*, A. Schöne, 1875.

Syncellus = Syncellus or George the Monk, in *Corpus Scriptorum Historicorum Byzantinorum*, W. Dindorf, 1829.

NOTE

THE editor wishes to acknowledge with gratitude the valuable help ungrudgingly given to him in all Egyptological matters by Professor Percy E. Newberry (Liverpool and Cairo) and by Professor Battiscombe Gunn (Oxford); but neither of these Egyptologists must be held responsible for the final form in which their contributions appear, except where their names or initials are appended. Thanks are also due to Professor D. S. Margoliouth (Oxford), who very kindly revised the Latin translation of the Armenian Version of Eusebius, *Chronica*, by comparing it with the original Armenian as given in Aucher's edition : the footnotes show how much the text here printed has benefited from his revision.

In a work which brings before the mind's eye a long series of Kings of Egypt, the editor would have liked to refer interested readers to some book containing a collection of portraits of these kings; but it seems that, in spite of the convenience and interest which such a book would possess, no complete series of royal portraits has yet been published.[1] For a certain number of portrait-sketches (25 in all), skilfully created from existing mummies and ancient representations, see Winifred Brunton, *Kings and Queens of Ancient Egypt* (1924), and *Great Ones of Ancient Egypt* (1929).

[1] For portraits of some kings, see Petrie, *The Making of Egypt*, 1939, *passim*.

THE *AEGYPTIACA* OF MANETHO:
MANETHO'S *HISTORY OF EGYPT*

ΑΙΓΥΠΤΙΑΚΑ

ΤΟΜΟΣ ΠΡΩΤΟΣ

Fr. 1. Eusebius, *Chronica* I. (Armenian Version), p. 93 (Mai).

Ex Aegyptiacis Manethonis monumentis, qui in tres libros historiam suam tribuit,—de diis et de heroibus, de manibus et de mortalibus regibus qui Aegypto praefuerunt usque ad regem Persarum Darium.

1. Primus homo (deus) Aegyptiis Vulcanus[1] est, qui etiam ignis repertor apud eos celebratur. Ex eo Sol; [postea Sôsis[2];] deinde Saturnus; tum

---

[1] *Cf.* Joannes Lydus, *De Mensibus*, iv. 86 (Wünsch). On *Maius*, after speaking of Hephaestus, Lydus adds: κατὰ δὲ ἱστορίαν Μανέθων Αἰγυπτιακῶν ὑπομνημάτων ἐν τόμῳ τρίτῳ φησίν, ὅτι πρῶτος ἀνθρώπων * παρ' Αἰγυπτίοις ἐβασίλευσεν Ἥφαιστος ὁ καὶ εὑρέτης τοῦ πυρὸς αὐτοῖς γενόμενος· ἐξ οὗ Ἥλιος, οὗ Κρόνος, μεθ' ὃν Ὅσιρις, ἔπειτα Τυφών, ἀδελφὸς Ὀσίρεως. From this passage we see that Lydus gives the sequence "Hêphaestus, Hêlios (the Sun), Cronos, Osiris, Typhôn," omitting Sôsis as Eusebius does. After this passage in Lydus comes Fr. 84 Ἰστέον δὲ . . .

[2] From Joannes Antiochenus(Malalas),*Chron.*, 24(Migne, *Patrologia*, Vol. 97).

* Bracketed by Hopfner, *Fontes Historiae Religionis*, Bonn, 1922-3, p. 65.

2

THE *AEGYPTIACA* OF MANETHO: MANETHO'S *HISTORY OF EGYPT*

BOOK I.

Fr. 1 (*from the Armenian Version of Eusebius, Chronica*). DYNASTIES OF GODS, DEMIGODS, AND SPIRITS OF THE DEAD.

FROM the *Egyptian History* of Manetho, who composed his account in three books. These deal with the Gods, the Demigods, the Spirits of the Dead, and the mortal kings who ruled Egypt down to Darius, king of the Persians.

1. The first man (or god) in Egypt is Hephaestus,[1] who is also renowned among the Egyptians as the discoverer of fire. His son, Helios (the Sun), was succeeded by Sôsis: then follow, in turn, Cronos,

---

[1] The Pre-dynastic Period begins with a group of gods, "consisting of the Great Ennead of Heliopolis in the form in which it was worshipped at Memphis" (T. E. Peet, *Cambridge Ancient History*, i. p. 250). After summarizing §§ 1-3 Peet adds: "From the historical point of view there is little to be made of this". See Meyer, *Geschichte des Altertums* [5], I. ii. p. 102 f. for the Egyptian traditions of the Pre-dynastic Period. In the Turin Papyrus the Gods are given in the same order: (Ptah), Rê, (Shu), Geb, Osiris, Sêth (200 years), Horus (300 years), Thoth (3126 years), Ma'at, Har, . . . Total . . . . See Meyer, *Aeg. Chron.* p. 116, and *cf.* Fr. 3.

Osiris; exin Osiridis frater Typhon; ad extremum
Orus, Osiridis et Isidis filius.   Hi primi inter
Aegyptios rerum potiti sunt.   Deinceps continuata
successione delapsa est regia auctoritas usque ad
Bydin (Bitem) per annorum tredecim milia ac nongentos. Lunarem tamen annum intelligo, videlicet
xxx diebus constantem : quem enim nunc mensem
dicimus, Aegyptii olim anni nomine indigitabant.

2. Post deos regnarunt heroes annis MCCLV : rur-
susque alii reges dominati sunt annis MDCCCXVII :
tum alii triginta reges Memphitae annis MDCCXC :
deinde alii Thinitae decem reges annis CCCL.

3. Secuta est manium heroumque dominatio annis
MMMMMDCCCXIII.

4. Summa temporis in mille et myriadem [1] con-
surgit annorum, qui tamen lunares, nempe menstrui,

[1] Müller : mille myriadas Mai.

---

[1] The name Bydis (or Bites) seems to be the Egyptian
bity " king " (from *bit* " bee "), the title of the kings of
Lower Egypt : see the Palermo Stone, and *cf.* Herodotus,
iv. 155, " the Libyans call their king ' Battos ' " (P. E.
Newberry). Bitys appears in late times as a translator
or interpreter of Hermetical writings : see Iamblich.
De Mysteriis, viii. 5 (= Scott, *Hermetica*, iv. p. 34) where
the prophet Bitys is said to have translated [for King
Ammôn] a book (*The Way to Higher Things*, *i.e.* a treatise
on the theurgic or supernatural means of attaining to
union with the Demiurgus) which he found inscribed in
hieroglyphs in a shrine at Saïs in Egypt. *Cf.* the pseudo-
Manetho, App. I.

[2] There is no evidence that the Egyptian year was
ever equal to a month : there were short years (each of
360 days) and long years (see Fr. 49).

[3] See *Excerpta Latina Barbari* (Fr. 4) for the beginning
of this dynasty : " First, Anubis . . . ".

Osiris, Typhon, brother of Osiris, and lastly Orus, son of Osiris and Isis. These were the first to hold sway in Egypt. Thereafter, the kingship passed from one to another in unbroken succession down to Bydis (Bites) [1] through 13,900 years. The year I take, however, to be a lunar one, consisting, that is, of 30 days : what we now call a month the Egyptians used formerly to style a year.[2]

2. After the Gods, Demigods reigned for 1255 years,[3] and again another line of kings held sway for 1817 years : then came thirty more kings of Memphis,[4] reigning for 1790 years ; and then again ten kings of This, reigning for 350 years.

3. There followed the rule of Spirits of the Dead and Demigods,[5] for 5813 years.

4. The total [of the last five groups] amounts to 11,000 years,[6] these however being lunar periods, or

---

[4] Corroborated by the Turin Papyrus, Col. ii. : " of Memphis ".

[5] " Demigods " should be in apposition to " Spirits of the Dead " (νέκυες ἡμίθεοι), as in *Excerpta Latina Barbari* (Fr. 4) and Africanus (Fr. 6. 1). These are perhaps the *Shemsu Hor*, the Followers or Worshippers of Horus, of the Turin Papyrus : see H. R. Hall, *Cambridge Ancient History*, i. p. 265. Before King Mênês (Fr. 6), the king of Upper Egypt who imposed his sway upon the fertile Delta and founded the First Dynasty,—the *Shemsu Hor*, the men of the Falcon Clan whose original home was in the West Delta, had formed an earlier united kingdom by conquering Upper Egypt : see V. Gordon Childe, *New Light on the Most Ancient East*, 1934, p. 8, based upon Breasted, *Bull. Instit. Franç. Arch. Or.* xxx. (Cairo, 1930), pp. 710 ff., and Schäfer's criticism, *Orient. Literaturz.* 1932, p. 704.

[6] The exact total of the items given is 11,025 years. So also 24,900 *infra* is a round number for 24,925.

sunt. Sed revera dominatio, quam narrant Aegyptii,
deorum, heroum, et manium tenuisse putatur lunarium annorum omnino viginti quattuor milia et
nongentos,[1] ex quibus fiunt solares anni MMCCVI.

5. Atque haec si cum Hebraeorum chronologia
conferre volueris, in eandem plane sententiam con-
spirare videbis. Namque Aegyptus ab Hebraeis
Mestraïmus appellatur: Mestraïmus autem ⟨haud [2]⟩
multo post diluvium tempore exstitit. Quippe ex
Chamo, Noachi filio, post diluvium ortus est Aegyptus
sive Mestraïmus, qui primus ad Aegypti incolatum
profectus est, qua tempestate gentes hac illac spargi
coeperunt. Erat autem summa temporis ab
Adamo ad diluvium secundum Hebraeos annorum
MMCCXLII.

6. Ceterum[3] quum Aegyptii praerogativa antiqui-
tatis quadam seriem ante diluvium tenere se iactent
Deorum, Heroum, et Manium annorum plus viginti
milia regnantium, plane aequum est ut hi anni in

---

[1] Aucher's version runs: duae myriades quatuor millia
et DCCCC.

[2] haud: conj. approved by Karst.

[3] Petermann's version of the first sentence of this section runs as follows: Itaque placet (licet) Egiptiis, priscis
(primis) temporibus quae praecesserunt diluvium, se iactare
ob antiquitatem. Deos quosdam fuisse dicunt suos, semi-
deosque et manes. In menses redactis annis apud Hebraeos
enarratis, lunarium annorum myriades duas et amplius
etiam computant (computarunt), ita ut tot fere menses
fiant, quot anni apud Hebraeos comprehenduntur; scilicet
(id est) a protoplasto homine usque ad Mezrajim tempora
nostra computando ("And so, for the early times which
preceded the Flood, the Egyptians may well boast of their
antiquity. They say that certain Gods were theirs, as well
as Demigods and Spirits of the Dead. Having reduced to

months. But, in truth, the whole rule of which the Egyptians tell — the rule of Gods, Demigods, and Spirits of the Dead—is reckoned to have comprised in all 24,900 lunar years, which make 2206[1] solar years.

5. Now, if you care to compare these figures with Hebrew chronology, you will find that they are in perfect harmony. Egypt is called Mestraïm [2] by the Hebrews; and Mestraïm lived ⟨not⟩ long after the Flood. For after the Flood, Cham (or Ham), son of Noah, begat Aegyptus or Mestraïm, who was the first to set out to establish himself in Egypt, at the time when the tribes began to disperse this way and that. Now the whole time from Adam to the Flood was, according to the Hebrews, 2242 years.

6. But, since the Egyptians claim by a sort of prerogative of antiquity that they have, before the Flood, a line of Gods, Demigods, and Spirits of the Dead, who reigned for more than 20,000 years, it clearly follows that these years should be reckoned

[1] Boeckh, *Manetho und die Hundssternperiode*, p. 85, corrects this to 2046.

[2] Mestraïm : the Mizraïm of *O.T. Genesis* x. 6 : Arabic *Miṣrun,* Cuneiform *Muṣri, Miṣri* (Egypt). Mizraïm is a dual name-form, perhaps to be explained in reference to the two great native divisions of Egypt, Upper and Lower.

---

months the years recorded by the Hebrews, they reckon 20,000 lunar years and even more than that number, so that it comes to practically as many months as the years of Hebrew chronology, *i.e.* reckoning our times * from the creation of man to Mezraïm.")

* Karst emends this to "Biblical times".

menses tot convertantur quot ab Hebraeis memo-
rantur anni: nempe ut qui menses continentur in
memoratis apud Hebraeos annis, ii totidem intelli-
gantur Aegyptiorum lunares anni, pro ea temporum
summa, quae a primo condito homine ad Mestraī-
mum usque colligitur. Sane Mestraīmus generis
Aegyptiaci auctor fuit, ab eoque prima Aegyptiorum
dynastia manare credenda est.

7. Quodsi temporum copia adhuc exuberet, re-
putandum est plures fortasse Aegyptiorum reges
una eademque aetate exstitisse; namque et Thini-
tas regnavisse aiunt et Memphitas et Saītas et
Aethiopes eodemque tempore alios.[1] Videntur
praeterea alii quoque alibi imperium tenuisse:
atque hae dynastiae suo quaeque in nomo [2] semet
continuisse: ita ut haud singuli reges successivam
potestatem acceperint, sed alius alio loco eadem
aetate regnaverit. Atque hinc contigit, ut tantus
numerus annorum confieret. Nos vero, his omissis,
persequamur singillatim Aegyptiorum chronologiam.

(Continued in Fr. 7(b).)

[1] Petermann renders: ac interim (iuxta eosdem) alios
quoque, "and others too, besides these".
[2] The Armenian version here confuses νόμος "law" and
νομός "nome": the Latin translation corrects this blunder.

---

[1] For the contemporaneous existence of a number of
petty kingdoms in Egypt, see the Piankhi *stele*, Breasted,
Ancient Records, iv. §§ 830, 878, and the passage from
Artapanus, *Concerning the Jews*, quoted on p. 73 n. 3.
T. Nicklin (in his *Studies in Egyptian Chronology*, 1928-29,

as the same number of months as the years
recorded by the Hebrews : that is, that all the
months contained in the Hebrew record of years,
should be reckoned as so many lunar years of the
Egyptian calculation, in accordance with the total
length of time reckoned from the creation of man
in the beginning down to Mestraïm. Mestraïm was
indeed the founder of the Egyptian race ; and from
him the first Egyptian dynasty must be held to
spring.

7. But if the number of years is still in excess, it
must be supposed that perhaps several Egyptian
kings ruled at one and the same time ; for they say
that the rulers were kings of This, of Memphis, of
Saïs, of Ethiopia, and of other places at the same
time. It seems, moreover, that different kings held
sway in different regions, and that each dynasty was
confined to its own nome : thus it was not a succession
of kings occupying the throne one after the other, but
several kings reigning at the same time in different
regions.[1] Hence arose the great total number of
years. But let us leave this question and take up
in detail the chronology of Egyptian history.

(Continued in Fr. 7(b).)

p. 39) says : " The Manethonian Dynasties are not lists
of rulers over all Egypt, but lists partly of more or less
independent princes, partly of princely lines from which
later sprang rulers over all Egypt. (Cf. the Scottish
Stuarts, or the Electors of Hanover.) Some were mere
Mayors of the Palace or princelets maintaining a pre-
carious independence, or even more subordinate Governors
of nomes, from whom, however, descended subsequent
monarchs. (Cf. the Heptarchy in England.) "

Fr. 2.   Syncellus, p. 73.

1. Μετὰ δὲ ταῦτα καὶ περὶ ἐθνῶν Αἰγυπτιακῶν πέντε ἐν τριάκοντα δυναστείαις ἱστορεῖ τῶν λεγομένων παρ' αὐτοῖς θεῶν καὶ ἡμιθέων καὶ νεκύων καὶ θνητῶν, ὧν καὶ Εὐσέβιος ὁ Παμφίλου μνησθεὶς ἐν τοῖς Χρονικοῖς αὐτοῦ φησὶν οὕτως·

2. " Αἰγύπτιοι δὲ θεῶν καὶ ἡμιθέων καὶ παρὰ τούτοις νεκύων καὶ θνητῶν ἑτέρων βασιλέων πολλὴν καὶ φλύαρον συνείρουσι μυθολογίαν· οἱ γὰρ παρ' αὐτοῖς παλαιότατοι σεληναίους ἔφασκον εἶναι τοὺς[1] ἐνιαυτοὺς ἐξ ἡμερῶν τριάκοντα συνεστῶτας, οἱ δὲ μετὰ τούτους ἡμίθεοι ὥρους ἐκάλουν τοὺς ἐνιαυτοὺς τοὺς[2] τριμηνιαίους."

3. Καὶ ταῦτα μὲν ὁ Εὐσέβιος μεμφόμενος αὐτοῖς τῆς φλυαρίας εὐλόγως συνέγραψεν, ὃν ὁ Πανόδωρος οὐ καλῶς, ὡς οἶμαι, ἐν τούτῳ μέμφεται, λέγων ὅτι ἠπόρησε διαλύσασθαι τὴν ἔννοιαν τῶν συγγραφέων, ἣν αὐτὸς καινότερόν τι δοκῶν κατορθοῦν λέγει·

4. "'Επειδὴ ἀπὸ τῆς τοῦ Ἀδὰμ πλάσεως ἕως[3] τοῦ Ἐνώχ, ἤτοι τοῦ καθολικοῦ κοσμικοῦ ͵ασπβ' ἔτους, οὔτε μηνὸς οὔτε ἐνιαυτοῦ ἀριθμὸς ἡμερῶν ἐγνωρίζετο, οἱ δὲ ἐγρήγοροι, κατελθόντες ἐπὶ τοῦ καθολικοῦ

---

[1] MSS. εἶναι τοὺς ͵τψ' μηνιαίους τοὺς ἐνιαυτούς : ͵τψ' μηνιαίους τοὺς secl. Scaliger.
[2] MSS. τοὺς ψ' τριμηνιαίους : ψ' delet m.
[3] ἕως add. m.

Fr. 2 (*from Syncellus*).

Thereafter [1] Manetho tells also of five Egyptian tribes which formed thirty dynasties, comprising those whom they call Gods, Demigods, Spirits of the Dead, and mortal men. Of these Eusebius, " son " of Pamphilus, gives the following account in his *Chronica :* " Concerning Gods, Demigods, Spirits of the Dead, and mortal kings, the Egyptians have a long series of foolish myths. The most ancient Egyptian kings, indeed, alleged that their years were lunar years consisting of thirty days, whereas the Demigods who succeeded them gave the name *hôroi* to years which were three months long." So Eusebius wrote with good reason, criticizing the Egyptians for their foolish talk ; and in my opinion Panodôrus [2] is wrong in finding fault with Eusebius here, on the ground that Eusebius failed to explain the meaning of the historians, while Panodôrus thinks he himself succeeds by a somewhat novel method, as follows :

" From the creation of Adam, indeed, down to Enoch, *i.e.* to the general cosmic year 1282, the number of days was known in neither month nor year ; but the Egregori (or ' Watchers '),[3] who had

[1] This passage follows after Appendix I., p. 210.

[2] Panodôrus (*fl. c.* 395-408 A.D.) and his contemporary Annianus were Egyptian monks who wrote on Chronology with the purpose of harmonizing Chaldean and Egyptian systems with that of the Jews. Panodôrus used (and perhaps composed) the *Book of Sôthis* (App. IV.).

[3] Ἐγρήγοροι, " Watchers, Angels "—in *Enoch*, 179, of the angels who fell in love with the daughters of men. The Greek word Ἐγρήγοροι is a mispronunciation of the Aramaic word used in *Enoch*, 179.

κοσμικοῦ χιλιοστοῦ ἔτους, συναναστραφέντες τοῖς ἀνθρώποις ἐδίδαξαν αὐτοὺς τοὺς κύκλους τῶν δύο φωσ-
τήρων δωδεκαζῳδίους εἶναι ἐκ μοιρῶν τριακοσίων
ἑξήκοντα, οἱ δὲ ἀποβλέψαντες εἰς τὸν περιγειότερον,
μικρότερον καὶ εὐδηλότερον τριακονθήμερον σελη-
νιακὸν κύκλον ἐθέσπισαν εἰς ἐνιαυτὸν ἀριθμεῖσθαι,
διὰ τὸ καὶ τὸν τοῦ ἡλίου κύκλον ἐν τοῖς αὐτοῖς
δώδεκα ζῳδίοις πληροῦσθαι ἐν ἰσαρίθμοις μοίραις
τξ′. ὅθεν συνέβη τὰς βασιλείας τῶν παρ᾽ αὐτοῖς
βασιλευσάντων θεῶν γενεῶν ἕξ, ἐν δυναστείαις
ἕξ, κατ᾽ ἔτη[1] ἐν σεληνιακοῖς τριακονθημέροις κύκλοις
παρ᾽ αὐτοῖς ἀριθμεῖσθαι· ἃ καὶ συνῆξαν σελήνια α′
,αππε′ ἔτη, ἡλιακὰ ͵ϛκθ′· ταῦτα δὲ συναριθμούμενα
τοῖς πρὸ τῆς τούτων βασιλείας ἡλιακοῖς ,ανη′ ἔτεσι
συνάγουσιν ὁμάδα ἐτῶν ͵βκζ′.'' ὁμοίως δὲ κατὰ
τὰς δύο δυναστείας τῶν ἐννέα ἡμιθέων τῶν
μηδέποτε γεγονότων ὡς γεγονότων ἔτη σιδ′ καὶ
ἥμισυ σπουδάζει συνιστᾶν ἀπὸ τῶν ωνη′ ὡρῶν,[2]
ἤτοι τρόπων, ὡς γίνεσθαί φησι, σὺν ͵ϛκθ′, ͵αρπγ′[3]
καὶ ἥμισυ ἔτη, καὶ συναπτόμενα τοῖς ἀπὸ Ἀδὰμ
μέχρι τῆς τῶν θεῶν βασιλείας ,ανη′ ἔτεσι συνάγειν
ἔτη ͵βρμβ′ ἕως τοῦ κατακλυσμοῦ.

5. Καὶ ταῦτα μὲν ὁ Πανόδωρος τὰς κατὰ θεοῦ
καὶ τῶν θεοπνεύστων γραφῶν Αἰγυπτιακὰς συγ-
γραφὰς συμφωνεῖν αὐταῖς ἀγωνίζεται δεικνύναι,
μεμφόμενος τὸν Εὐσέβιον, μὴ εἰδὼς ὅτι καθ᾽ ἑαυτοῦ
καὶ τῆς ἀληθείας ἀποδέδεικται ταῦτα αὐτοῦ τὰ

---

[1] MSS. ἔτη alone: κατ᾽ ἔτη m.

[2] ωνή ὡρῶν or ὅρων m.: ὠνιώρων MSS.: ἐνιαυσίων ὡρῶν Scaliger.

[3] ,αρπγ′ m.: ,αρνγ′ MSS.

descended to earth in the general cosmic year 1000, held converse with men, and taught them that the orbits of the two luminaries, being marked by the twelve signs of the Zodiac, are composed of 360 parts. Observing the moon's orbit which is nearer the earth, smaller, and more conspicuous, as it has a period of thirty days, men decided that it should be reckoned as a year, since the orbit of the sun also was filled by the same twelve signs of the Zodiac with an equal number of parts, 360. So it came to pass that the reigns of the Gods who ruled among them for six generations in six dynasties were reckoned in years each consisting of a lunar cycle of thirty days. The total in lunar years is 11,985, or 969 solar years. By adding these to the 1058 [1] solar years of the period before their reign, they reach the sum total of 2027 years." Similarly, in the two dynasties of nine Demigods,—these being regarded as real, although they never existed,—Panodôrus strives to make up 214½ years out of 858 *hôroi* (periods of three months) or *tropoi*, so that with the 969 years they make, he says, 1183½, and these, when added to the 1058 years from the time of Adam to the reign of the Gods, complete a total of 2242 years down to the Flood.

Thus Panodôrus exerts himself to show that the Egyptian writings against God and against our divinely inspired Scriptures are really in agreement with them. In this he criticizes Eusebius, not understanding that these arguments of his, which are incapable of proof or of reasoning, have been proved

---

[1] See Intro. p. xxx.

ἀναπόδεικτά τε καὶ ἀσυλλόγιστα, εἴ γε... οὔτε
Βαβυλὼν ἢ Χαλδαϊκὴ πρὸ τοῦ κατακλυσμοῦ οὔτε
ἡ Αἴγυπτος πρὸ τοῦ Μεστρὲμ ἐβασιλεύθη, οἶμαι δ'
ὅτι οὐδ' ᾠκίσθη . . .

Fr. 3.   Syncellus, p. 32.

Περὶ τῆς τῶν Αἰγυπτίων ἀρχαιολογίας.

Μανεθῶ ὁ Σεβεννύτης ἀρχιερεὺς τῶν ἐν Αἰγύπτῳ
μιαρῶν ἱερῶν μετὰ Βήρωσσον γενόμενος ἐπὶ Πτολεμαίου τοῦ Φιλαδέλφου γράφει τῷ αὐτῷ Πτολεμαίῳ,
ψευδηγορῶν καὶ αὐτὸς ὡς ὁ Βήρωσσος, περὶ δυναστειῶν ϛ', ἤτοι θεῶν τῶν μηδέποτε γεγονότων ϛ',[1]
οἳ, φησὶ, διαγεγόνασιν ἐπὶ ἔτη α' ͵απϙε'. ὧν
πρῶτος, φησὶ, θεὸς Ἥφαιστος ἔτη ͵θ ἐβασίλευσε.
ταῦτα τὰ ͵θ ἔτη πάλιν τινὲς τῶν καθ' ἡμᾶς ἱστορικῶν
ἀντὶ μηνῶν σεληνιακῶν λογισάμενοι καὶ μερίσαντες
τὸ τῶν ἡμερῶν πλῆθος τῶν αὐτῶν ͵θ σεληνίων παρὰ
τὰς τριακοσίας ἑξήκοντα πέντε ἡμέρας τοῦ ἐνιαυτοῦ
συνῆξαν ἔτη ψκζ ⌐δ', ξένον τι δοκοῦντες κατωρ-
θωκέναι, γελοίων δὲ μᾶλλον εἰπεῖν ἄξιον τὸ ψεῦδος
τῇ ἀληθείᾳ συμβιβάζοντες.

Πρώτη δυναστεία[2] Αἰγυπτίων.

α'   ἐβασίλευσεν Ἥφαιστος ἔτη ψκζ ⌐δ'.[3]
β'   Ἥλιος Ἡφαίστου, ἔτη π' ϛ'.
γ'   Ἀγαθοδαίμων, ἔτη νϛ' ⌐ιβ'.

[1] MS. A ζ'.
[2] MS. A has πρώτη δυναστεία after Ἥφαιστος.
[3] Müller : MSS. ψκδ' ⌐δ' (724¾).

against himself and against truth, since indeed . . .
neither Babylon nor Chaldea was ruled by kings
before the Flood, nor was Egypt before Mestrem,
and in my opinion it was not even inhabited before
that time. . . .

Fr. 3 (*from Syncellus*).

On the Antiquity of Egypt.

Manetho of Sebennytus, chief priest of the accursed
temples of Egypt, who lived later than Bêrôssos in
the time of Ptolemy Philadelphus, writes to this
Ptolemy, with the same utterance of lies as Bêrôssos,
concerning six dynasties or six gods who never
existed : these, he says, reigned for 11,985 years.
The first of them, the god Hêphaestus, was king for
9000 years. Now some of our historians, reckoning
these 9000 years as so many lunar months, and
dividing the number of days in these 9000 lunar
months by the 365 days in a year, find a total of
$727\frac{3}{4}$ years. They imagine that they have attained
a striking result, but one must rather say that it is
a ludicrous falsehood which they have tried to pit
against Truth.

The First Dynasty of Egypt.

1. Hêphaestus reigned for $727\frac{3}{4}$ years.
2. Hêlios (the Sun), son of Hêphaestus, for $80\frac{1}{6}$
   years.
3. Agathodaemôn, for $56\frac{7}{12}$ years.

15

δ′   Κρόνος, ἔτη μ′ ὑ.
ε′   Ὄσιρις καὶ Ἶσις, ἔτη λε′.
ϛ′   Τύφων, ἔτη κθ′.

ζ′   Ὧρος ἡμίθεος, ἔτη κε′.
η′   Ἄρης ἡμιθεος, ἔτη κγ′.
θ′   Ἄνουβις ἡμίθεος, ἔτη ιζ′.
ι′   Ἡρακλῆς ἡμίθεος, ἔτη ιε′.
ια′   Ἀπόλλων ἡμίθεος, ἔτη κε′.
ιβ′   Ἄμμων ἡμίθεος, ἔτη λ′.
ιγ′   Τιθοῆς ἡμίθεος, ἔτη κζ′.
ιδ′   Σῶσος ἡμίθεος, ἔτη λβ′.
ιε′   Ζεὺς ἡμίθεος, ἔτη κ′.

Fr. 4.   *Excerpta Latina Barbari* (Schöne, p. 215).

Egyptiorum regnum invenimus vetustissimum
omnium regnorum; cuius initium sub Manethono [1]
dicitur memoramus scribere. Primum [2] deorum qui
ab ipsis scribuntur faciam regna sic:

Ifestum [*i.e.* Hephaestum] dicunt quidam deum
regnare in Aegypto annos sexcentos LXXX: post
hunc Solem Iphesti annos LXXVII: post istum

---

[1] ὑπὸ Μανέθωνος Scaliger.
[2] Frick (*Chronica Minora*, i., 1893, p. 286) restores the
original Greek as follows: πρῶτον θεῶν τῶν παρ' αὐτοῖς
γραφομένων ποιήσω βασιλείας οὕτως. α′ Ἥφαιστόν φασί τινες
θεὸν βασιλεῦσαι ἐν Αἰγύπτῳ ἔτη χπ′.

---

[1] Total, 969 years.
[2] Total, 214 years. Total for Gods and Demigods,
1183 years. See Fr. 2.

4. Cronos, for 40½ years.
5. Osiris and Isis, for 35 years.
6. Typhôn, for 29 years.[1]

Demigods :

7. Ôrus, for 25 years.
8. Arês, for 23 years.
9. Anubis, for 17 years.
10. Hêraclês, for 15 years.
11. Apollô, for 25 years.
12. Ammôn, for 30 years.
13. Tithoês,* for 27 years.
14. Sôsus, for 32 years.
15. Zeus, for 20 years.[2]

Fr. 4 [3] (*from Excerpta Latina Barbari*).

In the kingdom of Egypt we have the oldest of
all kingdoms, and we are minded to record its beginning, as it is given by Manetho. First, I shall put
down as follows the reigns of the Gods, as recorded
by the Egyptians. Some say that the god Hêphaestus reigned in Egypt for 680 years : after him,
Sol [Hêlios, the Sun], son of Hêphaestus, for 77

---

[3] This extract made by an anonymous and ignorant
scribe depends chiefly upon Africanus. See Weill, *La
fin du moyen empire égyptien*, pp. 640, 642 f., 655 f.
Gelzer and Bauer have inferred that the Greek account
translated by Barbarus was either the work of the
Egyptian monk Annianus (see Fr. 2, p. 11 n. 2) or at
least a source derived from him (Laqueur, *R.-E.* xiv. 1,
1081).

* For the divinity Tithoês in two inscriptions of Coptos,
see O. Guéraud in *Ann. Serv. Antiq.*, 35 (1935), pp. 5 f.

17

Sosinosirim[1] annos CCCXX: post hunc Oron
ptoliarchum annos XXVIII: post hunc Tyfona
annos XLV.[2] Colliguntur deorum regna anni mille
DL.

Deinceps Mitheorum[3] regna sic:

Prota[4] Anube S[amusim, qui etiam Aegyptiorum
scripturas conposuit] annos LXXXIII.

[Post hunc Apiona grammaticus qui secundum
Inachum interpraetatur annos LXVII quem sub
Argios initio regnaverunt.]

---

[1] Corrected by the first hand from Sisinosirim: Sosin,
Osirim Scaliger. Barbarus probably intended: post istum
Sosin, post hunc Osirim. *Cf.* Cedren., i. p. 36, 2: καὶ μετ'
αὐτὸν Σῶσις, εἶτα Ὄσιρις.

[2] After XLV the digit I or II seems to have been erased.

[3] Frick restores: Ἑξῆς Ἡμιθέων βασιλεῖαι οὕτως· αʹ πρῶτα
Ἄνουβις ἔτη πγʹ. βʹ μετὰ τοῦτον Ἀμουσίν ⟨φασί τινες βασιλεῦσαι, ὃν⟩ Ἀπίων ὁ γραμματικὸς ὁ καὶ τὰς Αἰγυπτίων γραφὰς συνθεὶς
κατὰ Ἴναχον ἑρμηνεύει τὸν ἐπ' Ἀργείων ἀρχῆς βασιλεύσαντα ἔτη
ξζʹ.

μετὰ ταῦτα τοὺς Νεκύων βασιλέας ἡρμήνευσεν Ἡμιθέους καλῶν
καὶ αὐτούς . . . κρατίστους καλῶν ἔτη ‚βρʹ.

[4] πρῶτα. Along with the reign of the demigod Anubis,
Barbarus has preserved a note by Africanus referring to
Amôsis: see Fr. 52. This note was, for some reason, transferred from its original place between Potestas XVI. and
XVII. See Unger, *Manetho,* pp. 163 f. This mangled
sentence, as interpreted by Unger, Gelzer, and Frick,
attests the value of the tradition preserved by Barbarus.

---

[1] The actual total of the items given is 1150 years.

[2] The translation follows the restored Greek original:
see note 3 on the text.

years : next, Sosinosiris [Sôsis and Osiris], for 320 years : then Orus the Ruler, for 28 years ; and after him, Typhon, for 45 years. Total for the reigns of the Gods, 1550 years.[1]

Next come the reigns of the Demigods, as follows : first, Anubes [2] for 83 years ; then after him, Amusis, some say, was king. About him, Apiôn the grammarian,[3] who composed a history of Egypt, explained that he lived in the time of Inachus [4] who was king at the founding of Argos . . . for 67 years.[5]

---

[3] Apiôn the grammarian, born in Upper Egypt, lived at Rome in the time of Tiberius, Gaius, and Claudius : Tiberius called him by the nickname of " cymbalum mundi ". As leader of the anti-Jewish movement, Apiôn was later attacked by Josephus in his *Contra Apionem*.

The quotation from Apiôn appears to derive in part from the *History* of Ptolemy of Mendês : see Tatian, *Or. adversus Graecos*, § 38, in Migne, *Patrologia Graeca*, vi. 880-882, and in Müller, *F.H.G.* iv. p. 485 (quoted in *F.H.G.* ii. p. 533). (Ptolemy of Mendês dated the Exodus to the reign of Amôsis, who was contemporary with Inachus. Apiôn in the fourth volume of his *Aegyptiaca* (in five volumes) stated that Auaris was destroyed by Amôsis.) Much matter must have been common to the works of Ptolemy of Mendês and Apiôn : cf. Africanus in Eusebius, *Praepar. Evang.* x. 10, " Apiôn says that in the time of Inachus Moses led out the Jews ". Cf. Fr. 52, 1 ; 53, 9.

[4] The founder of the First Dynasty of kings of Argos, Inachus is said to have died twenty generations before the Fall of Troy, *i.e. circa* 1850 B.C. Aegyptus and Danaus were fifth in descent from Inachus : cf. Fr. 50, § 102.

[5] This appears to be the length of the reign of Amôsis, not of Inachus. Cf. Fr. 52, 1, where Africanus as recorded by Syncellus omits the number of years.

19

I. Post hec[1] Ecyniorum[2] reges interpraetavit, Imitheus[2] vocans et ipsos[3] . . . annos duo milia C, fortissimos vocans.

II. Mineus et pronepotes ipsius VII regnaverunt annos CCLIII.[4]

III. Bochus et aliorum octo annos CCCII.

IV. Necherocheus et aliorum VII annos CCXIV.

V. Similiter aliorum XVII annos CCLXXVII.

VI. Similiter aliorum XXI annos CCLVIII.

VII. Othoi et aliorum VII annos CCIII.

VIII. Similiter et aliorum XIV annos CXL.

IX. Similiter et aliorum XX annos CCCCIX.

X. Similiter et aliorum VII annos CCIV.

Hec[5] finis de primo tomo Manethoni habens tempora annorum duo milia C.

XI. Potestas Diopolitanorum annos LX.

XII. Potestas Bubastanorum annos CLIII.

[1] For *haec*.

[2] These words are perversions of Νεκύων and Ἡμιθέους respectively : see p. 18 n. 3.

[3] In the lacuna here, there would be an account of the mortal kings to whom the number 2100 (2300) belongs.

[4] *Cf.* Fr. 6, Dynasty I.   [5] For *haec*.

---

[1] The totals given by Barbarus are generally those of Africanus. Barbarus omits Manetho's Dynasty VII.; and Potestas X. is explained by Gelzer (*Sextus Julius Africanus*, p. 199) as being Manetho's X. + XI. + Ammenemes (16 years) = 244 years. Total, 2300.

[2] The actual total of the items given is 2260 years.

[3] Potestas XI. is Manetho's Dynasty XII. Barbarus therefore gives Dynasties XII.-XVIII.: the totals (corrected by Meyer, *Aeg. Chron.* 99, n. 2) are—XII. 160, XIII. 453, XIV. 184, XV. 284, XVI. 518, XVII. 151,

I. Thereafter he [Manetho] gave an account of the kings who were Spirits of the Dead, calling them also Demigods, . . . who reigned for 2100 years : he called them " very brave " (Heroes).

    II. Mineus and seven of his descendants reigned for 253 years.[1]

    III. Bochus and eight other kings reigned for 302 years.

    IV. Necherocheus and seven other kings for 214 years.

    V. Similarly seventeen other kings for 277 years.

    VI. Similarly twenty-one other kings for 258 years.

    VII. Othoi and seven other kings for 203 years.

    VIII. Similarly fourteen other kings for 140 years.

    IX. Similarly twenty other kings for 409 years.

    X. Similarly seven other kings for 204 years.

Here ends the First Book of Manetho, which contains a period of 2100 years.[2]

    XI.[3] A dynasty of kings of Diospolis, for 60 years.

    XII. A dynasty of kings of Bubastus, for 153 years.

XVIII. 262 (+ XIX. 209). Sum total for Book II. 2221 years : *cf.* Fr. 55 Africanus, 56 Eus. (Arm.), 2121 years.

    The names of Potestates XII.-XVII., or Dynasties XIII.-XVIII., come from some other source than Manetho : the Tanites of Potestas XIII. or Dynasty XIV. appear to correspond with the Hyksôs, just as in the *Book of Sôthis* (App. IV.) ; while others may be local dynasties of the Hyksôs age. The kings of Hermupolis (Potestas XVII.) apparently denote the kings of the Eighteenth Dynasty, whose names indicate the cult of the Moon-deities 'Ioḥ and Thôth of Hermupolis (Meyer, *Gesch.*[5] I. ii. p. 326).

XIII. Potestas Tanitorum annos CLXXXIV.
XIV. Potestas Sebennitorum annos CCXXIV.
XV. Potestas Memfitorum annos CCCXVIII.
XVI. Potestas Iliopolitorum annos CCXXI.
XVII. Potestas Ermupolitorum annos CCLX.

Usque ad septimam decimam potestatem secundum scribitur tomum,[1] ut docet numerum habentem annos mille quingentos XX. Haec sunt potestates Aegyptiorum.

Fr. 5. MALALAS, *Chronographia*, p. 25 (MIGNE, *Patrologia Graeca*, Vol. 97).

Ταῦτα δὲ τὰ παλαιὰ καὶ ἀρχαῖα βασίλεια τῶν Αἰγυπτίων Μανέθων συνεγράψατο· ἐν οἷς συγγράμμασιν αὐτοῦ ἐμφέρεται ἄλλως λέγεσθαι τὰς ἐπωνυμίας τῶν πέντε πλανητῶν ἀστέρων. Τὸν γὰρ λεγόμενον Κρόνον ἀστέρα ἐκάλουν τὸν λάμποντα, τὸν δὲ Διὸς τὸν φαέθοντα, τὸν δὲ Ἄρεος τὸν πυρώδη, τὸν δὲ Ἀφροδίτης τὸν κάλλιστον, τὸν δὲ Ἑρμοῦ τὸν στίλβοντα· ἅτινα μετὰ ταῦτα Σωτάτης ὁ σοφώτατος ἡρμήνευσε. Cf. id., p. 59: Αἰγυπτίων δὲ ἐβασίλευσε πρῶτος βασιλεὺς τῆς φυλῆς τοῦ Χάμ, υἱοῦ Νῶε, Φαραὼ ὁ καὶ Ναραχὼ

---

[1] MS. totum. Frick restores the original Greek as follows: μέχρι τῆς ιζʹ δυναστείας ὁ δεύτερος γράφεται τόμος, ὡς δηλοῖ ὁ ἀριθμός, ἔχων ἔτη ‚αφκʹ.

---

[1] The actual total of the items given is 1420 years.
[2] 4407 codd.

XIII. A dynasty of kings of Tanis, for 184 years.
XIV. A dynasty of kings of Sebennytus, for 224 years.
XV. A dynasty of kings of Memphis, for 318 years.
XVI. A dynasty of kings of Hêliopolis, for 221 years.
XVII. A dynasty of kings of Hermupolis, for 260 years.

The Second Book continues the record down to the Seventeenth Dynasty, and comprises 1520 years.[1] These are the Egyptian dynasties.

Fr. 5 (*from the Chronicle of Malalas*).

[After recording the reigns of Hêphaestus (1680 days), Hêlios (4477 [2] days), Sôsis, Osiris, Hôrus, and Thulis, Malalas adds :]

These ancient reigns of early Egyptian kings are recorded by Manetho, and in his writings it is stated that the names of the five planets are given in other forms : Cronos [Saturn] they used to call the shining star ; Zeus [Jupiter], the radiant star [Phaethôn] ; Arês [Mars], the fiery star ; Aphroditê [Venus], the fairest ; Hermês [Mercury], the glittering star. These names were later explained by the wise Sôtatês [? Sôtadês or Palaephatus [3]].

The first king of Egypt belonged to the tribe of Cham [Ham], Noah's son ; he was Pharaôh, who was also called Narachô.

---

[3] Palaephatus of Egypt, or Athens, wrote on Egyptian theology and mythology, *c.* 200 B.C.,—more than seven centuries earlier than Malalas himself (*c.* A.D. 491-578).

23

καλούμενος. Τὰ οὖν πρὸ τούτου παλαιὰ βασίλεια
Αἰγυπτίων ἐξέθετο Μανέθων ὁ σοφώτατος, ὡς
προείρηται.

Fr. 6. Syncellus, p. 99.

Ἐπειδὴ δὲ τῶν ἀπὸ Μεστραῒμ Αἰγυπτιακῶν
δυναστειῶν[1] οἱ χρόνοι ἕως Νεκταναβῶ χρειώδεις
τυγχάνουσιν ἐν πολλοῖς τοῖς περὶ τὰς χρονικὰς
καταγινομένοις ζητήσεις, αὐταὶ δὲ παρὰ Μανεθῶ
ληφθεῖσαι τοῖς ἐκκλησιαστικοῖς ἱστορικοῖς δια-
πεφωνημένως κατά τε τὰς αὐτῶν προσηγορίας καὶ
τὴν ποσότητα τῶν χρόνων τῆς βασιλείας ἐκδέδον-
ται, ἐπὶ τίνος τε αὐτῶν Ἰωσὴφ ἡγεμόνευσε τῆς
Αἰγύπτου καὶ μετ' αὐτὸν ὁ θεόπτης Μωϋσῆς τῆς
τοῦ Ἰσραὴλ ἐξ Αἰγύπτου πορείας ἡγήσατο, ἀναγ-
καῖον ἡγησάμην δύο τῶν ἐπισημοτάτων ἐκδόσεις
ἐκλέξασθαι καὶ ταύτας ἀλλήλαις παραθέσθαι,
Ἀφρικανοῦ τέ φημι καὶ τοῦ μετ' αὐτὸν Εὐσεβίου
τοῦ Παμφίλου καλουμένου, ὡς ἂν τὴν ἐγγίζουσαν
τῇ γραφικῇ ἀληθείᾳ δόξαν ὀρθῶς ἐπιβάλλων τις[2]
καταμάθοι, τοῦτο πρό γε πάντων εἰδὼς ἀκριβῶς,
ὅτι Ἀφρικανὸς μὲν εἴκοσιν ἔτη προστίθησιν ἐν τοῖς
ἀπὸ Ἀδὰμ ἕως τοῦ κατακλυσμοῦ χρόνοις, καὶ ἀντὶ
͵βσμβ' ͵βσξβ' ἔτη βούλεται εἶναι, ὅπερ οὐ δοκεῖ
καλῶς ἔχειν. Εὐσέβιος δὲ ͵βσμβ' ὑγιῶς ἔθετο καὶ
ὁμοφώνως τῇ γραφῇ. ἐν δὲ τοῖς ἀπὸ τοῦ κατακλυσμοῦ ἀμφότεροι διήμαρτον ἕως τοῦ Ἀβραὰμ

---

[1] δυναστειῶν Bunsen : ἐτῶν MSS.   [2] τις add. m.

Now, the ancient reigns in Egypt before King Narachô were set forth by the wise Manetho, as has already been mentioned.

Fr. 6 (*from Syncellus*).

Since a knowledge of the periods of the Egyptian dynasties from Mestraïm [1] down to Nectanabô [2] is on many occasions needful to those who occupy themselves with chronological investigations, and since the dynasties taken from Manetho's *History* are set forth by ecclesiastical historians with discrepancies in respect both to the names of the kings and the length of their reigns, and also as to who was king when Joseph was governor of Egypt, and in whose reign thereafter Moses,—he who saw God,— led the Hebrews in their exodus from Egypt, I have judged it necessary to select two of the most famous recensions and to set them side by side—I mean the accounts of Africanus and of the later Eusebius, the so-called " son " of Pamphilus,—so that with proper application one may apprehend the opinion which approaches nearest to Scriptural truth. It must, above all, be strictly understood that Africanus increases by 20 years the period from Adam to the Flood, and instead of 2242 years he makes it out to be 2262 years, which appears to be incorrect. On the other hand, Eusebius keeps to the sound reckoning of 2242 years in agreement with Scripture. In regard to the period from the Flood down to Abraham and Moses, both have gone astray by 130

[1] See p. 7 n. 2.
[2] Nectanabô or Nectanebus, the last king of Dynasty XXX.

καὶ Μωϋσέως ἔτεσι ρλ' τοῦ δευτέρου Καϊνᾶν υἱοῦ
Ἀρφαξὰδ καὶ γενεᾷ μιᾷ, τῇ ιγ', παρὰ τῷ θείῳ
εὐαγγελιστῇ Λουκᾷ, ἀπὸ Ἀδὰμ κειμένη. ἀλλ' ὁ
μὲν Ἀφρικανὸς ἐν τοῖς ἀπὸ Ἀδὰμ προστεθεῖσιν
αὐτῷ καὶ ἐπὶ τὸν κατακλυσμὸν ἔτεσιν κ' προαφήρ-
παξε ταῦτα, καὶ ἐν τοῖς τοῦ Καϊνᾶν καὶ τῶν μετέ-
πειτα ρι' μόνα λείπεται. διὸ καὶ ἕως Ἀβραὰμ
πρώτου ἔτους ,γσβ' ἔτη ἐστοιχείωσεν. ὁ δὲ
Εὐσέβιος ὁλοκλήρως τὰ ρλ' ὑφελών, ,γρπδ' ἕως
πρώτου ἔτους Ἀβραὰμ ἐξέδωκε.

ΚΑΤΑ ΑΦΡΙΚΑΝΟΝ.

Περὶ τῶν [μετὰ τὸν κατακλυσμὸν]¹
Αἰγύπτου δυναστειῶν, ὡς ὁ Ἀφρικανός.

α' Μετὰ νέκυας τοὺς ἡμιθέους πρώτη βασιλεία²
καταριθμεῖται βασιλέων ὀκτώ, ὧν πρῶτος

---

¹ Bracketed by Müller.   ² δυναστεία Boeckh.

---

[1] Arphaxad, son of Shem : O.T. Genesis x. 22. " Arphaxad " is probably a Mesopotamian name (W. F.
Albright, The Archaeology of Palestine and the Bible²,
1932-3, p. 139).

[2] N.T. Luke iii. 36.

[3] Eusebius reckoned 2242 years from Adam to the
Flood, and 942 years from the Flood to Abraham.

[4] Dynasties I. and II., the Thinites : c. 3200–c. 2780 B.C.
Note.—The dates which have been adopted throughout
this book are those of Eduard Meyer, except where another
authority is specified. Meyer's revised dates (as in
Die Ältere Chronologie . . ., 1931) may conveniently be
found in G. Steindorff's chapter on Ancient History in
Baedeker⁶, pp. ci. ff. In the Cambridge Ancient History,
vol. i., H. R. Hall gives for the dynasties a series of dates

years belonging to the second Caïnan, son of
Arphaxad,[1] even one generation, the thirteenth, from
Adam, as it is recorded by the divine evangelist
Luke.[2] But Africanus, in the 20 years which he
added between Adam and the Flood, anticipated
this ; and in the period of Caïnan and his successors,
only 110 years remain. Hence, down to the first
year of Abraham he reckoned 3202 years ; but
Eusebius, completely omitting those 130 years, gave
3184 years [3] as far as Abraham's first year.

DYNASTY I.

ACCORDING TO AFRICANUS.

Here is the account which Africanus gives of the
dynasties of Egypt [after the Flood].

1. In succession to the spirits of the Dead, the
   Demigods,—the first royal house [4] numbers
   eight kings, the first of whom Mênês [5] of

which differ from those of Breasted and the German
School : he assigns earlier dates to the first twelve
dynasties, e.g. Dynasty I. c. 3500 B.C. A. Scharff, on the
other hand, dates the beginning of Dynasty I. c. 3000 B.C.
(Journ. of Eg. Arch. xiv., 1928, pp. 275 f.).

Dynasty I. For the identifications of Manetho's
kings with monumental and other evidence, see Meyer,
Geschichte des Altertums [5], I. ii. p. 140 : he identifies (1)
Mênês, (2) Atoti I., II., III., (5) Usaphaïs, (6) Miebis.

(3) Kenkenês and (5) Usaphaïs are two names of the
same king : see Newberry and Wainwright, "King Udymu
(Den) and the Palermo Stone" in Ancient Egypt, 1914,
p. 148 ff.

[5] On Mênês (c. 3200 B.C.) see P. E. Newberry in Winifred
Brunton's Great Ones of Ancient Egypt, 1929 : Min in Herodotus, ii. 4.

Μήνης Θινίτης ἐβασίλευσεν ἔτη ξβ´ · ὃς
ὑπὸ ἱπποποτάμου διαρπαγεὶς διεφθάρη.

β´ Ἄθωθις υἱός, ἔτη νζ´, ὁ τὰ ἐν Μέμφει βασίλεια οἰκοδομήσας · οὗ φέρονται βίβλοι ἀνα-
τομικαί, ἰατρὸς γὰρ ἦν.

γ´ Κενκένης υἱός, ἔτη λα´.

δ´ Οὐενέφης υἱός, ἔτη κγ´ · ἐφ᾽ οὗ λιμὸς κατέσχε τὴν Αἴγυπτον μέγας. οὗτος τὰς
περὶ Κωχώμην ἤγειρε πυραμίδας.

ε´ Οὐσαφαῖδος υἱός, ἔτη κ´.

ϛ´ Μιεβιδὸς υἱός, ἔτη κϛ´.

ζ´ Σεμέμψης υἱός, ἔτη ιη´ · ἐφ᾽ οὗ φθορὰ
μεγίστη κατέσχε τὴν Αἴγυπτον.

η´ Βιηνεχὴς υἱός, ἔτη κϛ´.

Ὁμοῦ, ἔτη σνγ´.

Τὰ τῆς πρώτης δυναστείας οὕτω πως καὶ Εὐσέβιος ὡς ὁ Ἀφρικανὸς ἐξέθετο.

---

[1] This (Anc. Egyptian *Theny*), near Girga, about 310
miles S. of Cairo (Baedeker⁸, p. 231), the capital of the
nome of This, and the seat of the First and Second Dynasties. The cemetery of the First Dynasty kings was
near Abydos : see Petrie, *Royal Tombs*, i. and ii., and
Baedeker ⁸, p. 260.

[2] For a representation of a king fighting with a hippopotamus, see a seal-impression in Petrie, *Royal Tombs*,
II. vii. 6 ; and for a hippopotamus-hunt, see a year-name
of Udymu, Schäfer, *Palermo Stone*, p. 20, No. 8.

With the whole story, *cf.* the miraculous deliverance
of Mênas by a crocodile in Diodorus Siculus, i. 89.

[3] Building of palace at Memphis—by Min or Mênês,
Herodotus, ii. 99, Josephus, *Ant.* viii. 6, 2, 155 ; by his
son Athôthis, says Manetho ; by Uchoreus, Diod. i. 50.

This[1] reigned for 62 years. He was carried
off by a hippopotamus[2] and perished.

2. Athôthis, his son, for 57 years. He built the
   palace at Memphis;[3] and his anatomical
   works[4] are extant, for he was a physician.

3. Kenkenês, his son, for 31 years.

4. Uenephês, his son, for 23 years. In his reign a
   great famine seized Egypt. He erected the
   pyramids near Kôchômê.[5]

5. Usaphaidos,[6] his son, for 20 years.

6. Miebidos,[6] his son, for 26 years.

7. Semempsês, his son, for 18 years. In his reign
   a very great calamity befell Egypt.

8. Biênechês, his son, for 26 years.

Total, 253 years.[7]

Eusebius also sets out the details of the First
Dynasty in much the same way as Africanus.

---

[4] For the later study of anatomy (including, perhaps,
the practice of vivisection) by kings of Ptolemaic Egypt,
see G. Lumbroso, *Glossario, s.v. Ἀνατομική.*

[5] Kôchômê has been identified with Sakkâra, and excavations carried out there in the Archaic Cemetery from
1935 by W. B. Emery (assisted by Zaki Saad) have gone
far to confirm Manetho. Several tombs which date from
the First Dynasty were discovered at Sakkâra in 1937 and
1938. One of these, the tomb of Nebetka under the 5th
king of Dynasty I., was found to contain in its interior
a stepped-pyramid construction of brickwork : during the
building the form of the tomb was altered to a palace-
façade mastaba.

[6] These forms are really the genitives of the names
Usaphaïs and Miebis.

[7] The actual total of the items given is 263 years.

29

Fr. 7 (a). *Syncellus*, p. 102. *ΚΑΤΑ ΕΥΣΕΒΙΟΝ*.

Περὶ τῶν [μετὰ τὸν κατακλυσμὸν][1]
Αἰγυπτίων δυναστειῶν, ὡς Εὐσέβιος.

Μετὰ νέκυας καὶ τοὺς ἡμιθέους πρώτην δυναστείαν καταριθμοῦσι βασιλέων ὀκτώ· ὧν γέγονε
Μήνης, ὃς διασήμως αὐτῶν ἡγήσατο. ἀφ' οὗ
τοὺς ἐξ ἑκάστου γένους βασιλεύσαντας ἀναγρά-
ψομεν ὧν[2] ἡ διαδοχὴ τοῦτον ἔχει τὸν τρόπον·

α' Μήνης Θινίτης καὶ οἱ τούτου ἀπόγονοι [ιζ',
    ἐν ἄλλῳ δὲ][3] ζ'. ὃν Ἡρόδοτος Μῆνα
    ὠνόμασεν, ἐβασίλευσεν ἔτεσιν ξ'. οὗτος
    ὑπερόριον στρατείαν ἐποιήσατο καὶ ἔνδοξος
    ἐκρίθη, ὑπὸ[4] δὲ ἱπποποτάμου ἡρπάσθη.
β' Ἄθωθις ὁ τούτου υἱὸς ἦρξεν ἔτεσιν κζ', καὶ
    τὰ ἐν Μέμφει βασίλεια ᾠκοδόμησεν, ἰατρι-
    κήν τε ἐξήσκησε καὶ βίβλους ἀνατομικὰς
    συνέγραψε.
γ' Κενκένης ὁ τούτου υἱός, ἔτη λθ'.
δ' Οὐενέφης, ἔτη μβ'· ἐφ' οὗ λιμὸς κατέσχε
    τὴν χώραν, ὃς καὶ τὰς πυραμίδας τὰς περὶ
    Κωχώμην ἤγειρε.
ε' Οὐσαφάϊς,[5] ἔτη κ'.
ϛ' Νιεβάϊς,[6] ἔτη κϛ'.

---

[1] Bracketed by Müller.   [2] Vulgo ἀναγραψαμένων.
[3] Bracketed by Gelzer.   [4] ἴσπου A, ἵππου B.
[5] Οὐσαφαής A.   [6] Νιεβαής A.

Fr. 7 (a) (*from Syncellus*). ACCORDING TO EUSEBIUS.[1]

Here is the account which Eusebius gives of the Egyptian dynasties [after the Flood].

In succession to the Spirits of the Dead and the Demigods, the Egyptians reckon the First Dynasty to consist of eight kings. Among these was Mênês, whose rule in Egypt was illustrious. I shall record the rulers of each race from the time of Mênês ; their succession is as follows :

1. Mênês of This, with his [17, or in another copy] 7 descendants,—the king called Mên by Herodotus,—reigned for 60 years. He made a foreign expedition and won renown, but was carried off by a hippopotamus.
2. Athôthis, his son, ruled for 27 years. He built the palace at Memphis ; he practised medicine and wrote anatomical books.
3. Kenkenês, his son, for 39 years.
4. Uenephês, for 42 years. In his reign famine seized the land. He built the pyramids near Kôchôme.
5. Usaphaïs, for 20 years.
6. Niebaïs, for 26 years.

---

[1] The version (transmitted to us by Syncellus) which Eusebius gives of the *Epitome* of Manetho shows considerable differences from Africanus, both in the names of kings and in the length of their reigns. Peet (*Egypt and the Old Testament*, pp. 25 f.) says : " The astonishing variations between their figures are an eloquent testimony to what may happen to numbers in a few centuries through textual corruption." Petrie (*History of Egypt*, i. p. viii) compares the corruptions in such late Greek chronicles as those of the Ptolemies (c.v./A.D.).

ζ΄ Σεμέμψης, ἔτη ιη΄ · ἐφ᾽ οὗ πολλὰ παράσημα
ἐγένετο καὶ μεγίστη φθορά.
η΄ Οὐβιένθης, ἔτη κϛ΄.
Οἱ πάντες ἐβασίλευσαν ἔτη σνβ΄.

(b) EUSEBIUS, *Chronica* I. (Armenian Version),
pp. 94 sqq.

Post manes atque heroas primam dynastiam
numerant VIII regum, quorum primus fuit Menes,[1]
gloria regni administrandi praepollens : a quo exorsi
singulas regnantium familias diligenter scribemus,
quarum successiva series ita contexitur :

Menes Thinites eiusque posteri septem (quem
Herodotus Mina nuncupavit). Hic annis
XXX regnavit. Idem et extra regionis
suae fines cum exercitu progressus est, et
gloria rerum gestarum inclaruit. Ab hippo-
potamo genio[2] raptus est.

Athothis, huius filius, regno potitus est annis
XXVII. Is regia sibi palatia Memphi con-
struxit, et medicam item artem coluit, quin
et libros de ratione secandorum corporum
scripsit.

Cencenes eius filius, annis XXXIX.

Vavenephis, annis XLII, cuius aetate fames
regionem corripuit. Is pyramidas prope Cho
oppidum[3] excitavit.

[1] Corr. edd. : MSS. Memes.
[2] Müller conjectures the Greek original to have been :
ὑπὸ δαίμονος δὲ ἱπποποτάμου. But the Armenian text, liter-
ally translated, is : "by a horse-shaped river-monster"
(Karst, Margoliouth).

7. Semempsês, for 18 years. In his reign there
     were many portents and a very great calamity.
8. Ubienthês, for 26 years.

The total of all reigns, 252 years.[1]

(b) Armenian Version of Eusebius.

In succession to the Spirits of the Dead and the
Demigods, the Egyptians reckon the First Dynasty
to consist of eight kings. The first of these was
Mênês, who won high renown in the government of
his kingdom. Beginning with him, I shall carefully
record the royal families one by one : their succession
in detail is as follows :

Mênês of This (whom Herodotus named Min) and
     his seven descendants. He reigned for 30
     years, and advanced with his army beyond
     the frontiers of his realm, winning renown by
     his exploits. He was carried off by a hippo-
     potamus god (?).[2]
Athothis, his son, held the throne for 27 years. He
     built for himself a royal palace at Memphis,
     and also practised the art of medicine, writing
     books on the method of anatomy.
Cencenes, his son, for 39 years.
Vavenephis, for 42 years. In his time famine
     seized the land. He reared pyramids near
     the town of Cho.

---

[1] The actual total of the items given is 258 years.
[2] See note 2 on the text.

[3] Apparently = Χῶ κώμην, for Κωχώμην.

Usaphaïs, annis XX.

Niebaïs, annis XXVI.

Mempses, annis XVIII.   Sub hoc multa prodigia
    itemque maxima lues acciderunt.

Vibenthis,[1] annis XXVI.

Summa dominationis annorum CCLII.

Fr. 8.   *Syncellus*, p. 101.   *ΚΑΤΑ ΑΦΡΙΚΑΝΟΝ.*

Δευτέρα δυναστεία Θινιτῶν βασιλέων
ἐννέα, ὧν πρῶτος Βοηθός, ἔτη λη′ · ἐφ' οὗ χάσμα
κατὰ Βούβαστον ἐγένετο καὶ ἀπώλοντο πολλοί.

β′ Καιέχως, ἔτη λθ′ · ἐφ' οὗ οἱ βόες Ἄπις ἐν
    Μέμφει καὶ Μνεῦις ἐν Ἡλιουπόλει καὶ ὁ
    Μενδήσιος τράγος ἐνομίσθησαν εἶναι θεοί.

[1] One MS. (G) has Vibethis.

_____

[1] Karst gives 270 years as the total transmitted in the
Armenian version.   The total of the items as given above
is 228 years.

[2] Dynasty II.—to c. 2780 B.C.   For identifications with
the Monuments, etc., see Meyer, *Geschichte* [5], I. ii. p. 146 :
he identifies (1) Boêthos, (2) Kaiechôs or Kechôus, (3)
Binôthris, (4) Tlas, (5) Sethenês, (7) Nephercherês,
(8) Sesôchris.   For (1) to (5), see G. A. Reisner, *The
Development of the Egyptian Tomb*, 1936, p. 123.

[3] Bubastus or Bubastis (Baedeker [8], p. 181), near Zagazig
in the Delta : Anc. Egyptian *Per-Baste*, the *Pi-beseth* of

Usaphaïs, for 20 years.

Niebaïs, for 26 years.

Mempses, for 18 years.   In his reign many portents and a great pestilence occurred.

Vibenthis, for 26 years.

Total for the dynasty, 252 years.[1]

Dynasty II.

Fr. 8 (*from Syncellus*).   According to Africanus.

The Second Dynasty [2] consists of nine kings of This.   The first was Boêthos, for 38 years.   In his reign a chasm opened at Bubastus,[3] and many perished.

2. Kaiechôs, for 39 years.   In his reign the bulls,[4] Apis at Memphis and Mnevis at Heliopolis, and the Mendesian goat were worshipped as gods.

Ezekiel xxx. 17.   See also Herodotus, ii. 60, 137 f.   The kings of Dynasty XXII. resided at Bubastis.

Earthquakes have always been rare in Egypt (Euseb., *Chron. Graec.* p. 42, l. 25; Pliny, *H.N.* ii. 82); but Bubastis is situated in an unstable region: see H. G. Lyons in *Cairo Scientific Journal*, i. (1907), p. 182.   It stands on an earthquake line, which runs to Crete.   A deep boring made at Bubastis failed to reach rock.

[4] The worship of Apis is earlier even than Dynasty II.: see Palermo Stone, Schäfer, p. 21, No. 12 (in reign of Udymu).   For Apis, see Herodotus, ii. 153, and Diod. Sic. i. 84, 85 (where all three animals are mentioned).   The goat was a cult animal in very early times: *cf.* Herodotus, ii. 46.

35

γ΄ Βίνωθρις, ἔτη μζ΄· ἐφ᾽ οὗ ἐκρίθη τὰς
     γυναῖκας βασιλείας γέρας ἔχειν.
δ΄ Τλάς, ἔτη ιζ΄.
ε΄ Σεθένης, ἔτη μα΄.
ϛ΄ Χαίρης, ἔτη ιζ΄.
ζ΄ Νεφερχέρης, ἔτη κε΄· ἐφ᾽ οὗ μυθεύεται
     τὸν Νεῖλον μέλιτι κεκραμένον ἡμέρας ἕν-
     δεκα ῥυῆναι.
η΄ Σέσωχρις, ἔτη μη΄, ὃς ὕψος εἶχε πηχῶν ε΄,
     παλαιστῶν [1] γ΄.
θ΄ Χενερής, ἔτη λ΄.
Ὁμοῦ, ἔτη τβ΄.

Ὁμοῦ πρώτης καὶ δευτέρας δυναστείας [μετὰ τὸν
κατακλυσμὸν] ἔτη φνε΄ κατὰ τὴν δευτέραν ἔκδοσιν
Ἀφρικανοῦ.

Fr. 9.   Syncellus, p. 103.   ΚΑΤΑ ΕΥΣΕΒΙΟΝ.

Δευτέρα δυναστεία βασιλέων ἐννέα.

Πρῶτος Βῶχος, ἐφ᾽ οὗ χάσμα κατὰ Βούβαστον
ἐγένετο, καὶ πολλοὶ ἀπώλοντο.

Μεθ᾽ ὃν δεύτερος Καιχῶος,[2] ὅτε καὶ ὁ Ἆπις καὶ
ὁ Μνεῦις, ἀλλὰ καὶ ὁ Μενδήσιος τράγος θεοὶ
ἐνομίσθησαν.

---

[1] Boeckh, Bunsen : MSS. πλάτος.
[2] Müller : MSS. μεθ᾽ ὃν καὶ δεύτερος Χῶος.

3. Binôthris, for 47 years.   In his reign it was
   decided that women [1] might hold the kingly
   office.
4. Tlas, for 17 years.
5. Sethenês, for 41 years.
6. Chairês, for 17 years.
7. Nephercherês, for 25 years.   In his reign, the
   story goes, the Nile flowed blended with
   honey for 11 days.
8. Sesôchris, for 48 years :   his stature was 5 cubits,
   3 palms.[2]
9. Chenerês, for 30 years.

Total, 302 years.

Total for the First and Second Dynasties [after the
Flood], 555 years, according to the second edition of
Africanus.

Fr. 9 (*from Syncellus*).   ACCORDING TO EUSEBIUS.

The Second Dynasty consisted of nine kings.
First came Bôchos, in whose reign a chasm opened
at Bubastus, and many perished.

He was succeeded by Kaichôos (or Chôos), in
whose time Apis and Mnevis and also the Mendesian
goat were worshipped as gods.

---

[1] No queens' names are recorded in the Royal Lists
of Abydos and Karnak.   Herodotus (ii. 100) records
one queen :   Diod. Sic. i. 44 (from Hecataeus) reckons
the number of Egyptian queens as five.

[2] The stature of each king is said to be noted in the
records mentioned by Diodorus Siculus, i. 44, 4.   *Cf.
infra*, Fr. 35, No. 3, App. II. No. 6 (p. 216).

γ' Βίοφις, ἐφ' οὗ ἐκρίθη καὶ τὰς γυναῖκας
βασιλείας γέρας ἔχειν. καὶ μετὰ τούτους
ἄλλοι τρεῖς, ἐφ' ὧν οὐδὲν παράσημον
ἐγένετο.

ζ' Ἐπὶ δὲ τοῦ ἑβδόμου μυθεύεται τὸν Νεῖλον
μέλιτι κεκραμένον ἡμέραις ἕνδεκα ῥυῆναι.

η' Μεθ' ὃν Σέσωχρις <, ἔτη> μη', ὃς λέγεται
γεγονέναι ὕψος ἔχων πηχῶν ε', παλαιστῶν
γ' τὸ μέγεθος.

θ' Ἐπὶ δὲ τοῦ θ' οὐδὲν ἀξιομνημόνευτον ὑπῆρχεν.
Οἳ καὶ ἐβασίλευσαν ἔτεσι σϟζ'.

Ὁμοῦ πρώτης καὶ δευτέρας δυναστείας ἔτη φμθ'
κατὰ τὴν ἔκδοσιν Εὐσεβίου.

Fr. 10.   EUSEBIUS, *Chronica* I. (Armenian Version),
p. 96.

Secunda dynastia regum IX.

Primus Bochus : sub eo specus ingens Bubasti
subsedit multosque mortales hausit.

Post eum Cechous, quo tempore [1] Apis et Mnevis
atque Mendesius hircus dii esse putabantur.

Deinde Biophis, sub quo lege statutum est, ut
feminae quoque regiam dignitatem obtinerent.

Tum alii tres, quorum aetate nullum insigne
facinus patratum est.

Sub septimo mythici aiunt flumen Nilum melle
simul et aqua fluxisse undecim diebus.

[1] Müller : MS. idemque.

3. Biophis, in whose reign it was decided that women also might hold the kingly office. In the reigns of the three succeeding kings, no notable event occurred.

7. In the seventh reign, as the story goes, the Nile flowed blended with honey for 11 days.

8. Next, Sesôchris was king for 48 years : the greatness of his stature is said to have been 5 cubits 3 palms.

9. In the ninth reign there happened no event worthy of mention. These kings ruled for 297 years.

Total for the First and Second Dynasties, 549 years, according to the recension of Eusebius.

Fr. 10. Armenian Version of Eusebius.

The Second Dynasty consisted of nine kings.

First came Bôchus, in whose reign a huge hole opened at Bubastus, and swallowed up many persons.

He was succeeded by Cechous, in whose time Apis and Mnevis and the Mendesian goat were worshipped as gods.

Next came Biophis, in whose reign it was decreed by law that women also might hold the royal office.

In the reigns of the three succeeding kings, no notable event occurred.

Under the seventh king fabulists tell how the river Nile flowed with honey as well as water for 11 days.

Postea Sesochris annis XLVIII, quem aiunt quin-
que cubitos altum, tres vero palmos latum fuisse.

Sub nono tandem nihil memoria dignum actum
est.

Hi regnaverunt annis CCXCVII.

Fr. 11.   *Syncellus*, p. 104.   *ΑΦΡΙΚΑΝΟΥ.*

Τρίτη δυναστεία Μεμφιτῶν βασιλέων
ἐννέα, ὧν α' Νεχερώφης,[1] ἔτη κη'· ἐφ' οὗ
Λίβυες ἀπέστησαν Αἰγυπτίων, καὶ τῆς σελήνης παρὰ
λόγον αὐξηθείσης διὰ δέος ἑαυτοὺς παρέδοσαν.

β' Τόσορθρος, ἔτη κθ', ‹ἐφ' οὗ 'Ιμούθης[2]›.
οὗτος 'Ασκληπιὸς ‹παρὰ τοῖς[2]› Αἰγυπτίοις

¹ Νεχορόφης A.   ² Conj. Sethe.

---

¹ For this absurd perversion of the Greek words, see
p. 36 n. 1: πλάτος was added, perhaps as a corruption
of παλαιστῶν, and replaced μέγεθος in the Greek version of
Eusebius.

² The Old Kingdom, Dynasties III.-V.: c. 2780–c. 2420 B.C.
Dynasty III., c. 2780–c. 2720 B.C.   For identifications with
monumental and other evidence, see Meyer, *Geschichte* ⁵,
I. ii. p. 174 : he identifies (2) Tosorthos (Zoser I.—" the
Holy "), and holds that (1) Necherôphês is one name
of Kha'sekhemui, (6) Tosertasis may be Zoser II. Atoti,
and (9) Kerpherês may be Neferkerê' II.

³ Zoser was not the first builder with hewn stone : his
predecessor, Kha'sekhemui, used squared blocks of limestone for building purposes ; see Petrie, *Royal Tombs*,
ii. p. 13.   Granite blocks had already formed the floor
of the tomb of Udymu (Dynasty I.).

Two tombs of Zoser are known : (1) a mastaba at Bêt
Khallâf near This (Baedeker ⁸, p. 231), see J. Garstang,
Mahâsna and Bêt Khallâf; and (2) the famous Step

Next, Sesochris ruled for 48 years : he is said to have been 5 cubits high and 3 palms broad.[1]

Finally, under the ninth king no memorable event occurred.

These kings reigned for 297 years.

DYNASTY III.

Fr. 11 (*from Syncellus*). THE ACCOUNT OF AFRI-
CANUS.

The Third Dynasty [2] comprised nine kings of Memphis.

1. Necherôphês, for 28 years. In his reign the
   Libyans revolted against Egypt, and when
   the moon waxed beyond reckoning, they
   surrendered in terror.

2. Tosorthros,[3] for 29 years. ⟨In his reign lived
   Imuthês,[4]⟩ who because of his medical skill
   has the reputation of Asclepios among the

Pyramid at Sakkâra, which was the work o. the great architect Imhotep (Baedeker [8], p. 156 f.).

[4] If the emendation in the text be not accepted, the statement would surely be too inaccurate to be attributed to Manetho. The Egyptian Asclepios was Imouth or Imhotep of Memphis, physician and architect to King Zoser, afterwards deified : on Philae (now for the most part submerged) Ptolemy II. Philadelphus built a little temple to Imhotep. See Sethe, *Untersuchungen*, ii. 4 (1902) : J. B. Hurry, *Imhotep* (Oxford, 1926).

One of the Oxyrhynchus Papyri, edited by Grenfell and Hunt, P. Oxy. XI. 1381, of ii./A.D., has for its subject the eulogy of Imuthês-Asclepius : the fragment pre-served is part of the prelude. See G. Manteuffel, *De Opusculis Graecis Aegypti e papyris, ostracis, lapidibusque collectis*, 1930, No. 3.

κατὰ τὴν ἰατρικὴν νενόμισται, καὶ τὴν διὰ
ξεστῶν λίθων οἰκοδομίαν εὕρατο· ἀλλὰ καὶ
γραφῆς ἐπεμελήθη.

γ′ Τύρεις,[1] ἔτη ζ′.
δ′ Μέσωχρις, ἔτη ιζ′.
ε′ Σώϋφις, ἔτη ις′.
ς′ Τοσέρτασις, ἔτη ιθ′.
ζ′ Ἄχης, ἔτη μβ′.
η′ Σήφουρις, ⟨ἔτη⟩ λ′.
θ′ Κερφέρης, ἔτη κς′.

Ὁμοῦ, ἔτη σιδ′.
Ὁμοῦ τῶν τριῶν δυναστειῶν κατὰ Ἀφρικανὸν
ἔτη ψξθ′.

Fr. 12 (a).   Syncellus, p. 106.   ΚΑΤΑ ΕΥΣΕΒΙΟΝ.

Τρίτη δυναστεία Μεμφιτῶν βασιλέων
ὀκτώ,

α′ Νεχέρωχις, ἐφ᾽ οὗ Λίβυες ἀπέστησαν Αἰγυπτίων, καὶ τῆς σελήνης παρὰ λόγον αὐξηθείσης διὰ δέος ἑαυτοὺς παρέδοσαν.
β′ Μεθ᾽ ὃν Σέσορθος . . ., ὃς Ἀσκληπιὸς παρὰ
Αἰγυπτίοις ἐκλήθη διὰ τὴν ἰατρικήν. οὗτος
καὶ τὴν διὰ ξεστῶν λίθων οἰκοδομὴν εὕρατο,
ἀλλὰ καὶ γραφῆς ἐπεμελήθη.

Οἱ δὲ λοιποὶ ἓξ οὐδὲν ἀξιομνημόνευτον ἔπραξαν.
Οἳ καὶ ἐβασίλευσαν ἔτεσιν ρη′.
Ὁμοῦ τῶν τριῶν δυναστειῶν κατὰ τὸν Εὐσέβιον
ἔτη ψμζ′.

[1] Τύρις Α.

Egyptians, and who was the inventor of the art of building with hewn stone. He also devoted attention to writing.

3. Tyreis (or Tyris), for 7 years.
4. Mesôchris, for 17 years.
5. Sôÿphis, for 16 years.
6. Tosertasis, for 19 years.
7. Achês, for 42 years.
8. Sêphuris, for 30 years.
9. Kerpherês, for 26 years.

Total, 214 years.

Total for the first three dynasties, according to Africanus, 769 years.

Fr. 12 (a). (*from Syncellus*). ACCORDING TO EUSEBIUS.

The Third Dynasty consisted of eight kings of Memphis :

1. Necherôchis, in whose reign the Libyans revolted against Egypt, and when the moon waxed beyond reckoning, they surrendered in terror.
2. He was succeeded by Sesorthos . . . : he was styled Asclepios in Egypt because of his medical skill. He was also the inventor of the art of building with hewn stone, and devoted attention to writing as well.

The remaining six kings achieved nothing worthy of mention. These eight kings reigned for 198 years.

Total for the first three dynasties, according to Eusebius, 747 years.

(b) Eusebius, *Chronica* I. (Armenian Version),
p. 96.

Tertia dynastia Memphitarum regum VIII.

Necherochis, sub quo Libyes ab Aegyptiis defecerunt : mox intempestive [1] crescente luna territi ad obsequium reversi sunt.

Deinde Sosorthus . . ., qui ob medicam artem Aesculapius ab Aegyptiis vocitatus est. Is etiam sectis lapidibus aedificiorum struendorum auctor fuit : libris praeterea scribendis curam impendit.

Sex reliqui nihil commemorandum gesserunt. Regnatum est annis CXCVII.

Fr. 14. *Syncellus*, p. 105. *ΚΑΤΑ ΑΦΡΙΚΑΝΟΝ.*

Τετάρτη δυναστεία Μεμφιτῶν συγγενείας ἑτέρας βασιλεῖς η'.

---

[1] intempestive, Margoliouth ; importune, Aucher ; immaniter, Mai.

---

[1] Dynasty IV., c. 2720–c. 2560 B.C. For identifications with monumental and other evidence, see Meyer, *Geschichte* ⁵, I. ii. p. 181 : he identifies (1) Sôris (Snofru), (2) Suphis I. (Cheops, Khufu), then after Dedefrê' (not mentioned by Manetho), (3) Suphis II. (Chephren), (4) Mencherês (Mycerinus), and finally (an uncertain identification). (7) Sebercherês (Shepseskaf). For (3) Chephren and

(b) Armenian Version of Eusebius.

The Third Dynasty consisted of eight kings of Memphis :

Necherochis, in whose reign the Libyans revolted against Egypt : later when the moon waxed unseasonably, they were terrified and returned to their allegiance.

Next came Sosorthus . . . : he was styled Aesculapius by the Egyptians because of his medical skill. He was also the inventor of building with hewn stone ; and in addition he devoted care to the writing of books.

The six remaining kings did nothing worthy of mention. The reigns of the whole dynasty amount to 197 years.

Dynasty IV.

Fr. 14 (*from Syncellus*). According to Africanus.

The Fourth Dynasty [1] comprised eight kings of Memphis, belonging to a different line :

(4) Mycerinus, Diodorus i. 64 gives the good variants (3) Chabryês and (4) Mencherinus. On the Chronology of Dynasty IV. see Reisner, *Mycerinus* (*cf. infra*, note 2), pp. 243 ff. Reisner reads the name Dedefrê in the form Radedef, and identifies it with Ratoisês.

The Greek tales of the oppression of Egypt by Cheops and Chephren, etc., are believed to be the inventions of dragomans. *Cf.* Herodotus, ii. 124 (contempt for the gods), 129 (Mycerinus), with How and Wells's notes. Africanus has, moreover, acquired as a treasure the " sacred book " of Cheops.

α΄ Σῶρις, ἔτη κθ΄.

β΄ Σοῦφις, ἔτη ξγ΄ · ὃς τὴν μεγίστην ἤγειρε
πυραμίδα, ἥν φησιν Ἡρόδοτος[1] ὑπὸ Χέοπος
γεγονέναι. οὗτος δὲ καὶ ὑπερόπτης εἰς
θεοὺς ἐγένετο καὶ τὴν ἱερὰν συνέγραψε
βίβλον, ἣν ὡς μέγα χρῆμα ἐν Αἰγύπτῳ
γενόμενος ἐκτησάμην.

γ΄ Σοῦφις, ἔτη ξς΄.

δ΄ Μεγχέρης, ἔτη ξγ΄.

ε΄ Ῥατοίσης, ἔτη κε΄.

ϛ΄ Βίχερις, ἔτη κβ΄.

ζ΄ Σεβερχέρης, ἔτη ζ΄.

η΄ Θαμφθίς, ἔτη θ΄.

Ὁμοῦ, ἔτη σοζ΄.[2]

Ὁμοῦ τῶν δ΄ δυναστειῶν τῶν [μετὰ τὸν κατα-
κλυσμὸν] ἔτη ͵αμϛ΄ κατ᾽ Ἀφρικανόν.

---

[1] Hdt. ii. 124.　　　　[2] σοδ΄ A.

---

[1] On the Pyramids of Giza, see Baedeker [8], pp. 133 ff. ;
Noel F. Wheeler, " Pyramids and their Purpose,"
Antiquity, 1935, pp. 5-21, 161-189, 292-304 ; and for
the fourth king of Dynasty IV. see G. A. Reisner,
Mycerinus: The Temples of the Third Pyramid at Giza,
1931. Notwithstanding their colossal dimensions and
marvellous construction, the Pyramids have not escaped
detraction : Frontinus (*De Aquis*, i. 16) contrasts " the

1. Sôris, for 29 years.
2. Suphis [I.], for 63 years. He reared the Great
   Pyramid,[1] which Herodotus says was built
   by Cheops. Suphis conceived a contempt
   for the gods : he also composed the Sacred
   Book, which I acquired in my visit to Egypt [2]
   because of its high renown.
3. Suphis [II.], for 66 years.
4. Mencherês, for 63 years.
5. Ratoisês, for 25 years.
6. Bicheris, for 22 years.
7. Sebercherês, for 7 years.
8. Thamphthis, for 9 years.

Total, 277 years.[3]
Total for the first four dynasties [after the Flood],
1046 years according to Africanus.

idle pyramids " with " the indispensable structures " of
the several aqueducts at Rome ; and Pliny (*H.N.* 36, 8,
§ 75) finds in the pyramids " an idle and foolish ostenta-
tion of royal wealth ". But the pyramids have, at any
rate, preserved the names of their builders, especially
Cheops, to all future ages, although, as Sir Thomas Browne
characteristically wrote (*Urn-Burial*, Chap. 5): " To . . .
be but pyramidally extant is a fallacy of duration " . . .
" Who can but pity the founder of the Pyramids ? "
The modern Egyptologist says : " The Great Pyramid
is the earliest and most impressive witness . . . to the
final emergence of organized society from prehistoric
chaos and local conflict " (J. H. Breasted, *History of
Egypt*, p. 119).
   [2] Africanus went from Palestine to Alexandria, attracted
by the renown of the philosopher Heraclas, Bishop of
Alexandria : see Eusebius, *Hist. Eccl.* vi. 31, 2.
   [3] The MS. A gives as total 274 : the items add to 284.

Fr. 15. *Syncellus*, p. 106. *ΚΑΤΑ ΕΥΣΕΒΙΟΝ.*

Τετάρτη δυναστεία βασιλέων ιζ' Μεμφιτῶν συγγενείας ἑτέρας βασιλείας.

῏Ων τρίτος Σοῦφις, ὁ τὴν μεγίστην πυραμίδα
ἐγείρας, ἥν φησιν ῾Ηρόδοτος ὑπὸ Χέοπος γεγονέναι,
ὃς καὶ ὑπερόπτης εἰς θεοὺς γέγονεν, ὡς μετανοή-
σαντα αὐτὸν τὴν ἱερὰν συγγράψαι βίβλον, ἥν ὡς
μέγα χρῆμα Αἰγύπτιοι περιέπουσι. τῶν δὲ λοιπῶν
οὐδὲν ἀξιομνημόνευτον ἀνεγράφη. οἳ καὶ ἐβασίλευσαν ἔτεσιν υμη'.

῾Ομοῦ τῶν δ' δυναστειῶν [μετὰ τὸν κατακλυσμὸν]
,αρϟε' κατὰ Εὐσέβιον.

Fr. 16. Eusebius, *Chronica* I. (Armenian Version),
p. 97.

Quarta dynastia Memphitarum regum XVII ex
alia regia familia, quorum tertius, Suphis, maximae
pyramidis auctor, quam quidem Herodotus a Cheope
structam ait : qui in deos ipsos superbiebat ; tum
facti poenitens sacrum librum [1] conscribebat, quem
Aegyptii instar magni thesauri habere se putant.
De reliquis regibus nihil memorabile litteris man-
datum est. Regnatum est annis CCCCXLVIII.

[1] libros Sacrarii (Aucher), " the sanctuary books,"
" books for the shrine."

Fr. 15 (*from Syncellus*). ACCORDING TO EUSEBIUS.

The Fourth Dynasty comprised seventeen kings of Memphis belonging to a different royal line.

Of these the third was Suphis, the builder of the Great Pyramid, which Herodotus says was built by Cheops. Suphis conceived a contempt for the gods, but repenting of this, he composed the Sacred Book, which the Egyptians hold in high esteem.

Of the remaining kings no achievement worthy of mention has been recorded.

This dynasty reigned for 448 years.

Total for the first four dynasties [after the Flood], 1195 years according to Eusebius.

Fr. 16.   ARMENIAN VERSION OF EUSEBIUS.

The Fourth Dynasty consisted of seventeen kings of Memphis belonging to a different royal line. The third of these kings, Suphis, was the builder of the Great Pyramid, which Herodotus declares to have been built by Cheops. Suphis behaved arrogantly towards the gods themselves : then, in penitence, he composed the Sacred Book in which the Egyptians believe they possess a great treasure. Of the remaining kings nothing worthy of mention is recorded in history. The reigns of the whole dynasty amount to 448 years.

Fr. 18.   *Syncellus*, p. 107.   *ΚΑΤΑ ΑΦΡΙΚΑΝΟΝ.*

Πέμπτη δυναστεία βασιλέων η' ἐξ Ἐλεφαντίνης.

α' Οὐσερχέρης, ἔτη κη'.
β' Σεφρής, ἔτη ιγ'.
γ' Νεφερχέρης, ἔτη κ'.
δ' Σισίρης, ἔτη ζ'.
ε' Χέρης, ἔτη κ'.
ϛ' Ῥαθούρης, ἔτη μδ'.
ζ' Μενχέρης, ἔτη θ'.
η' Τανχέρης,[1] ἔτη μδ'.
θ' Ὄννος,[2] ἔτη λγ'.

Ὁμοῦ, ἔτη σμη'. γίνονται σὺν τοῖς προτεταγμένοις ͵αμϛ' ἔτεσι τῶν τεσσάρων δυναστειῶν ἔτη
͵ασϟδ'.

Fr. 19 (a).   *Syncellus*, p. 109.   *ΚΑΤΑ ΕΥΣΕΒΙΟΝ.*

Πέμπτη δυναστεία βασιλέων τριάκοντα
ἑνὸς ἐξ Ἐλεφαντίνης. ὧν πρῶτος Ὀθόης.
οὗτος ὑπὸ τῶν δορυφόρων ἀνῃρέθη.

[1] Τατχέρης corr. Lepsius.   [2] Ὄβνος A.

---

[1] Dynasty V. c. 2560–c. 2420 B.C. For identifications with
monumental and other evidence, see Meyer, *Geschichte*[5],
I. ii. p. 203 : his list runs (1) Userkaf, (2) Sahurēʿ, (3)
Nefererkerēʿ Kakai, (4) Nefrefrēʿ or Shepseskerēʿ, (5)
Khaʿneferrēʿ, (6) Neweserrēʿ Ini, (7) Menkeuhor (Akeuhor),
(8) Dedkerēʿ Asosi, (9) Unas.

DYNASTY V.

Fr. 18 (*from Syncellus*). ACCORDING TO AFRICANUS.

The Fifth Dynasty [1] was composed of eight kings of Elephantine :

1. Usercherês, for 28 years.
2. Sephrês, for 13 years.
3. Nephercherês, for 20 years.
4. Sisirês, for 7 years.
5. Cherês, for 20 years.
6. Rathurês, for 44 years.
7. Mencherês, for 9 years.
8. Tancherês (? Tatcherês), for 44 years.
9. Onnus, for 33 years.
Total, 248 years.[2]

Along with the aforementioned 1046 years of the first four dynasties, this amounts to 1294 years.

Fr. 19 (a) (*from Syncellus*). ACCORDING TO EUSEBIUS.

The Fifth Dynasty consisted of thirty-one kings of Elephantine. Of these the first was Othoês,[3] who was murdered by his bodyguard.

---

[2] The items total 218 years ; but if the reign of Othoês, the first king of Dynasty VI. is added, the total will then be 248 years.

[3] In the chronology of Eusebius, Dynasty V. is suppressed : the kings whom he mentions belong to Dynasty VI.

ʽΟ δὲ δʹ Φίωψ, ἑξαέτης ἀρξάμενος, ἐβασίλευσε
μέχρις ἐτῶν ἑκατόν. γίνονται οὖν σὺν τοῖς προτεταγμένοις ͵αρϟεʹ ἔτεσι τῶν τεσσάρων δυναστειῶν
⟨ἔτη⟩ ͵ασϟεʹ.

(b) Eusebius, *Chronica* I. (Armenian Version),
p. 97.

Quinta dynastia regum XXXI Elephantinorum,
quorum primus Othius, qui a satellitibus suis occisus
est.   Quartus Phiops, qui regiam dignitatem a sexto
aetatis anno ad centesimum usque tenuit.

Fr. 20.   *Syncellus*, p. 108.   ΚΑΤΑ ΑΦΡΙΚΑΝΟΝ.

Ἕκτη δυναστεία βασιλέων ἐξ Μεμφιτῶν.
αʹ ʼΟθόης,[1] ἔτη λʹ, ὃς ὑπὸ τῶν δορυφόρων
     ἀνῃρέθη.
βʹ Φιός, ἔτη νγʹ.
γʹ Μεθουσοῦφις, ἔτη ζʹ.

[1] ʽΟθώης A.

---

[1] Karst translates the Armenian as referring to the
sixtieth year—" began to rule at the age of 60 " ; but
Aucher's Armenian text has the equivalent of *sexennis*,
" six years old " (Margoliouth).

The fourth king, Phiôps, succeeding when six years old, reigned until his hundredth year. Thus, along with the aforementioned 1195 years of the first four dynasties, this amounts to 1295 years.

(b) ARMENIAN VERSION OF EUSEBIUS.

The Fifth Dynasty consisted of thirty-one kings of Elephantine. Of these the first was Othius, who was killed by his attendants. The fourth king was Phiôps, who held the royal office from his sixth [1] right down to his hundredth year.

DYNASTY VI.

Fr. 20 (*from Syncellus*).   ACCORDING TO AFRICANUS.

The Sixth Dynasty [2] consisted of six kings of Memphis :

1. Othoês, for 30 years : he was murdered by his bodyguard.
2. Phius, for 53 years.
3. Methusuphis, for 7 years.

---

[2] Dynasties VI.-VIII., the last Memphites, *c.* 2420– *c.* 2240 B.C.   Dynasty VI. Meyer (*Geschichte* [5], I. ii. p. 236) identifies as follows : (1) Othoês (Teti or Atoti), then after Userkerê', (2) Phius (Pepi I.), (3) Methusuphis (Merenrê' I.), (4) Phiôps (Pepi II.), (5) Menthesuphis (Merenrê' II.), (6) Nitôcris.   Sethe (*Sesostris*, p. 3) draws attention to the intentional differentiation of the same family-name—Phius for Pepi I., and Phiôps for Pepi II. : so also (3) Methusuphis and (5) Menthesuphis, and *cf. infra* on Psametik in Dynasty XXVI.   Are these variations due to Manetho or to his source ?

δ' Φίωψ, ἑξαέτης ἀρξάμενος βασιλεύειν, διε-
γένετο μέχρι ἐτῶν ρ'.

ε' Μενθεσοῦφις, ἔτος ἕν.

ς' Νίτωκρις, γεννικωτάτη καὶ εὐμορφοτάτη
τῶν κατ' αὐτὴν γενομένη, ξανθὴ τὴν χροιάν,
ἣ τὴν τρίτην ἤγειρε πυραμίδα, ἐβασίλευσεν
ἔτη ιβ'.

'Ομοῦ, ἔτη σγ'. γίνονται σὺν τοῖς προτεταγμένοις ,ασϟδ' τῶν ε' δυναστειῶν ἔτη ,αυϟζ'.

Fr. 21 (a).   Syncellus, p. 109.   ΚΑΤΑ ΕΥΣΕΒΙΟΝ.

Ἕκτη δυναστεία.

Γυνὴ Νίτωκρις ἐβασίλευσε, τῶν κατ' αὐτὴν
γεννικωτάτη καὶ εὐμορφοτάτη, ξανθή τε τὴν χροιὰν
ὑπάρξασα, ἣ καὶ λέγεται τὴν τρίτην πυραμίδα
ᾠκοδομηκέναι.

---

[1] The remarkable descriptions of social disorganization
and anarchy, addressed to an aged king in the Leiden
Papyrus of Ipuwer and known as The Admonitions of an
Egyptian Sage, are, according to Erman, to be associated
with the end of this reign : see A. Erman, " Die Mahnworte
eines ägyptischen Propheten " in Sitz. der preuss. Akad.
der Wissenschaften, xlii., 1919, p. 813.

[2] Nitôcris is doubtless the Neit-oḳre(t) of the Turin
Papyrus : the name means " Neith is Excellent " (cf.
App. II. Eratosthenes, No. 22, Ἀθηνᾶ νικηφόρος), and was
a favourite name under the Saïte Dynasty (Dyn. XXVI.),
which was devoted to the worship of Neith.   See
Herodotus, ii. 100, 134, Diod. Sic. I. 64. 14 (if Rhodôpis
is to be identified with Nitôcris), Strabo 17, 1. 33 (a
Cinderella-like story), Pliny, N.H. 36. 12. 78, and G. A.
Wainwright, Sky-Religion, pp. 41 ff.

A queen's reign ending the Dynasty is followed by a
period of confusion, just as after Dyn. XII. when Queen

4. Phiôps, who began to reign at the age of six, and continued until his hundredth year.[1]

5. Menthesuphis, for 1 year.

6. Nitôcris,[2] the noblest and loveliest of the women of her time, of fair complexion, the builder of the third pyramid, reigned for 12 years.

Total, 203 years.[3] Along with the aforementioned 1294 years of the first five dynasties, this amounts to 1497 years.

Fr. 21 (a) (*from Syncellus*). According to Eusebius.

The Sixth Dynasty.

There was a queen Nitôcris, the noblest and loveliest of the women of her time ; she had a fair complexion, and is said to have built the third pyramid.

Scemiophris (Sebeknofrurê') closes the line : *cf.* perhaps, in Dyn. IV., Thamphthis, of whom nothing is known.

In 1932 Professor Selim Hassan discovered at Giza the tomb of Queen Khentkawes, a tomb of monumental dimensions, the so-called fourth or " false " pyramid. Khentkawes was the daughter of Mycerinus ; and, disregarding the chronological difficulty, H. Junker, in *Mitteilungen des Deutschen Instituts für Ägyptische Altertumskunde in Kairo*, iii. 2 (1932), pp. 144-149, put forward the theory that the name Nitôcris is derived from Khentkawes, and that Manetho refers here to the so-called fourth pyramid, which merits the description (Fr. 21(b)),— " with the aspect of a mountain ". See further B. van de Walle in *L'Antiquité Classique*, 3 (1934), pp. 303-312.

[3] The correct total is 197 years : the reign of Phiôps is reckoned at 100, instead of 94 years (the Turin Papyrus gives 90 + x years).

Οἱ καὶ ἐβασίλευσαν [1] ἔτη τρία· ἐν ἄλλῳ σγ'.

Γίνονται σὺν τοῖς προτεταγμένοις ,ασϟε' τῶν πέντε δυναστειῶν ἔτη ,αυϟη'.

Σημειωτέον ὁπόσον Εὐσέβιος Ἀφρικανοῦ λείπεται ἀκριβείας ἔν τε τῇ τῶν βασιλέων ποσότητι καὶ ταῖς τῶν ὀνομάτων ὑφαιρέσεσι καὶ τοῖς χρόνοις, σχεδὸν τὰ Ἀφρικανοῦ αὐταῖς λέξεσι γράφων.

(b) Eusebius, *Chronica* I. (Armenian Version), p. 97.

Sexta dynastia. Femina quaedam Nitocris regnavit, omnium aetatis suae virorum fortissima et mulierum formosissima, flava rubris genis. Ab hac tertia pyramis excitata dicitur, speciem collis prae se ferens.

Ab his quoque regnatum est annis CCIII.

Fr. 23. *Syncellus*, p. 108. ΚΑΤΑ ΑΦΡΙΚΑΝΟΝ.

Ἑβδόμη δυναστεία Μεμφιτῶν βασιλέων ο', οἱ ἐβασίλευσαν ἡμέρας ο'.

Fr. 24 (a). *Syncellus*, p. 109. ΚΑΤΑ ΕΥΣΕΒΙΟΝ.

Ἑβδόμη δυναστεία Μεμφιτῶν βασιλέων πέντε, οἱ ἐβασίλευσαν ἡμέρας οε'.

[1] ἢ καὶ ἐβασίλευσεν m.

These rulers (or this ruler) reigned for three years : in another copy, 203 years. Along with the aforementioned 1295 years of the first five dynasties, this amounts to 1498 years.

(Syncellus adds) : It must be noted how much less accurate Eusebius is than Africanus in the number of kings he gives, in the omission of names, and in dates, although he practically repeats the account of Africanus in the same words.

(b) Armenian Version of Eusebius.

The Sixth Dynasty. There was a queen Nitôcris, braver than all the men of her time, the most beautiful of all the women, fair-skinned with red cheeks. By her, it is said, the third pyramid was reared, with the aspect of a mountain.

The united reigns of all the kings amount to 203 years.

Dynasty VII.

Fr. 23 (*from Syncellus*). According to Africanus.

The Seventh Dynasty [1] consisted of seventy kings of Memphis, who reigned for 70 days.

Fr. 24 (a) (*from Syncellus*). According to Eusebius.

The Seventh Dynasty consisted of five kings of Memphis, who reigned for 75 days.

[1] Dynasty VII.—a mere interregnum, or per'od of confusion until one king gained supreme power.

57

(b) Eusebius, *Chronica* I. (Armenian Version),
p. 97.

Septima dynastia Memphitarum regum V, qui
annis LXXV dominati sunt.

Fr. 25.   *Syncellus*, p. 108.   ΚΑΤΑ ΑΦΡΙΚΑΝΟΝ.

'Ογδόη δυναστεία Μεμφιτῶν βασιλέων
κζ', οἳ ἐβασίλευσαν ἔτη ρμς'. γίνονται σὺν
τοῖς προτεταγμένοις ἔτη ,αχλθ' τῶν ὀκτὼ δυναστειῶν.

Fr. 26 (a).   *Syncellus*, p. 110.   ΚΑΤΑ ΕΥΣΕΒΙΟΝ.

'Ογδόη δυναστεία Μεμφιτῶν βασιλέων
πέντε, οἳ ἐβασίλευσαν ἔτη ἑκατόν. γίνονται
σὺν τοῖς προτεταγμένοις ἔτη ,αφλη' τῶν ὀκτὼ
δυναστειῶν.

(b) Eusebius, *Chronica* I. (Armenian Version),
p. 97.

Octava dynastia Memphitarum regum V,[1] quorum
dominatio annos centum occupavit.

[1] V Aucher : aliter Mai.

---

[1] Dynasty VIII., according to Barbarus (Fr. 4) fourteen
kings for 140 years :   according to Meyer, probably eighteen
kings who reigned for 146 years.

[*Footnote continued on opposite page.*

(b) ARMENIAN VERSION OF EUSEBIUS.

The Seventh Dynasty consisted of five kings of Memphis, who held sway for 75 years.

DYNASTY VIII.

Fr. 25 (*from Syncellus*). ACCORDING TO AFRICANUS.

The Eighth Dynasty [1] consisted of twenty-seven kings of Memphis, who reigned for 146 years.   Along with the aforementioned reigns, this amounts to 1639 years for the first eight dynasties.

Fr. 26 (a) (*from Syncellus*). ACCORDING TO EUSEBIUS.

The Eighth Dynasty consisted of five kings of Memphis, who reigned for 100 years.   Along with the aforementioned reigns, this amounts to 1598 years for the first eight dynasties.

(b) ARMENIAN VERSION OF EUSEBIUS.

The Eighth Dynasty consisted of five [2] kings of Memphis, whose rule lasted for 100 years.

" The Turin Papyrus closes the first great period of Egyptian history at the end of what appears to be Manetho's VIIIth Dynasty (the last Memphites) " : it reckons 955 years from Dynasty I. to Dynasties VII. and VIII. (H. R. Hall in *C.A.H.* i. pp. 298, 170).   See A. Scharff in *J. Eg. Arch.* xiv., 1928, p. 275.
  [2] So Aucher, Petermann, and Karst.

Fr. 27.   *Syncellus*, p. 110.   *ΚΑΤΑ ΑΦΡΙΚΑΝΟΝ*.

Ἐνάτη   δυναστεία   Ἡρακλεοπολιτῶν
βασιλέων ιθ', οἳ ἐβασίλευσαν ἔτη υθ'· ὧν
ὁ πρῶτος Ἀχθόης, δεινότατος τῶν πρὸ αὐτοῦ
γενόμενος, τοῖς ἐν πάσῃ Αἰγύπτῳ κακὰ εἰργάσατο,
ὕστερον δὲ μανίᾳ περιέπεσε καὶ ὑπὸ κροκοδείλου
διεφθάρη.

Fr. 28 (a).   *Syncellus*, p. 111.   *ΚΑΤΑ ΕΥΣΕΒΙΟΝ*.

Ἐνάτη   δυναστεία   Ἡρακλεοπολιτῶν
βασιλέων τεσσάρων, οἳ ἐβασίλευσαν ἔτη
ἑκατόν· ὧν πρῶτος Ἀχθώης,[1] δεινότατος τῶν
πρὸ αὐτοῦ γενόμενος, τοῖς ἐν πάσῃ Αἰγύπτῳ κακὰ
εἰργάσατο, ὕστερον δὲ μανίᾳ περιέπεσε καὶ ὑπὸ
κροκοδείλου διεφθάρη.

(b) Eusebius, *Chronica* I. (Armenian Version),
p. 97.

Nona dynastia Heracleopolitarum regum IV, annis
C.   Horum primus Ochthôis saevissimus regum fuit

---

[1] *Ἄχθος* A vulgo.

---

[1] Dynasties IX. and X. *c.* 2240–*c.* 2100 B.C.—two series
of nineteen kings, both from Hêracleopolis (Baedeker [8], p.
218), near the modern village of Ahnâsia (Ancient Egyptian
Hat-nen-nesut), 77 miles S. of Cairo, *c.* 9 miles S. of the
entrance to the Fayûm.

The Turin Papyrus gives eighteen kings for Dynasties
IX. and X. as opposed to Manetho's thirty-eight.

[*Footnote continued on opposite page.*

Dynasty IX.

Fr. 27 (*from Syncellus*). According to Africanus.

The Ninth Dynasty [1] consisted of nineteen kings of Hêracleopolis, who reigned for 409 years. The first of these, King Achthoês, [2] behaving more cruelly than his predecessors, wrought woes for the people of all Egypt, but afterwards he was smitten with madness, and was killed by a crocodile. [3]

Fr. 28 (a) (*from Syncellus*). According to Eusebius.

The Ninth Dynasty consisted of four kings of Hêracleopolis, who reigned for 100 years. The first of these, King Achthôês, behaving more cruelly than his predecessors, wrought woes for the people of all Egypt, but afterwards he was smitten with madness, and was killed by a crocodile.

(b) Armenian Version of Eusebius.

The Ninth Dynasty consisted of four kings of Heracleopolis, reigning for 100 years. The first of these, King Ochthôis, [4] was more cruel than all his

---

Manetho's account of Dynasty IX. is best preserved by Africanus. Barbarus has almost the same figures—twenty kings for 409 years.

[2] Achthoês: in the Turin Papyrus Akhtôi (Meyer, *Geschichte* [5], I. ii. p. 247—three kings of this name). Meyer conjectures that the "cruelty" of Achthoês may be violent or forcible oppression of the feudal nobility.

[3] *Cf.* p. 28 n. 3.

[4] Okhthovis (Petermann's translation), -ov- representing the long o.

qui sibi praecesserant, universamque Aegyptum diris calamitatibus affecit. Idem denique vesania correptus est et a crocodilo peremptus.

Fr. 29.   *Syncellus*, p. 110.   *KATA AΦPIKANON*.

Δεκάτη δυναστεία 'Ηρακλεοπολιτῶν βασιλέων ιθ', οἳ ἐβασίλευσαν ἔτη ρπε'.

Fr. 30 (a).   *Syncellus*, p. 112.   *KATA EΥΣEBION*.

Δεκάτη δυναστεία 'Ηρακλεοπολιτῶν βασιλέων ιθ', οἳ ἐβασίλευσαν ἔτη ρπε'.

(b) EUSEBIUS, *Chronica* I. (Armenian Version), p. 97.

Decima dynastia Heracleopolitarum regum XIX, annis CLXXXV.

Fr. 31.   *Syncellus*, p. 110.   *KATA AΦPIKANON*.

'Ενδεκάτη δυναστεία Διοσπολιτῶν βασιλέων ις', οἳ ἐβασίλευσαν ἔτη μγ'. μεθ' οὓς 'Αμμενέμης, ἔτη ις'.

Μέχρι τοῦδε τὸν πρῶτον τόμον καταγήοχε Μανεθῶ.

'Ομοῦ βασιλεῖς ρϟβ', ἔτη ͵βτ', ἡμέραι ο'.

---

[1] The Middle Kingdom, Dynasties XI.-XIII.: *c.* 2100– *c.* 1700 B.C.

[*Footnote continued on opposite page.*

predecessors, and visited the whole of Egypt with dire disasters.   Finally, he was seized with madness, and devoured by a crocodile.

DYNASTY X.

Fr. 29 (*from Syncellus*).   ACCORDING TO AFRICANUS.

The Tenth Dynasty consisted of nineteen kings of Hêracleopolis, who reigned for 185 years.

Fr. 30 (a) (*from Syncellus*).   ACCORDING TO EUSEBIUS.

The Tenth Dynasty consisted of nineteen kings of Hêracleopolis, who reigned for 185 years.

(b) ARMENIAN VERSION OF EUSEBIUS.

The Tenth Dynasty consisted of nineteen kings of Heracleopolis, who reigned for 185 years.

DYNASTY XI.

Fr. 31 (*from Syncellus*).   ACCORDING TO AFRICANUS.

The Eleventh Dynasty [1] consisted of sixteen kings of Diospolis [or Thebes], who reigned for 43 years.   In succession to these, Ammenemês [2] ruled for 16 years.
Here ends the First Book of Manetho.
Total for the reigns of 192 kings, 2300 years 70 days.

Dynasty XI. (*c.* 2100–*c.* 2000 B.C.) with its seat at Thebes: sixteen kings of Thebes ruling for only 43 years (Manetho): Turin Papyrus gives six kings with more than 160 years.
[2] Ammenemês is Amenemhêt I. : see pp. 66 f., nn. 1, 2.

Fr. 32 (a).   *Syncellus*, p. 112.   ΚΑΤΑ ΕΥΣΕΒΙΟΝ.

'Ενδεκάτη δυναστεία Διοσπολιτῶν βασιλέων
ιϛ', οἳ ἐβασίλευσαν ἔτη μγ'. μεθ' οὓς 'Αμμενέμης, ἔτη ιϛ'.

Μέχρι τοῦδε τὸν πρῶτον τόμον καταγήοχεν ὁ
Μανεθῶ. 'Ομοῦ βασιλεῖς ρϟβ', ἔτη ͵βτ', ἡμέραι
οθ'.

(b) EUSEBIUS, *Chronica* I. (Armenian Version),
p. 97.

Undecima dynastia Diospolitarum regum XVI,
annis XLIII.   Post hos Ammenemes annis XVI.

Hactenus primum librum Manetho produxit.
Sunt autem reges CXCII, anni MMCCC.

Fr. 32 (a) (*from Syncellus*). ACCORDING TO
EUSEBIUS.

The Eleventh Dynasty consisted of sixteen kings
of Diospolis [or Thebes], who reigned for 43 years.   In
succession to these, Ammenemês ruled for 16 years.
Here ends the First Book of Manetho.
Total for the reigns of 192 kings, 2300 years 79 days.

(b) ARMENIAN VERSION OF EUSEBIUS.

The Eleventh Dynasty consisted of sixteen kings
of Diospolis [or Thebes], who reigned for 43 years.   In
succession to these, Ammenemes ruled for 16 years.
Here ends the First Book of Manetho.
Total for the reigns of 192 kings, 2300 years.

ΤΟΜΟΣ ΔΕΥΤΕΡΟΣ.

Fr. 34.　*Syncellus,* p. 110.　*ΚΑΤΑ ΑΦΡΙΚΑΝΟΝ.*

Δευτέρου τόμου Μανεθῶ.
Δωδεκάτη δυναστεία Διοσπολιτῶν βασιλέων ἑπτά.

α′ Σεσόγχοσις,[1] Ἀμμανέμου υἱός, ἔτη μϛ′.
β′ Ἀμμανέμης, ἔτη λη′, ὃς ὑπὸ τῶν ἰδίων
　　εὐνούχων ἀνῃρέθη.
γ′ Σέσωστρις,[2] ἔτη μη′, ὃς ἅπασαν ἐχειρώ-
　　σατο τὴν Ἀσίαν ἐν ἐνιαυτοῖς ἐννέα, καὶ
　　τῆς Εὐρώπης τὰ μέχρι Θρᾴκης, πανταχόσε

---

[1] γεσονγόσις (for Σεσόγχοσις) B : Σεσόγχωρις m.
[2] A : Σέσοστρις B.

---

[1] Dynasty XII. c. 2000-1790 B.C. (Meyer, *Geschichte* [5],
I. ii. p. 270). Including Ammenemês whom Manetho
places between Dynasty XI. and Dynasty XII., there are
eight rulers in Dynasty XII.—(1) Ammenemês (Amenemhêt
I.), (2) Sesonchôsis (Senwosret or Sesôstris I.), (3) Ammanemês (Amenemhêt II.), (4) Sesôstris II. (omitted by
Manetho), (5) Sesôstris (Senwosret III.), (6) Manetho's
Lamarês and Amerês (Amenemhêt III., Nema'trê'),
(7) Ammenemês (Amenemhêt IV.), (8) Scemiophris
(Queen Sebeknofrurê'). For (5), the great Sesôstris
(1887-1850 B.C.) of Herodotus, ii. 102, Diod. Sic. I. 53 ff.,
see Sethe, *Unters. zur Gesch.* . . . *Aeg.* ii. 1, and Meyer, *Geschichte* [5], I. ii. p. 268. The name of Amenemhêt bespeaks
his Theban origin : he removed the capital further north
to Dahshûr, a more central position—" Controller of the
Two Lands," as its Egyptian name means. Thus the
kings of Dynasty XII. are kings who came from Thebes,
but ruled at Dahshûr.

[*Footnote continued on opposite page.*

BOOK II.

DYNASTY XII.

Fr. 34 (*from Syncellus*).   ACCORDING TO AFRICANUS.

From the Second Book of Manetho.

The Twelfth Dynasty [1] consisted of seven kings of Diospolis.

1. Sesonchosis, son of Ammanemês, for 46 years.
2. Ammanemês, for 38 years : he was murdered by his own eunuchs.[2]
3. Sesôstris, for 48 years : in nine years he sub-dued the whole of Asia, and Europe as far as Thrace, everywhere erecting memorials of

---

In Dynasty XII. the conquests of Dynasty VI. in the south were extended ; and Sesôstris III. was the first Egyptian king to conquer Syria.   Among works of peace the great irrigation schemes in the Fayûm perpetuated the name of Amenemhêt III. in "Lake Moeris". (See G. Caton-Thompson and E. W. Gardner, *The Desert Fayûm*, 1934.)   Manetho mentions his building of the Labyrinth : it is significant that after the reign of Sesôstris III. and his wide foreign conquests, his son should have built the Labyrinth.   Vases of the Kamares type from Crete have been found at Kahûn, not far from the Labyrinth.

[2] See A. de Buck (*Mélanges Maspero*, vol. i., 1935, pp. 847-52) for a new interpretation of the purpose of *The Instruction of Amenemmes* : in this political pamphlet the dead king speaks from the tomb in support of his son Sesostris, now holding the throne in spite of strong opposition, and violently denounces the ungrateful ruffians who murdered him.   It seems probable that Manetho's note here refers to the death of Ammenemês I. (Battiscombe Gunn).

μνημόσυνα ἐγείρας τῆς τῶν ἐθνῶν σχέσεως,[1]
ἐπὶ μὲν τοῖς γενναίοις ἀνδρῶν, ἐπὶ δὲ τοῖς
ἀγεννέσι γυναικῶν μόρια ταῖς στήλαις ἐγχαράσσων, ὡς [2] ὑπὸ Αἰγυπτίων μετὰ Ὄσιριν
πρῶτον νομισθῆναι.

δ΄ Λαχάρης,[3] ἔτη η΄, ὃς τὸν ἐν Ἀρσινοΐτῃ
λαβύρινθον ἑαυτῷ τάφον κατεσκεύασε.

ε΄ Ἀμερής,[4] ἔτη η΄.

ϛ΄ Ἀμμενέμης,[5] ἔτη η΄.

ζ΄ Σκεμίοφρις, ἀδελφή, ἔτη δ΄.

Ὁμοῦ, ἔτη ρξ΄.

Fr. 35.   *Syncellus*, p. 112.   ΚΑΤΑ ΕΥΣΕΒΙΟΝ.

Δευτέρου τόμου Μανεθῶ.

Δωδεκάτη δυναστεία Διοσπολιτῶν βασιλέων ἑπτά. ὧν ὁ πρῶτος Σεσόγχωσις,[6]
Ἀμμενέμου υἱός, ἔτη μϛ΄.

[1] κατασχέσεως m.	[2] m. : ὃς MSS.
[3] Λαμάρης Meyer.	[4] Ἀμμερής A.
[5] Ἀμενέμης B.	[6] B : Σεσόγχωρις A.

---

[1] See *Agyptische Inschriften aus den Museen zu Berlin*,
i. p. 257, for a *stele* at Semneh with an inscription in which
the great Sesôstris pours contempt upon his enemies, the
Nubians.

[2] For the sexual symbols represented upon pillars, see
Hdt. ii. 102, 106, Diod. Sic. I. 55. 8 : *cf.* the representation
of mutilated captives on one of the walls of the Ramesseum,
Diod. Sic. I. 48. 2.   It has been suggested that Herodotus,
who saw the pillars of Sesostris in Palestine, may possibly
have mistaken an Assyrian for an Egyptian relief.

his conquest of the tribes.[1] Upon *stelae* [pillars] he engraved for a valiant race the secret parts of a man, for an ignoble race those of a woman.[2] Accordingly he was esteemed by the Egyptians as the next in rank to Osiris.

4. Lacharês (Lamarês),[3] for 8 years : he built the Labyrinth [4] in the Arsinoïte nome as his own tomb.

5. Amerês, for 8 years.

6. Ammenemês, for 8 years.

7. Scemiophris, his sister, for 4 years.

Total, 160 years.

Fr. 35 (*from Syncellus*). ACCORDING TO EUSEBIUS.

From the Second Book of Manetho.

The Twelfth Dynasty consisted of seven kings of Diospolis. The first of these, Sesonchosis, son of Ammenemês, reigned for 46 years.

[3] For other names of Amenemhêt III., see note on Marês, App. II., No. 35, p. 224.

[4] The Labyrinth is correctly attributed by Manetho to Amenemhêt III., who built it as his mortuary temple (contrast Herodotus, ii. 148, who assigns this monument to the Dodecarchy). The Fayûm was a place of great importance during this dynasty, from Amenemhêt I. onwards.

The description of the nome as " Arsinoïte " has often been suspected as a later interpolation ; but if " Arsinoïte " was used by Manetho himself, it gives as a date in his life the year 256 B.C. when Ptolemy Philadelphus commemorated Queen Arsinoe (d. 270 B.C.) in the new name of the nome. (*Cf.* Intro. p. xvi for a possible reference to Manetho, the historian of Egypt, in 241 B.C.)

β' Ἀμμανέμης, ἔτη λη', ὃς ὑπὸ τῶν ἰδίων
εὐνούχων ἀνῃρέθη.

γ' Σέσωστρις,[1] ἔτη μη', ὃς λέγεται γεγονέναι
πηχῶν δ', παλαιστῶν γ', δακτύλων β'. ὃς
πᾶσαν ἐχειρώσατο τὴν Ἀσίαν ἐν ἐνιαυτοῖς
ἐννέα, καὶ τῆς Εὐρώπης τὰ μέχρι Θρᾴκης,
πανταχόσε μνημόσυνα ἐγείρας τῆς τῶν
ἐθνῶν κατασχέσεως, ἐπὶ μὲν τοῖς γενναίοις
ἀνδρῶν, ἐπὶ δὲ τοῖς ἀγεννέσι γυναικῶν
μόρια ταῖς στήλαις ἐγχαράσσων, ὡς[2] καὶ
ὑπὸ τῶν Αἰγυπτίων ⟨πρῶτον⟩[3] μετὰ
Ὄσιριν νομισθῆναι.

Μεθ' ὃν Λάμαρις, ἔτη η', ὃς τὸν ἐν Ἀρσενοΐτῃ[4]
λαβύρινθον ἑαυτῷ τάφον κατεσκεύασεν.

Οἱ δὲ τούτου διάδοχοι ἐπὶ ἔτη μβ', οἳ πάντες
ἐβασίλευσαν ἔτεσι σμέ.

Fr. 36. Eusebius, *Chronica* I. (Armenian Version), p. 98.

E Manethonis secundo libro.

Duodecima dynastia Diospolitarum regum VII,
quorum primus Sesonchosis Ammenemis filius annis
XLVI.

Ammenemes annis XXXVIII, qui a suis eunuchis
interemptus est.

Sesostris annis XLVIII, cuius mensura fertur
cubitorum quattuor, palmarumque trium cum digitis

---

[1] A : Σέσοστρις B.   [2] m : ὃς MSS.   [3] m.

2. **Ammanemês**, for 38 years : he was murdered by his own eunuchs.
3. **Sesôstris**, for 48 years : he is said to have been 4 cubits 3 palms 2 fingers' breadths in stature. In nine years he subdued the whole of Asia, and Europe as far as Thrace, everywhere erecting memorials of his conquest of the tribes. Upon *stelae* [pillars] he engraved for a valiant race the secret parts of a man, for an ignoble race those of a woman. Accordingly he was esteemed by the Egyptians as the next in rank to Osiris.

Next to him Lamaris reigned for 8 years : he built the Labyrinth in the Arsinoïte nome as his own tomb.

His successors ruled for 42 years, and the reigns of the whole dynasty amounted to 245 years.[1]

Fr. 36. Armenian Version of Eusebius.

From the Second Book of Manetho.
The Twelfth Dynasty consisted of seven kings of Diospolis. The first of these, Sesonchosis, son of Ammenemês, reigned for 46 years.

2. **Ammenemês**, for 38 years : he was murdered by his own eunuchs.
3. **Sesôstris**, for 48 years : he is said to have been 4 cubits 3 palms 2 fingers' breadth in

---

[1] The items given add to 182 years.

⁴ This variant spelling with -ε- for -ι- appears to be a mere scribal error due to confusion with words beginning ἀρσεν-.

duobus. Is universam Asiam annorum novem spa-
tio sibi subdidit, itemque Europae partem usque ad
Thraciam.   Idem et suae in singulas gentes dominationis monumenta ubique constituit ; apud gentes
quidem strenuas virilia, apud vero imbelles feminea
pudenda ignominiae causa columnis insculpens.
Quare is ab Aegyptiis proximos post Osirin honores
tulit.

Secutus est Lampares, annis VIII.   Hic in
Arsinoïte labyrinthum cavernosum sibi tumulum
fecit.

Regnaverunt successores eius annis XLII.

Summa universae dominationis annorum CCXLV.

Fr. 38.   *Syncellus*, p. 113.   ΚΑΤΑ ΑΦΡΙΚΑΝΟΝ.

Τρισκαιδεκάτη δυναστεία Διοσπολιτῶν βασιλέων
ξ', οἳ ἐβασίλευσαν ἔτη υνγ'.[1]

Fr. 39 (a).   *Syncellus*, p. 114.   ΚΑΤΑ ΕΥΣΕΒΙΟΝ.

Τρισκαιδεκάτη δυναστεία Διοσπολιτῶν βασιλέων
ξ', οἳ ἐβασίλευσαν ἔτη υνγ'.

[1] B : ρπδ' A.

---

[1] The Armenian has a word here for " sufferings " or
" torments " (Margoliouth) : Karst expresses the general
meaning as—" he engraved their oppression through (or,
by means of) . . ."

[2] Karst translates this word by " das höhlenwendelgang-
förmige ".

[3] Dynasty XIII., 1790–c. 1700 B.C. In the Turin Papyrus there is a corresponding group of sixty kings : see
the list in Meyer, *Geschichte* [5], I. ii. pp. 308 f., one of them

72

stature. In nine years he subdued the whole
of Asia, and Europe as far as Thrace. Everywhere he set up memorials of his subjugation of
each tribe : among valiant races he engraved
upon pillars a man's secret parts, among un-
warlike races a woman's, as a sign of disgrace.[1]
Wherefore he was honoured by the Egyptians
next to Osiris.

His successor, Lampares, reigned for 8 years : in
the Arsinoïte nome he built the many-chambered [2]
Labyrinth as his tomb.

The succeeding kings ruled for 42 years.

Total for the whole dynasty, 245 years.

DYNASTY XIII.

Fr. 38 (*from Syncellus*). ACCORDING TO AFRICANUS.

The Thirteenth Dynasty [3] consisted of sixty kings
of Diospolis, who reigned for 453 years.

Fr. 39 (a) (*from Syncellus*). ACCORDING TO EUSEBIUS.

The Thirteenth Dynasty consisted of sixty kings
of Diospolis, who reigned for 453 years.

being a name ending in -mes, perhaps Dedumes, the king
Τουτίμαιος of Fr. 42.   The twenty-fifth king in the Turin
Papyrus, Col. VII., Kha'neferrê' Sebekhotp IV., is probably the King Chenephrês of whom Artapanus (i./B.C.)
says that he was " king of the regions above Memphis
(for there were at that time many kings in Egypt) " in
the lifetime of Moses (Artapanus, *Concerning the Jews*,
quoted by Euseb., *Praepar. Evang.* ix. 27 : see also
Clement of Alexandria, *Strom.* i. 23, 154).

73

(b) Eusebius, *Chronica* I. (Armenian Version),
p. 99.

Tertia decima dynastia Diospolitarum regum LX,
qui regnarunt annis CCCCLIII.

Fr. 41 (a).   *Syncellus*, p. 113.   *ΚΑΤΑ ΑΦΡΙΚΑΝΟΝ.*

Τεσσαρεσκαιδεκάτη δυναστεία Ξοϊτῶν βασιλέων
ος', οἳ ἐβασίλευσαν ἔτη ρπδ'.[1]

(b) *Syncellus*, p. 114.   *ΚΑΤΑ ΕΥΣΕΒΙΟΝ.*

Τεσσαρεσκαιδεκάτη δυναστεία Ξοϊτῶν βασιλέων
ος', οἳ ἐβασίλευσαν ἔτη ρπδ' · ἐν ἄλλῳ υπδ'.

(c) Eusebius, *Chronica* I. (Armenian Version),
p. 99.

Quarta   decima   dynastia   Xoïtarum [2]   regum
LXXVI, qui regnarunt annis CCCCLXXXIV.

[1] B on y : a lacuna in A.
[2] Aucher : Khsojitarum (Petermann's translation).

---

[1] Dynasties XIV.-XVII., the Hyksôs Age : *c.* 1700-
1580 B.C.

Dynasty XIV.   Nothing is known of the kings of
Dynasty XIV., whose seat was at Xoïs (Sakha) in
the West Delta—an island and town in the Sebennytic
nome (Strabo, 17. 1. 19).   They were not rulers of Upper
Egypt, but probably of the West Delta only.   At this
period there was, it is probable, another contemporary
dynasty in Upper Egypt (Dynasty XVII. of Manetho).

In the Turin Papyrus there is a long series of rulers'
names corresponding to this dynasty ; but the number

(b) ARMENIAN VERSION OF EUSEBIUS.

The Thirteenth Dynasty consisted of sixty kings of Diospolis, who reigned for 453 years.

DYNASTY XIV.

Fr. 41 (a) (*from Syncellus*). ACCORDING TO AFRICANUS.

The Fourteenth Dynasty [1] consisted of seventy-six kings of Xoïs, who reigned for 184 years.

(b) ACCORDING TO EUSEBIUS.

The Fourteenth Dynasty consisted of seventy-six kings of Xoïs, who reigned for 184 years,—in another copy, 484 years.

(c) ARMENIAN VERSION OF EUSEBIUS.

The Fourteenth Dynasty consisted of seventy-six kings of Xoïs, who reigned for 484 years.

given by Manetho (76) was not approximated in the Papyrus which shows between twenty and thirty names of kings. Not one of these names is preserved on the Monuments, nor on the Karnak Tablet. The kings of Dynasty XIV., and even the last kings of Dynasty XIII., reigned simultaneously with the Hyksôs kings : *cf.* the double series of kings in Dynasty XVII. In the Royal Lists of Abydos and Sakkâra the rulers of Dynasties XIII.-XVII. are altogether omitted. The Royal List of Karnak gives a selection of about thirty-five names of Dynasties XIII.-XVII., omitting Dynasty XIV. and the Hyksôs.

Fr. 42. Josephus, *Contra Apionem*, I. 14, §§ 73–92.[1]

73 Ἄρξομαι δὴ πρῶτον ἀπὸ τῶν παρ' Αἰγυπτίοις
γραμμάτων. αὐτὰ μὲν οὖν οὐχ οἷόν τε παρα-
τίθεσθαι τἀκείνων, Μανεθὼς[2] δ' ἦν τὸ γένος Αἰγύπτιος, ἀνὴρ τῆς Ἑλληνικῆς μετεσχηκὼς παιδείας,
ὡς δῆλός ἐστιν· γέγραφεν γὰρ Ἑλλάδι φωνῇ τὴν
πάτριον ἱστορίαν ἐκ δέλτων[3] ἱερῶν, ὥς φησιν

---

[1] For §§ 73-75, 82-90, see Eusebius, *Praepar. Evang.* x. 13:
for §§ 73-105, see Eusebius, *Chron.* i. pp. 151-8, Schöne
(Arm.).

[2] Eus.: Μανέθων L, Lat. (same variation elsewhere).

[3] δέλτων Gutschmid (*sacris libris* Lat.: *sacris monumentis*
Eus. *Arm.*, *cf.* § 226): τε τῶν L.

---

[1] The invasion of the Hyksôs took place at some time
in Dynasty XIII.: hence the succeeding anarchy in a
period of foreign domination. The later Egyptians looked
back upon it as the Jews did upon the Babylonian
captivity, or the English upon the Danish terror. The
keen desire of the Egyptians to forget about the Hyksôs
usurpation accounts in part for our ignorance of what
actually happened: " it is with apparent unwillingness
that they chronicle any events connected with it " (Peet,
Egypt and the Old Testament, p. 69). In Egyptian texts
the " infamous " (Hyksôs) were denoted as 'Amu,—a
title also given to the Hittites and their allies by Ramessês
II. in the poem of the Battle of Kadesh (ed. Kuentz, § 97).
Perhaps they were combined with Hittites who in 1925
B.C. brought the kingdom of Babel to an end. It is
certain that with the Hyksôs numerous Semites came into
Egypt: some of the Hyksôs kings have Semitic names.
For the presence of an important Hurrian element among
the Hyksôs, see E. A. Speiser, "Ethnic Movements,"
in *Ann. of Amer. Sch. of Or. Res.* xiii. (1932), p. 51. The

THE HYKSÔS AGE, c. 1700–c. 1580 B.C.[1]

Fr. 42 (*from* Josephus, *Contra Apionem*, i. 14, §§ 73-92).

[Josephus is citing the records of neighbouring nations in proof of the antiquity of the Jews.]

I will begin with Egyptian documents. These I cannot indeed set before you in their ancient form ; but in Manetho we have a native Egyptian who was manifestly imbued with Greek culture. He wrote in Greek the history of his nation, translated, as he himself tells us, from sacred tablets ; [2] and on many

Hyksôs brought with them from Asia their tribal god, which was assimilated by the Egyptians to Sêth, the god of foreign parts, of the desert, and of the enemy.

In the first half of the second millennium B.C. the Hyksôs ruled a great kingdom in Palestine and Syria (Meyer, *Geschichte*[5], i. § 304) ; and when their power was broken down by the arrival of hostile tribes, King Amôsis took advantage of their plight to drive the Hyksôs out of Egypt (A. Jirku, " Aufstieg und Untergang der Hyksôs," in *Journ. of the Palestine Orient. Soc.* xii., 1932, p. 60).

A dim tradition of Hyksôs-rule is possibly preserved in Herodotus, ii. 128. Perhaps " the shepherd Philitis " in that passage is connected with " Philistines," a tribe which may have formed part of these invaders. There is confusion between two periods of oppression of the common people,—under the pyramid-builders and under the Hyksôs. For a translation of the Egyptian records which illustrate the Hyksôs period, see Battiscombe Gunn and Alan H. Gardiner, *J. Eg. Arch.* v., 1918, pp. 36-56, " The Expulsion of the Hyksôs ".

[2] The word " tablets " is a probable emendation, since Manetho would naturally base his *History* upon temple-archives on stone as well as on papyrus : *cf.* the Palermo Stone, the Turin Papyrus, etc. (Intro. pp. xxiii ff.).

αὐτός, μεταφράσας, ὃς¹ καὶ πολλὰ τὸν Ἡρόδοτον
ἐλέγχει τῶν Αἰγυπτιακῶν ὑπ᾽ ἀγνοίας ἐψευσμένον.
74 οὗτος δὴ τοίνυν ὁ Μανεθὼς ἐν τῇ δευτέρᾳ τῶν
Αἰγυπτιακῶν ταῦτα περὶ ἡμῶν γράφει· παραθή-
σομαι δὲ τὴν λέξιν αὐτοῦ καθάπερ αὐτὸν ἐκεῖνον
παραγαγὼν μάρτυρα·
75   " Τουτίμαιος.² ἐπὶ τούτου οὐκ οἶδ᾽ ὅπως ὁ ³ θεὸς
ἀντέπνευσεν, καὶ παραδόξως ἐκ τῶν πρὸς ἀνατολὴν
μερῶν ἄνθρωποι τὸ γένος ἄσημοι καταθαρρήσαντες
ἐπὶ τὴν χώραν ἐστράτευσαν καὶ ῥᾳδίως ἀμαχητὶ
76 ταύτην κατὰ κράτος εἷλον, καὶ τοὺς ἡγεμονεύσαν-
τας ἐν αὐτῇ χειρωσάμενοι τὸ λοιπὸν τάς τε πόλεις
ὠμῶς ἐνέπρησαν καὶ τὰ τῶν θεῶν ἱερὰ κατέσ-
καψαν, πᾶσι δὲ τοῖς ἐπιχωρίοις ἐχθρότατά πως
ἐχρήσαντο, τοὺς μὲν σφάζοντες, τῶν δὲ καὶ τὰ
77 τέκνα καὶ γυναῖκας εἰς δουλείαν ἄγοντες. πέρας
δὲ καὶ βασιλέα ἕνα ἐξ αὐτῶν ἐποίησαν, ᾧ ὄνομα

¹ ὃς Eus.: om. L.
² Gutschmid: τοῦ Τίμαιος ὄνομα L, Eus. (ὄνομα probably a
gloss: ἄνεμος Gutschmid).
³ ὁ Eus. (perhaps a survival of Ancient Egyptian usage):
om. L: Meyer conj. θεός τις.

---

¹ Cf. Manetho, Fr. 88.
² This account of the Hyksôs invasion is obviously
derived from popular Egyptian tales, the characteristics
of which are deeply imprinted upon it.   Meyer (Geschichte ⁵,
I. ii. p. 313) quotes from papyri and inscriptions passages
of similar style and content, e.g. Pap. Sallier I. describing
the war with the Hyksôs, and mentioning " Lord Apôpi
in Auaris," and an inscription of Queen Hatshepsut from
the Speos Artemidos, referring to the occupation of

points of Egyptian history he convicts Herodotus [1]
of having erred through ignorance. In the second
book of his *History of Egypt*, this writer Manetho
speaks of us as follows. I shall quote his own words,
just as if I had brought forward the man himself as a
witness : [2]

"Tutimaeus.[3] In his reign, for what cause I
know not, a blast of God smote us ; and un-
expectedly, from the regions of the East, invaders
of obscure race marched in confidence of victory
against our land. By main force they easily seized
it without striking a blow ; [4] and having overpowered
the rulers of the land, they then burned our cities
ruthlessly, razed to the ground the temples of the
gods, and treated all the natives with a cruel hos-
tility, massacring some and leading into slavery the
wives and children of others. Finally, they appointed as king one of their number whose name was

Auaris. See Breasted, *Ancient Records*, i. § 24, ii. §§ 296 ff.
Meyer adds that he would not be surprised if Manetho's
description reappeared word for word one day in a hieratic
papyrus. *Cf.* § 75 ὁ θεός : § 76 the crimes of the Hyksôs
(Fr. 54, § 249, those of the Solymites and their polluted
allies) : § 77 the upper and lower lands : §§ 78, 237 religious tradition to explain the name of Auaris and its
dedication to Typhôn : § 99 hollow phrases about military
expeditions of Sethôs : § 237 the form of the phrase ὡς
χρόνος ἱκανὸς διῆλθεν, and many other passages. See also
Weill, *La fin du moyen empire égyptien*, pp. 76 ff.

[3] See Fr. 38, n. 3.

[4] The success of the Hyksôs may have been due to
superior archery and to the use of horse-drawn chariots,
previously unknown in Egypt (Maspero, *Hist. Anc.* ii.
p. 51 ; Petrie, *Hyksos and Israelite Cities*, p. 70 ; H. R.
Hall, *Anc. Hist. of Near East* [8], p. 213), as well as to superior
weapons of bronze (H. R. Hall, *C.A.H.* i. p. 291 n., 312 f.).

ἦν Σάλιτις.¹ καὶ οὗτος ἐν τῇ Μέμφιδι κατεγίνετο,
τήν τε ἄνω καὶ κάτω χώραν δασμολογῶν καὶ
φρουρὰν ἐν τοῖς ἐπιτηδειοτάτοις καταλείπων²
τόποις. μάλιστα δὲ καὶ τὰ πρὸς ἀνατολὴν ἠσφα-
λίσατο μέρη, προορώμενος, Ἀσσυρίων ποτὲ μεῖζον
78 ἰσχυόντων, ἐσομένην ἐπιθυμίᾳ³ τῆς αὐτοῦ βασιλείας ἔφοδον. εὑρὼν δὲ ἐν νομῷ τῷ Σαΐτῃ⁴
πόλιν ἐπικαιροτάτην, κειμένην μὲν πρὸς ἀνατολὴν
τοῦ Βουβαστίτου ποταμοῦ, καλουμένην δ' ἀπό
τινος ἀρχαίας θεολογίας Αὔαριν, ταύτην ἔκτισέν

---

¹ *Silitis* Eus. *Arm.*: Σαΐτης Fr. 43, 48, 49.
² *Ed. pr.*: καταλιπὼν L.   ³ Bekker: ἐπιθυμίαν L.
⁴ Conj. Σεθροΐτῃ Manetho, Fr. 43, 48, 49.

---

[1] The name may be Semitic (*cf.* Hebr. *shallīṭ*), but it
has not been found on the monuments. Possibly it is
not strictly a proper name, but rather a title like " prince,"
" general " : " sultan " comes from the same root.
[2] *Cf.* § 90. Manetho regards as historically true the
Greek tales of the great Assyrian Empire of Ninus and
Semiramis. The period referred to here is much earlier
than the time when Assyria began to harass the Mediter-
ranean regions.
[3] If " Saïte " is correct here, it has nothing to do with
the famous Saïs, but is probably used for " Tanite ":
cf. Herodotus, ii. 17, Strabo, 17, 1, 20 (P. Montet in *Revue
Biblique*, xxxix. 1930). The Sethroïte nome (Fr. 43, 45,
49) is in the extreme E. of the Delta, adjoining the Tanite
nome. For Sethroê see H. Junker, *Zeit. f. äg. Sprache* 75.
1939, p. 78.
[4] For Bubastis see Fr. 8 n. 2. The Bubastite branch is
the farthest E., the next being the Tanitic.
[5] Auaris, in Ancient Egyptian *Hetwaʻret*, "town of the
desert strip," but this meaning does not explain the
" religious tradition ". (The older interpretations, " house
of the flight," " house of the leg," were attached to the
Seth-Typhôn legend : *cf.* n. 3 *infra*.) Tanis was a strong-

Salitis.[1] He had his seat at Memphis, levying
tribute from Upper and Lower Egypt, and always
leaving garrisons behind in the most advantageous
positions.   Above all, he fortified the district to the
east, foreseeing that the Assyrians,[2] as they grew
stronger, would one day covet and attack his kingdom.

" In the Saïte [Sethroïte] nome [3] he found a city
very favourably situated on the east of the Bubastite
branch [4] of the Nile, and called Auaris [5] after an

hold of the Hyksôs : in *O.T. Numbers* xiii. 22, " Now
Hebron (in S. Palestine) was built seven years before Zoan
in Egypt," Zoan is Tanis (Dja'net), and the statement
probably refers to the Hyksôs age. Sethe cautiously
said, " Seth is the god of the Hyksôs cities, Tanis and
Auaris ".   But in *Revue Biblique*, xxxix., 1930, pp. 5-28,
Pierre Montet, the excavator of Tanis, brought forward
reasons to identify Auaris and Pi-Ra'messes with Tanis ;
and Alan H. Gardiner (*J. Eg. Arch.* xix., 1933, pp. 122-
128) gave further evidence for this view (p. 126) : " San
el-Hagar marks the site of the city successively called
Auaris, Pi-Ra'messe, and Tanis ".   In spite of the criticism of Raymond Weill (*J. Eg. Arch.* xxi., 1935, pp. 10-25),
who cited a hieroglyphic document (found in the temple
of Ptah in Memphis) in which Auaris and " the field (or
land) of Tanis " are separate, Pierre Montet (*Syria*, xvii.,
1936, pp. 200-202) maintains the identity of Auaris,
Pi-Ra'messes, and Tanis. [So does H. Junker, *Zeit. f. äg.
Sprache* 75. 1939, pp. 63-84.]

Meanwhile, a new identification of Pi-Ra'messês had
been suggested : by excavation M. Hamza (*Annales du
Service des Antiquités de l'Égypte*, xxx. 1930, p. 65) found
evidence tending to identify Pi-Ra'messês with the palace
of Ramessês II. at Tell el-Yahudîya, near Kantîr, *c.* 25
kilometres south of Tanis ; and William C. Hayes (*Glazed
Tiles from a Palace of Ramessês II. at Kantîr : The Metro-
politan Museum of Art Papers*, No. 3, 1937) supports this
theory that Kantîr was the Delta residence of the Ramesside kings of Egypt, pointing out that there is a practically

[*Footnote continued on page* 83.

τε καὶ τοῖς τείχεσιν ὀχυρωτάτην ἐποίησεν, ἐν-
οικίσας αὐτῇ καὶ πλῆθος ὁπλιτῶν εἰς εἴκοσι καὶ
79 τέσσαρας μυριάδας ἀνδρῶν προφυλακήν. ἔνθα δὲ [1]
κατὰ θέρειαν ἤρχετο, τὰ μὲν σιτομετρῶν καὶ
μισθοφορίαν παρεχόμενος, τὰ δὲ καὶ ταῖς ἐξοπ-
λισίαις πρὸς φόβον τῶν ἔξωθεν ἐπιμελῶς γυμνάζων.
ἄρξας δ' ἐννεακαίδεκα ἔτη, τὸν βίον ἐτελεύτησε.
80 μετὰ τοῦτον δὲ ἕτερος ἐβασίλευσεν τέσσαρα καὶ
τεσσαράκοντα ἔτη καλούμενος Βνών,[2] μεθ' ὃν
ἄλλος Ἀπαχνὰν [3] ἓξ καὶ τριάκοντα ἔτη καὶ μῆνας
ἑπτά, ἔπειτα δὲ καὶ Ἄπωφις [4] ἓν καὶ ἑξήκοντα καὶ
81 Ἰαννᾶς [5] πεντήκοντα καὶ μῆνα ἕνα, ἐπὶ πᾶσι δὲ
καὶ Ἄσσις [6] ἐννέα καὶ τεσσαράκοντα καὶ μῆνας δύο.
καὶ οὗτοι μὲν ἓξ ἐν αὐτοῖς ἐγενήθησαν πρῶτοι
ἄρχοντες, ποθοῦντες [7] ἀεὶ καὶ μᾶλλον [8] τῆς Αἰγύπτου
82 ἐξᾶραι τὴν ῥίζαν. ἐκαλεῖτο δὲ τὸ σύμπαν αὐτῶν [9]

---

[1] Hic autem Lat.: ἐνθάδε L.
[2] Manetho, Fr. 43, 48, 49: Βηών L.
[3] Apakhnan Eus.: Παχνὰν Fr. 43: Apachnas Lat.
[4] Aphosis Eus. Arm.: Ἄφοβις MSS., Fr. 43: Ἄφωφις Fr. 49.
[5] Ἰανίας ed. pr.: Samnas Lat.: Anan Eus. Arm.: Ἀννὰς or Ἀννὰν Gutschmid.
[6] Ases Lat.: Aseth Eus. (Gutschmid and Meyer hold Ἀσηθ to be the form used by Josephus).
[7] Ed. pr.: πορθοῦντες L.
[8] πολεμοῦντες ἀεὶ καὶ ποθοῦντες μᾶλλον MSS. Big. and Hafn. in Hudson.
[9] σύμπαν αὐτῶν Eus., omne genus eorum Lat.: om. L.

ancient religious tradition.[1] This place he rebuilt and fortified with massive walls, planting there a garrison of as many as 240,000 heavy-armed men to guard his frontier. Here he would come in summertime, partly to serve out rations and pay his troops, partly to train them carefully in manœuvres and so strike terror into foreign tribes. After reigning for 19 years, Salitis died; and a second king, named Bnôn,[2] succeeded and reigned for 44 years. Next to him came Apachnan, who ruled for 36 years and 7 months;[3] then Apôphis for 61, and Iannas for 50 years and 1 month; then finally Assis for 49 years and 2 months. These six kings, their first rulers, were ever more and more eager to extirpate the Egyptian stock. Their race as a whole was called

unbroken series of royal Ramesside monuments which cover a period of almost 200 years.

In 1906 Petrie discovered at Kantîr a vast fortified encampment of Hyksôs date and a Hyksôs cemetery : see Petrie, *Hyksôs and Israelite Cities*, pp. 3-16 (the earthwork ramparts of the camp were intended to protect an army of chariots).

[1] See Fr. 54, § 237, for its connexion with Seth-Typhon, to whom the tribal god of the Hyksôs was assimilated.

[2] Of these Hyksôs names Bnôn and Apachnan are unexplained. Apôpi (the name of several kings—at least three), and perhaps Asêth (Assis), seem to be pure Egyptian : Iannas is presumed to be Khian, whose cartouche turned up surprisingly and significantly on the lid of an alabastron in the Palace of Minos at Knossos in Crete, as well as on a basalt lion from Baghdad. On Khian, see Griffith in *Proc. of Soc. of Bibl. Arch.* xix. (1897), pp. 294 f., 297.

[3] In his *History* (and for short reigns in the *Epitome*, see *e.g.* Dynasty XXVII.) Manetho reckoned by months as well as by years, like the Turin Papyrus and the Palermo Stone : see Intro. pp. xxiv f.

ἔθνος 'Υκσώς,[1] τοῦτο δέ ἐστιν βασιλεῖς ποιμένες·
τὸ γὰρ ὗκ καθ' ἱερὰν γλῶσσαν βασιλέα σημαίνει,
τὸ δὲ σὼς ποιμήν ἐστι καὶ ποιμένες κατὰ τὴν
κοινὴν διάλεκτον, καὶ οὕτω συντιθέμενον γίνεται
'Υκσώς.   τινὲς δὲ λέγουσιν αὐτοὺς Ἄραβας εἶναι."

83 [ἐν [2] δ' ἄλλῳ ἀντιγράφῳ οὐ βασιλεῖς σημαίνεσθαι
διὰ τῆς τοῦ ὗκ προσηγορίας, ἀλλὰ τοὐναντίον αἰχμαλώτους δηλοῦσθαι ποιμένας·[3] τὸ γὰρ ὗκ πάλιν
Αἰγυπτιστὶ καὶ τὸ ἂκ δασυνόμενον αἰχμαλώτους
ῥητῶς μηνύειν.[4]]   καὶ τοῦτο μᾶλλον πιθανώτερόν
μοι φαίνεται καὶ παλαιᾶς ἱστορίας ἐχόμενον.

84 Τούτους τοὺς προκατωνομασμένους βασιλέας,
[καὶ] [5] τοὺς τῶν Ποιμένων καλουμένων καὶ τοὺς
ἐξ αὐτῶν γενομένους, κρατῆσαι τῆς Αἰγύπτου

---

[1] 'Υκουσσώς Eus. (*Hikkusin* Eus. *Arm.*): so also *infra*.
[2] The bracketed clause (already in Eus.) is apparently an
ancient gloss, derived from § 91: *cf.* the similar marginal
annotations to §§ 92, 98.
[3] ποιμένας Eus.: οὐ ποιμένας L.
[4] μηνύειν Holwerda: μηνύει L.
[5] Bracketed by Thackeray, Reinach.

---

[1] Hyksôs, " rulers of foreign lands " (Erman-Grapow,
Wörterbuch, iii. p. 171, 29).   Another form of the name,
Hykussôs, is preserved by Eusebius, but it is uncertain
whether the medial -u- is really authentic—the Egyptian
plural (Meyer).   *Hyk* = ruler of a pastoral people, a
sheikh.
   " The Hyksôs, like the foreign Kassite Dynasty in
Babylonia, adopted the higher culture of the conquered

Hyksôs,[1] that is 'king-shepherds': for *hyk* in the sacred language means 'king,' and *sôs* in common speech is 'shepherd' or 'shepherds': [2] hence the compound word 'Hyksôs'. Some say that they were Arabs." [3] In another copy [4] the expression *hyk*, it is said, does not mean "kings": on the contrary, the compound refers to "captive-shepherds".[5] In Egyptian *hyk*, in fact, and *hak* when aspirated expressly denote "captives".[6] This explanation seems to me the more convincing and more in keeping with ancient history.

These kings whom I have enumerated above, and their descendants, ruling over the so-called Shepherds, dominated Egypt, according to Manetho, for 511

country" (J. Garstang, *The Heritage of Solomon*, 1934, p. 62).

[2] This is correct: for the Egyptian word *š'sw*, " Bedouins," which in Coptic became *shôs*, " a herdsman," see Erman-Grapow, *Wörterbuch*, iv. p. 412, 10 (B.G.).

[3] In a papyrus (ii./iii. A.D.) quoted by Wilcken in *Archiv für Pap.* iii. (1906), pp. 188 ff. (*Chrestomathie*, I. ii. p. 322) ἄμμος ὑκσιωτική is mentioned—aloe [or cement (Preisigke)] from the land of the Hyksiôtae, apparently in Arabia. This gives some support to the statement in the text.

[4] Josephus, in revising this treatise just as he revised his *Antiquities*, appears to have used a second version of Manetho's *Aegyptiaca*. Did Josephus ever have before him Manetho's original work? Laqueur thinks it more probable that Josephus consulted revisions of Manetho made from the philo- or the anti-Semitic point of view: see Intro. p. xx. Since the third century B.C. an extensive literature on the origin of the Jews had arisen.

[5] This appears to be a Jewish explanation (§ 91), to harmonize with the story of Joseph.

[6] The reference here is to the Egyptian word *ḥ'ḳ*, " booty," " prisoners of war " (Erman-Grapow, *Wörterbuch*, iii. p. 33) (B.G.).

85 φησὶν ἔτη πρὸς τοῖς πεντακοσίοις ἔνδεκα. μετὰ
ταῦτα δὲ τῶν ἐκ τῆς Θηβαΐδος καὶ τῆς ἄλλης
Αἰγύπτου βασιλέων γενέσθαι φησὶν ἐπὶ τοὺς
Ποιμένας ἐπανάστασιν, καὶ πόλεμον[1] συρραγῆναι
86 μέγαν καὶ πολυχρόνιον. ἐπὶ δὲ βασιλέως, ᾧ
ὄνομα εἶναι Μισφραγμούθωσις,[2] ἡττημένους[3] φησὶ
τοὺς Ποιμένας[4] ἐκ μὲν τῆς ἄλλης Αἰγύπτου πάσης
ἐκπεσεῖν, κατακλεισθῆναι δ᾽ εἰς τόπον ἀρουρῶν
ἔχοντα μυρίων τὴν περίμετρον· Αὔαριν[5] ὄνομα τῷ
87 τόπῳ. τοῦτόν φησιν ὁ Μανεθὼς ἅπαντα τείχει
τε μεγάλῳ καὶ ἰσχυρῷ περιβαλεῖν τοὺς Ποιμένας,
ὅπως τήν τε κτῆσιν ἅπασαν ἔχωσιν ἐν ὀχυρῷ
88 καὶ τὴν λείαν τὴν ἑαυτῶν. τὸν δὲ Μισφραγμουθώσεως υἱὸν Θούμμωσιν[6] ἐπιχειρῆσαι μὲν αὐτοὺς
διὰ πολιορκίας ἑλεῖν κατὰ κράτος, ὀκτὼ καὶ
τεσσαράκοντα μυριάσι στρατοῦ προσεδρεύσαντα
τοῖς τείχεσιν· ἐπεὶ δὲ τῆς πολιορκίας[7] ἀπέγνω,

[1] + αὐτοῖς L, Lat.: om. Eus.
[2] Eus.: Ἀλισφραγμούθωσις L (Lat.): so also infra.
[3] Conj. Cobet: ἡττωμένους L.
[4] + ἐξ αὐτοῦ L: om. Eus.: ὑπ᾽ αὐτοῦ ed. pr.
[5] Αὔαριν L (Lat.): Αὔαρις Eus.
[6] Θούμμωσιν L: Θμούθωσιν Eus.
[7] L: τὴν πολιορκίαν Eus.

---

[1] This number of years, much too high for the length
of the Hyksôs sway in Egypt, may perhaps refer to the
whole period of their rule in Palestine and Syria : see
A. Jirku, in Journ. of the Palestine Orient. Soc. xii., 1932,
p. 51 n. 4.

[2] Misphragmuthôsis, i.e. Menkheperrê‘ (Tuthmôsis III.)
and his son Thummôsis, i.e. Tuthmôsis IV., are here said
to have driven out the Hyksôs. In Fr. 50, § 94, Tethmôsis
is named as the conqueror. In point of historical fact the

years.[1] Thereafter, he says, there came a revolt of the kings of the Thebaïd and the rest of Egypt against the Shepherds, and a fierce and prolonged war broke out between them. By a king whose name was Misphragmuthôsis,[2] the Shepherds, he says, were defeated, driven out of all the rest of Egypt, and confined in a region measuring within its circumference 10,000 arûrae,[3] by name Auaris. According to Manetho, the Shepherds enclosed this whole area with a high, strong wall, in order to safeguard all their possessions and spoils. Thummôsis, the son of Misphragmuthôsis (he continues), attempted by siege to force them to surrender, blockading the fortress with an army of 480,000 men. Finally, giving up the siege in despair, he concluded

victorious king was Amôsis, and he took Auaris by main force : the genuine Manetho must surely have given this name which is preserved by Africanus and Eusebius, as also by Apiôn in Tatian, *adv. Graecos*, § 38.   See p. 101 n. 2, and *cf.* Meyer, *Aeg. Chron.* pp. 73 f.

Weill, *La fin du moyen empire égyptien*, p. 95, explains the error by assuming that the exploit of the capture of Auaris was usurped by Tuthmôsis IV., as it was usurped earlier by Hatshepsut and later by Ramessês III.

Breasted (*C.A.H.* ii. p. 83) holds that, since with the catastrophic fall of Kadesh on the Orontes before the arms of Tuthmôsis III. the last vestige of the Hyksôs power disappeared, the tradition of late Greek days made Tuthmôsis III. the conqueror of the Hyksôs.   He points out that the name Misphragmuthôsis is to be identified with the two cartouche-names of Tuthmôsis III.: it is a corruption of " Menkheperrê' Tuthmôsis ".

[3] Lit. " with a circumference of 10,000 *arûrae* ".   The text (which cannot be attributed as it stands to Manetho —τὴν περίμετρον must be a later addition) implies a wrong use of *arûra* as a measure of length ; it is, in reality, a measure of area, about half an acre.

ποιήσασθαι συμβάσεις, ἵνα τὴν Αἴγυπτον ἐκλιπόντες
ὅποι βούλονται πάντες ἀβλαβεῖς ἀπέλθωσι. τοὺς
89 δὲ ἐπὶ ταῖς ὁμολογίαις πανοικησίᾳ μετὰ τῶν
κτήσεων οὐκ ἐλάττους μυριάδων ὄντας εἴκοσι καὶ
τεσσάρων ἀπὸ τῆς Αἰγύπτου τὴν ἔρημον εἰς Συρίαν
διοδοιπορῆσαι. φοβουμένους δὲ τὴν Ἀσσυρίων
90 δυναστείαν, τότε γὰρ ἐκείνους τῆς Ἀσίας κρατεῖν,
ἐν τῇ νῦν Ἰουδαίᾳ καλουμένῃ πόλιν οἰκοδομησα-
μένους τοσαύταις μυριάσιν ἀνθρώπων ἀρκέσουσαν,
Ἱεροσόλυμα ταύτην ὀνομάσαι.

91   Ἐν ἄλλῃ δέ τινι βίβλῳ τῶν Αἰγυπτιακῶν
Μανεθὼς τοῦτό φησι ⟨τὸ⟩[1] ἔθνος, τοὺς καλου-
μένους Ποιμένας, αἰχμαλώτους ἐν ταῖς ἱεραῖς
αὐτῶν βίβλοις γεγράφθαι, λέγων ὀρθῶς· καὶ
γὰρ τοῖς ἀνωτάτω προγόνοις ἡμῶν τὸ ποιμαίνειν
πάτριον ἦν, καὶ νομαδικὸν ἔχοντες τὸν βίον οὕτως
92 ἐκαλοῦντο Ποιμένες. αἰχμάλωτοί τε πάλιν οὐκ
ἀλόγως ὑπὸ τῶν Αἰγυπτίων ἀνεγράφησαν, ἐπειδή-
περ ὁ πρόγονος ἡμῶν Ἰώσηπος[2] ἑαυτὸν ἔφη πρὸς
τὸν βασιλέα τῶν Αἰγυπτίων αἰχμάλωτον εἶναι,

---

[1] Bekker : om. L.
[2] L (in margin): ἐν ἑτέρῳ ἀντιγράφῳ εὑρέθη οὕτως· κατήχθη
πραθεὶς παρὰ τῶν ἀδελφῶν εἰς Αἴγυπτον πρὸς τὸν βασιλέα τῆς
Αἰγύπτου, καὶ πάλιν ὕστερον τοὺς αὐτοῦ ἀδελφοὺς μετεπέμψατο
τοῦ βασιλέως ἐπιτρέψαντος.

---

[1] 240,000—the number of the garrison mentioned in
§ 78, where they are described as " hoplites ".
[2] On the origin of " Jeru-šalem," see A. Jirku in *Zeitschr.
d. Deutsch. Morgenl. Gesellschaft*, 90 (1936), pp. * 10 * f. :
the first part, Jeru-, is non-Semitic (*cf. O.T. Ezek.* xvi. 2,
45 : *2 Sam.* xxiv. 16, and the names Jeru-ba'al, Jeru-'el ;

a treaty by which they should all depart from Egypt
and go unmolested where they pleased. On these
terms the Shepherds, with their possessions and
households complete, no fewer than 240,000 persons,[1]
left Egypt and journeyed over the desert into Syria.
There, dreading the power of the Assyrians who were
at that time masters of Asia, they built in the land
now called Judaea a city large enough to hold all
those thousands of people, and gave it the name of
Jerusalem.[2]

In another book [3] of his *History of Egypt* Manetho
says that this race of so-called Shepherds is, in the
sacred books of Egypt, described as " captives " ;
and his statement is correct. With our remotest
ancestors, indeed, it was a hereditary custom to
feed sheep ; and as they lived a nomadic life, they
were called Shepherds.[4] On the other hand, in the
Egyptian records they were not unreasonably styled
Captives, since our ancestor Joseph told the king of
Egypt [5] that he was a captive, and later, with the

also, Jaru-wataš in an inscr. of Boghazköi) ; the second
part, Šalem, is a Canaanitish divine name, found in the
texts of Ras esh-Shamra. The name of the city occurs
in the El-Amarna Letters in the form " Urusalimmu,"
the oldest literary mention of Jerusalem.

[3] *Cf.* § 83 for the same information, there attributed to
" another copy ".

[4] *Cf. O.T. Genesis* xlvi. 32-34, xlvii. 3.

[5] In the Biblical narrative Joseph told the chief butler
or cup-bearer (*Genesis* xl. 15). The margin of the Florentine MS. has a note on this passage : " In another copy
(*i.e.* of the treatise *Against Apion*) the following reading
was found—' he was sold by his brethren and brought
down into Egypt to the king of Egypt ; and later, again,
with the king's consent, summoned his brethren to Egypt '."

καὶ τοὺς ἀδελφοὺς εἰς τὴν Αἴγυπτον ὕστερον
μετεπέμψατο, τοῦ βασιλέως ἐπιτρέψαντος.   ἀλλὰ
περὶ μὲν τούτων ἐν ἄλλοις ποιήσομαι τὴν ἐξέτασιν
ἀκριβεστέραν.

Fr. 43.   Syncellus, p. 113.   ΚΑΤΑ ΑΦΡΙΚΑΝΟΝ.

Πεντεκαιδεκάτη δυναστεία Ποιμένων.   ἦσαν
δὲ Φοίνικες ξένοι βασιλεῖς ς', οἳ καὶ Μέμφιν
εἷλον, οἳ καὶ ἐν τῷ Σεθροΐτῃ νομῷ πόλιν ἔκτισαν,
ἀφ' ἧς ὁρμώμενοι Αἰγυπτίους ἐχειρώσαντο.

᾽Ὧν πρῶτος Σαΐτης ἐβασίλευσεν ἔτη ιθ', ἀφ'
οὗ καὶ ὁ Σαΐτης νομός.[1]

β' Βνῶν, ἔτη μδ'.

γ' Παχνάν, ἔτη ξα'.

δ' Σταάν, ἔτη ν'.

ε' Ἄρχλης, ἔτη μθ'.

ς' Ἄφωφις,[2] ἔτη ξα'.

'Ομοῦ, ἔτη σπδ'.

[1] In B the words οἳ καὶ ἐν τῷ Σεθροΐτῃ νομῷ . . . ἐχειρώσαντο
come after ὁ Σαΐτης νομός.

[2] m.: Ἄφοβις MSS.

[1] The reference seems to be to Fr. 54, § 227 ff., but ἐν
ἄλλοις usually refers to a separate work.

[2] Africanus gives a less correct list than Josephus (cf.
the transposition of Apóphis to the end):   there is further
corruption in Eusebius (Fr. 48) and the Book of Sôthis
(App. IV.).

[3] This statement of the Phoenician origin of the Hyksôs
kings has generally been discredited until recently: now
the Ras esh-Shamra tablets, which imply a pantheon
strikingly similar to that of the Hyksôs, have shown that
the Hyksôs were closely related to the Phoenicians.

king's consent, summoned his brethren to Egypt.
But I shall investigate this subject more fully in
another place.[1]

Dynasty XV.

Fr. 43 (*from Syncellus*). According to Africanus.[2]

The Fifteenth Dynasty consisted of Shepherd Kings.
There were six foreign kings from Phoenicia,[3] who
seized Memphis : in the Sethroïte nome they founded
a town, from which as a base they subdued Egypt.

The first of these kings, Saïtês, reigned for 19
years : the Saïte nome [4] is called after him.

2. Bnôn, for 44 years.

3. Pachnan [Apachnan], for 61 years.

4. Staan,[5] for 50 years.

5. Archlês,[6] for 49 years.

6. Aphôphis,[7] (Aphobis), for 61 years.

Total, 284 years.

[4] See p. 80 n. 3. The Saïte nome proper, as opposed
to this " Tanite " nome, is mentioned in Egyptian texts
of the Old Kingdom. For the famous Saïs, the seat of
Dynasty XXVI. (now Sa El-Hagar, see Baedeker,[8] p. 36
—N.W. of Tanta on the right bank of the Rosetta branch),
the centre of the cult of Neith, " the metropolis of the
lower country " (Strabo, 17. 1, 18), *cf.* Herodotus, ii. 62 ;
Diod. i. 28, 4 (for its relation to Athens).

[5] For Iannas (in Josephus), the Khian of the Monuments,
see p. 83 n. 2.

[6] Archlês here, and in Eusebius (Fr. 48), corresponds
with Assis (or Aseth) in Josephus (Fr. 42, § 80) ; but the
change in the form of the name is extraordinary.

[7] The length of reign (61 years, as in Josephus) leads one
to believe that Africanus has transposed Apôphis from
the 4th place to the 6th ; but in point of fact the last
Hyksôs king whom we know by name was called Apepi.

Fr. 44 (a).   *Syncellus*, p. 114.   *ΚΑΤΑ ΕΥΣΕΒΙΟΝ.*

Πεντεκαιδεκάτη δυναστεία Διοσπολιτῶν βασιλέων, οἳ ἐβασίλευσαν ἔτη σν´.

(b) EUSEBIUS, *Chronica I.* (Armenian Version),
p. 99.

Quinta decima dynastia Diospolitarum regum, qui
regnarunt annis CCL.

Fr. 45.   *Syncellus*, p. 114.   *ΚΑΤΑ ΑΦΡΙΚΑΝΟΝ.*

῾Εκκαιδεκάτη δυναστεία Ποιμένες ἄλλοι βασιλεῖς
λβ´ · ἐβασίλευσαν ἔτη φιη´.

Fr. 46 (a).   *Syncellus*, p. 114.   *ΚΑΤΑ ΕΥΣΕΒΙΟΝ.*

῾Εκκαιδεκάτη δυναστεία Θηβαῖοι βασιλεῖς ε´,[1] οἳ
καὶ ἐβασίλευσαν ἔτη ρϟ´.

(b) EUSEBIUS, *Chronica I.* (Armenian Version),
p. 99.

Sexta decima dynastia Thebaeorum regum V, qui
regnarunt annis CXC.

[1] η´ Boeckh.

92

Fr. 44 (a) (*from Syncellus*). ACCORDING TO EUSEBIUS.

The Fifteenth Dynasty consisted of kings of Diospolis, who reigned for 250 years.

(b) ARMENIAN VERSION OF EUSEBIUS.

The Fifteenth Dynasty consisted of kings of Diospolis, who reigned for 250 years.

DYNASTY XVI.

Fr. 45 (*from Syncellus*). ACCORDING TO AFRICANUS.

The Sixteenth Dynasty were Shepherd Kings again, 32 in number : they reigned for 518 years.[1]

Fr. 46 (a) (*from Syncellus*). ACCORDING TO EUSEBIUS.

The Sixteenth Dynasty were kings of Thebes, 5 in number : they reigned for 190 years.

(b) ARMENIAN VERSION OF EUSEBIUS.

The Sixteenth Dynasty were kings of Thebes, 5 in number : they reigned for 190 years.

---

[1] Barbarus gives 318 years (p. 23, XV.) ; Meyer conjectures that the true number is 418 (*Aeg. Chron.* p. 99). Contrast Fr. 42, § 84 (511 years).

93

Fr. 47. *Syncellus*, p. 114. ΚΑΤΑ ΑΦΡΙΚΑΝΟΝ.

῾Επτακαιδεκάτη δυναστεία Ποιμένες ἄλλοι βασιλεῖς μγ' καὶ Θηβαῖοι ἢ[1] Διοσπολῖται μγ'.

῾Ομοῦ οἱ Ποιμένες καὶ οἱ Θηβαῖοι ἐβασίλευσαν
ἔτη ρνα'.

Fr. 48 (a). *Syncellus*, p. 114. ΚΑΤΑ ΕΥΣΕΒΙΟΝ.

῾Επτακαιδεκάτη δυναστεία Ποιμένες ἦσαν ἀδελφοὶ[2] Φοίνικες ξένοι βασιλεῖς, οἳ καὶ Μέμφιν εἷλον.

῏Ων πρῶτος Σαΐτης ἐβασίλευσεν ἔτη ιθ', ἀφ'
οὗ καὶ ὁ Σαΐτης νομὸς ἐκλήθη, οἳ καὶ ἐν τῷ
Σεθροΐτῃ νομῷ πόλιν ἔκτισαν, ἀφ' ἧς ὁρμώμενοι
Αἰγυπτίους ἐχειρώσαντο.

[1] Müller.
[2] A *lapsus calami* for δὲ (Meyer): Africanus (Fr. 43) preserves the true text: ἦσαν δὲ Φοίνικες . .

---

[1] See H. E. Winlock, "Tombs of the Seventeenth
Dynasty at Thebes," in *J. Eg. Arch.* x. pp. 217 ff.
[2] Barbarus gives 221 years (p. 23, XVI.). According to
Manetho the total length of the foreign usurpation probably was 929 years (260 in Josephus + 518 + 151).
Josephus (Fr. 42, § 84) gives 511 years. These statements,
even if based on actual traditions, have no weight as
compared with the certain *data* of the Monuments. The
almost complete lack of buildings of the Hyksôs time and
the close connexion of the Thebans of Dynasty XVII.

DYNASTY XVII

Fr. 47 (*from Syncellus*). ACCORDING TO AFRICANUS.

The Seventeenth Dynasty [1] were Shepherd Kings again, 43 in number, and kings of Thebes or Diospolis, 43 in number.

Total of the reigns of the Shepherd Kings and the Theban kings, 151 years.[2]

Fr. 48 (a) (*from Syncellus*). ACCORDING TO EUSEBIUS.

The Seventeenth Dynasty were Shepherds and brothers : [3] they were foreign kings from Phoenicia, who seized Memphis.

The first of these kings, Saïtês, reigned for 19 years : the Saïte nome [4] is called after him. These kings founded in the Sethroïte nome a town, from which as a base they subdued Egypt.

---

with those of Dynasty XIII. tend to show that the Hyksôs rule in the Nile Valley lasted for about a hundred and twenty years, c. 1700-1580 B.C. Under one of the Theban kings, Ta'o, who bore the epithet " The Brave," war with the Hyksôs broke out c. 1590 B.C. ; Kamose, the last king of Dynasty XVII., continued the war of independence, and Amôsis (of Dynasty XVIII.) finally expelled the usurpers.

[3] This must be a mistake of transcription : see note 2 on the text.

[4] See Fr. 42, § 78, n. 3, Fr. 43, n. 4.

β′ Βνῶν, ἔτη μ′.
γ′ [1] Ἄφωφις, ἔτη ιδ′.
Μεθ᾽ ὃν Ἄρχλης, ἔτη λ′.
Ὁμοῦ, ἔτη ργ′.

Κατὰ τούτους Αἰγυπτίων βασιλεὺς Ἰωσὴφ δείκνυται.

(b) Eusebius, *Chronica I.* (Armenian Version),
p. 99 sq.

Septima decima dynastia Pastorum, qui fratres
erant Phoenices exterique reges, et Memphin occuparunt.

Ex his primus Saïtes imperavit annis XIX, a quo
Saïtarum quoque nomos nomen traxit. Eidem in
Sethroïte nomo urbem condiderunt, unde incursione
facta Aegyptios perdomuerunt.

Secundus Bnon, annis XL.
Deinde Archles, annis XXX.
Aphophis, annis XIV.

Summa annorum CIII.
Horum aetate regnavisse in Aegypto Josephus
videtur.

[1] Om. A.

---

[1] See p. 95 n. 3.　　　　[2] See p. 80 n. 3.

2. Bnôn, for 40 years.
3. Aphôphis, for 14 years.

After him Archlês reigned for 30 years.
    Total, 103 years.

It was in their time that Joseph was appointed king of Egypt.

(b) ARMENIAN VERSION OF EUSEBIUS.

The Seventeenth Dynasty consisted of Shepherds, who were brothers [1] from Phoenicia and foreign kings: they seized Memphis.   The first of these kings, Saïtes, reigned for 19 years: from him, too, the Saïte nome [2] derived its name.   These kings founded in the Sethroïte nome a town from which they made a raid and subdued Egypt.

The second king was Bnon, for 40 years.
Next, Archles, for 30 years.
Aphophis, for 14 years.

    Total, 103 years.

It was in their time that Joseph appears to have ruled in Egypt.[3]

    The Armenian text of this sentence is rather difficult, but Professor Margoliouth, pointing out that the Armenian present infinitive is used here for the perfect, approves of this rendering.   Karst translates the Armenian in the following sense: "It is under these kings that Joseph arises, to rule over Egypt".

Fr. 49.   *Scholia in Platonis Timaeum*, 21 E
(Hermann).

Σαϊτικός· ἐκ τῶν Μανεθὼ Αἰγυπτιακῶν. Ἑπτακαιδεκάτη δυναστεία Ποιμένες· ἦσαν ἀδελφοὶ[1] Φοίνικες ξένοι βασιλεῖς, οἳ καὶ Μέμφιν εἷλον.

Ὧν πρῶτος Σ α ΐ τ η ς ἐβασίλευσεν ἔτη ιθ', ἀφ' οὗ καὶ ὁ Σαΐτης νομὸς ἐκλήθη· οἳ καὶ ἐν τῷ Σεθρωΐτῃ νομῷ πόλιν ἔκτισαν, ἀφ' ἧς ὁρμώμενοι Αἰγυπτίους ἐχειρώσαντο.

Δεύτερος τούτων Βνῶν, ἔτη μ'.

Τρίτος Ἀρχάης, ἔτη λ'.

Τέταρτος Ἄφωφις, ἔτη ιδ'.

Ὁμοῦ, ργ'.

Ὁ δὲ Σαΐτης προσέθηκε τῷ μηνὶ ὥρας ιβ', ὡς εἶναι ἡμερῶν λ', καὶ τῷ ἐνιαυτῷ ἡμέρας ς', καὶ γέγονεν ἡμερῶν τξέ.

---

[1] δὲ conj.: *cf.* Fr. 48 (a).

Fr. 49 (*from the Scholia to Plato*).

Saïtic, of Saïs.   From the *Aegyptiaca* of Manetho.
The Seventeenth Dynasty consisted of Shepherds :
they were brothers [1] from Phoenicia, foreign kings,
who seized Memphis.   The first of these kings, Saïtês,
reigned for 19 years : the Saïte nome [2] is called after
him.   These kings founded in the Sethrôïte nome a
town, from which as a base they subdued Egypt.

The second of these kings, Bnôn, reigned for 40
years ; the third, Archaês, for 30 years ; and the
fourth, Aphôphis, for 14 years.   Total, 103 years.

Saïtês added 12 hours to the month, to make its
length 30 days ; and he added 6 days to the year,
which thus comprised 365 days.[3]

---

[1] See p. 95 n. 3.   [2] See p. 80 n. 3.

[3] The addition of 5 days (not 6, as above) to the short
year of 360 days was made long before the Hyksôs age :
it goes back to at least the Pyramid Age, and probably
earlier.   The introduction of the calendar, making an
artificial reconciliation of the lunar and solar years, perhaps
as early as 4236 B.C., is believed to give the earliest fixed
date in human history : see V. Gordon Childe, *New Light
on the Most Ancient East*, 1934, pp. 5 f.

Fr. 50.   Josephus, *Contra Apionem*, I, 15, 16,
§§ 93–105.[1]

(Continued from Fr. 42.)

93   Νυνὶ δὲ τῆς ἀρχαιότητος ταύτης παρατίθεμαι
τοὺς Αἰγυπτίους μάρτυρας.   πάλιν οὖν τὰ τοῦ
Μανεθῶ[2] πῶς ἔχει πρὸς τὴν τῶν χρόνων τάξιν
94 ὑπογράψω.   φησὶ δὲ οὕτως·   '' μετὰ τὸ ἐξελθεῖν ἐξ
Αἰγύπτου τὸν λαὸν τῶν Ποιμένων εἰς Ἱεροσόλυμα,
ὁ ἐκβαλὼν αὐτοὺς ἐξ Αἰγύπτου βασιλεὺς Τέθμωσις
ἐβασίλευσεν μετὰ ταῦτα ἔτη εἰκοσιπέντε καὶ
μῆνας τέσσαρας καὶ ἐτελεύτησεν, καὶ παρέλαβεν
τὴν ἀρχὴν ὁ αὐτοῦ υἱὸς Χέβρων ἔτη δεκατρία.
95 μεθ' ὃν Ἀμένωφις εἴκοσι καὶ μῆνας ἑπτά.   τοῦ
δὲ ἀδελφὴ Ἀμεσσὶς[3] εἰκοσιὲν καὶ μῆνας ἐννέα.
τῆς δὲ Μήφρης δώδεκα καὶ μῆνας ἐννέα.   τοῦ
δὲ Μηφραμούθωσις εἰκοσιπέντε καὶ μῆνας δέκα.
96 τοῦ δὲ Θμῶσις[4] ἐννέα καὶ μῆνας ὀκτώ.   τοῦ δ'
Ἀμένωφις τριάκοντα καὶ μῆνας δέκα.   τοῦ δὲ

---

[1] §§ 94–105 are quoted by Theophilus, *Ad Autolycum*, III,
20 f.   §§ 103, 104 are quoted by Eusebius, *Praepar. Evang.*,
X, 13.
   [2] Niese : Μανέθωνος L.
   [3] Naber : Ἀμενσὶς Fr. 52 : Ἀμεσσὴς L.
   [4] Τυθμώσης Manetho, Fr. 51 : Τούθμωσις Fr. 52, 53.

---

[1] The New Kingdom : Dynasties XVIII.-XX.: c. 1580–
c. 1100 B.C.
   Dynasty XVIII. c. 1580–1310 B.C.
   For identifications with the monumental evidence which
is firmly established, see Meyer, *Geschichte*[2], ii. 1, p. 78 :
the names and order of the first nine kings are : (1) Amôsis

DYNASTIES, XVIII,[1] XIX.

Fr. 50 (*from* Josephus, *Contra Apionem*, i. 15, 16, §§ 93-105)—(*continued from* Fr. 42).

For the present I am citing the Egyptians as witnesses to this antiquity of ours. I shall therefore resume my quotations from Manetho's works in their reference to chronology. His account is as follows : " After the departure of the tribe of Shepherds from Egypt to Jerusalem, Tethmôsis,[2] the king who drove them out of Egypt, reigned for 25 years 4 months until his death, when he was succeeded by his son Chebrôn, who ruled for 13 years. After him Amenôphis reigned for 20 years 7 months ; then his sister Amessis for 21 years 9 months ; then her son Mêphrês for 12 years 9 months ; then his son Mêphramuthôsis for 25 years 10 months ; then his son Thmôsis for 9 years 8 months ; then his son Amenôphis

(Chebrôn is unexplained), (2) Amenôphis I., (3) Tuthmôsis I., (4) Tuthmôsis II., (5) Hatshepsut (apparently Manetho's Amessis or Amensis : the same length of reign, 21 years), (6) Tuthmôsis III. (corresponding to Mêphrês, *i.e.* Menkheperrê' or Meshperê', and Misphragmuthôsis, *i.e.* Menkheperrê' Thutmose), (7) Amenôphis II., (8) Tuthmôsis IV. (the order of these two being reversed by Manetho), (9) Amenôphis III. (Hôrus, the same length of reign, 36 years).

The remaining kings of the dynasty are : Amenôphis IV. (Akhnaten, see p. 123 n. 1), Semenkhkarê' (? Acenchêrês), Tût'ankhamon (? Chebrês), Ay (? Acherrês) : see *C.A.H.* ii. p. 702. On rulers Nos. 3, 4, 5 and 6, see Wm. F. Edgerton, *The Thutmosid Succession*, 1933.

For Dynasty XIX. see p. 148 n. 1.

[2] Tethmôsis = Amôsis : see note on Misphragmuthôsis, Fr. 42, § 86. For the scarab of Amôsis see Plate 1, 3.

Ὧρος τριακονταὲξ καὶ μῆνας πέντε. τοῦ δὲ
θυγάτηρ Ἀκεγχερὴς δώδεκα καὶ μῆνα ἕνα. τῆς
97 δὲ Ῥάθωτις ἀδελφὸς ἐννέα. τοῦ δὲ Ἀκεγχήρης
δώδεκα καὶ μῆνας πέντε. τοῦ δὲ Ἀκεγχήρης
ἕτερος δώδεκα καὶ μῆνας τρεῖς. τοῦ δὲ Ἁρμαῒς
τέσσαρα καὶ μῆνα ἕνα. τοῦ δὲ Ῥαμέσσης ἓν
καὶ μῆνας τέσσαρας. τοῦ δὲ Ἁρμέσσης Μιαμοῦν
ἑξηκονταὲξ καὶ μῆνας δύο. τοῦ δὲ Ἀμένωφις
98 δεκαεννέα καὶ μῆνας ἕξ. τοῦ δὲ Σέθως ὁ καὶ
Ῥαμέσσης,[1] ἱππικὴν καὶ ναυτικὴν ἔχων δύναμιν,
τὸν μὲν ἀδελφὸν Ἅρμαῒν ἐπίτροπον τῆς Αἰγύπτου
κατέστησεν,[2] καὶ πᾶσαν μὲν αὐτῷ τὴν ἄλλην βασιλικὴν περιέθηκεν ἐξουσίαν, μόνον δὲ ἐνετείλατο
διάδημα μὴ φορεῖν μηδὲ τὴν βασιλίδα μητέρα τε
99 τῶν τέκνων ἀδικεῖν, ἀπέχεσθαι δὲ καὶ τῶν ἄλλων
βασιλικῶν παλλακίδων. αὐτὸς δὲ ἐπὶ Κύπρον καὶ
Φοινίκην καὶ πάλιν Ἀσσυρίους τε καὶ Μήδους

---

[1] Eus.: Σέθωσις καὶ Ῥαμέσσης L.

[2] L (in margin): εὑρέθη ἐν ἑτέρῳ ἀντιγράφῳ οὕτως· μεθ' ὃν
Σέθωσις καὶ Ῥαμέσσης δύο ἀδελφοί· ὁ μὲν ναυτικὴν ἔχων δύναμιν
τοὺς κατὰ θάλατταν † ἀπαντῶντας καὶ διαχειρωμένους † (διαπειρω-
μένους Naber) ἐπολιόρκει· μετ' οὐ πολὺ δὲ καὶ τὸν Ῥαμέσσην
ἀνελών, Ἅρμαῒν ἄλλον αὐτοῦ ἀδελφὸν ἐπίτροπον τῆς Αἰγύπτου
καταστῆσαι (for κατέστησε).

---

[1] Howard Carter (Tutankhamen, iii. p. 3) points out that
monuments of Amenôphis III. are dated to his 37th year,
perhaps even to his 40th year; and he explains that
Manetho has given the length of his reign as sole ruler.
More commonly, the high figures assigned to the reigns of
kings may be explained by the assumption that over-
lapping co-regencies have been included.

[2] Miamûn = Mey-amûn, " beloved of Amûn ".

for 30 years 10 months;[1] then his son Ôrus for 36 years
5 months ; then his daughter Acenchĕrês for 12 years
1 month ; then her brother Rathôtis for 9 years ;
then his son Acenchêrês for 12 years 5 months, his
son Acenchêrês II. for 12 years 3 months, his son
Harmaïs for 4 years 1 month, his son Ramessês for
1 year 4 months, his son Harmessês Miamûn[2] for
66 years 2 months, his son Amenôphis for 19 years
6 months, and his son Sethôs, also called Ramessês,[3]
whose power lay in his cavalry and his fleet. This
king appointed his brother Harmaïs viceroy of Egypt,
and invested him with all the royal prerogatives,
except that he charged him not to wear a diadem,
nor to wrong the queen, the mother of his children,
and to refrain likewise from the royal concubines.
He then set out on an expedition against Cyprus and
Phoenicia and later against the Assyrians and the

[3] The margin of the Florentine MS. has a note here :
" The following reading was found in another copy :
' After him Sethôsis and Ramessês, two brothers. The
former, with a strong fleet, blockaded his murderous (?)
adversaries by sea. Not long after, he slew Ramessês and
appointed another of his brothers, Harmaïs, as viceroy of
Egypt.' " This is intended as a correction of the text of
Josephus, but it contains the error of the Florentine MS.
in the reading Σέθωσις καὶ 'Ραμέσσης. Sethôsis is the
Sesostris of Herodotus, ii. 102, where his naval expedition
in the " Red Sea " is described.

Meyer, *Aeg. Chron.* p. 91, considers the words " also
called Ramesses " an addition to Manetho. See § 245.

W. Struve (see p. 148 n. 1) would here emend Sethôs
into Sesôs, which was a name of Ramesês II. : according
to the monuments he reigned for 67 years (*cf.* Fr. 55, 2),
and his triumphant Asiatic campaigns were told by
Hecataeus of Abdera (Osymandyas in Diodorus Siculus,
i. 47 ff.).

στρατεύσας, ἅπαντας τοὺς μὲν δόρατι, τοὺς δὲ
ἀμαχητὶ φόβῳ δὲ τῆς πολλῆς δυνάμεως ὑποχειρίους
ἔλαβε, καὶ μέγα φρονήσας ἐπὶ ταῖς εὐπραγίαις ἔτι
καὶ θαρσαλεώτερον ἐπεπορεύετο τὰς πρὸς ἀνατολὰς
100 πόλεις τε καὶ χώρας καταστρεφόμενος. χρόνου
τε ἱκανοῦ γεγονότος, Ἅρμαῖς ὁ καταλειφθεὶς ἐν
Αἰγύπτῳ πάντα τἄμπαλιν οἷς ἀδελφὸς [1] παρῄνει
μὴ ποιεῖν ἀδεῶς ἔπραττεν· καὶ γὰρ τὴν βασιλίδα
βιαίως ἔσχεν καὶ ταῖς ἄλλαις παλλακίσιν ἀφειδῶς
διετέλει χρώμενος, πειθόμενος δὲ [2] ὑπὸ τῶν φίλων
101 διάδημα ἐφόρει καὶ ἀντῆρε τῷ ἀδελφῷ. ὁ δὲ
τεταγμένος ἐπὶ τῶν ἱερέων [3] τῆς Αἰγύπτου γράψας
βιβλίον ἔπεμψε τῷ Σεθώσει, δηλῶν αὐτῷ πάντα
καὶ ὅτι ἀντῆρεν ὁ ἀδελφὸς αὐτῷ Ἅρμαῖς. παρα-
χρῆμα οὖν ὑπέστρεψεν εἰς Πηλούσιον καὶ ἐκράτησεν
102 τῆς ἰδίας βασιλείας. ἡ δὲ χώρα ἐκλήθη ἀπὸ τοῦ
αὐτοῦ ὀνόματος Αἴγυπτος· λέγεται [4] γὰρ ὅτι ὁ
μὲν Σέθως ἐκαλεῖτο Αἴγυπτος, Ἅρμαῖς δὲ ὁ ἀδελφὸς
αὐτοῦ Δαναός.''

---

[1] ἀδελφὸς Gutschmid: ἀδελφὸς L.   [2] τε conj. Niese.
[3] ἱερέων L (perhaps an Ancient Egyptian formula): ἱερῶν
Hudson (sacra Lat., fana Eus.)—with this cf. Revenue Laws
of Ptolemy Philadelphus, 51⁹ (258 B.C.) οἱ ἐπὶ τῶν ἱερῶν τεταγ-
μένοι.   [4] λέγεται Gutschmid: λέγει L (dicit Lat.).

---

[1] A frequent title from the Old Kingdom onwards is
" overseer of the priests of Upper and Lower Egypt,''
later applied to the high priest of Amûn. The emendation ἱερῶν (for ἱερέων) is supported by a reference in a
papyrus of about the time of Manetho.
[2] See Fr. 54, § 274, n. 1 (pp. 140-141).
[3] With the return of Sethôs to a country in revolt, cf.
Herodotus, ii. 107 (return of Sesostris and the perilous

Medes; and he subjugated them all, some by the
sword, others without a blow and merely by the
menace of his mighty host.   In the pride of his conquests, he continued his advance with still greater
boldness, and subdued the cities and lands of the
East.   When a considerable time had elapsed,
Harmaïs who had been left behind in Egypt, reck-
lessly contravened all his brother's injunctions.   He
outraged the queen and proceeded to make free with
the concubines; then, following the advice of his
friends, he began to wear a diadem and rose in revolt
against his brother.   The warden of the priests of
Egypt [1] then wrote a letter which he sent to Sethôsis,
revealing all the details, including the revolt of his
brother Harmaïs.   Sethôsis forthwith returned to
Pêlusium [2] and took possession of his kingdom [3]; and
the land was named Aegyptus after him.   It is said
that Sethôs was called Aegyptus, and his brother
Harmaïs, Danaus." [4]

banquet), Diod. Sic. i. 57, 6-8.   The tale appears to be
a piece of folklore (Maspero, *Journ. des Savants*, 1901,
pp. 599, 665 ff.).   See Wainwright, *Sky-Religion*, p. 48.

[4] Danaus: *cf.* § 231.   See Meyer, *Aeg. Chron.* p. 75, for
the theory that the identification of Sethôs and Harmaïs
with Aegyptus and Danaus is due, not to Manetho, but to
a Jewish commentator or interpolator.

The tradition is that Danaus, a king of Egypt, was
expelled by his brother and fled to Argos with his fifty
daughters, and there "the sons of Aegyptus" were slain
by " the daughters of Danaus."   The legend appears to
have existed in Egypt as well as in Greece: see Diod. Sic.
i. 28. 2, 97. 2.   For attempts to explain the story in terms
of Aegean pre-history, see J. L. Myres, *Who Were the
Greeks ?* (1930), pp. 323 ff.; M. P. Nilsson, *The Mycenaean
Origin of Greek Mythology* (1932), p. 64.

103   Ταῦτα μὲν ὁ Μανεθώς. δῆλον δ' ἐστὶν ἐκ τῶν
εἰρημένων ἐτῶν, τοῦ χρόνου συλλογισθέντος, ὅτι
οἱ καλούμενοι Ποιμένες, ἡμέτεροι δὲ[1] πρόγονοι,
τρισὶ καὶ ἐνενήκοντα καὶ τριακοσίοις πρόσθεν ἔτεσιν
ἐκ τῆς Αἰγύπτου ἀπαλλαγέντες τὴν χώραν ταύτην
ἐπῴκησαν ἢ Δαναὸν εἰς Ἄργος ἀφικέσθαι· καίτοι
104 τοῦτον ἀρχαιότατον Ἀργεῖοι νομίζουσι. δύο τοίνυν
ὁ Μανεθὼς ἡμῖν τὰ μέγιστα μεμαρτύρηκεν ἐκ τῶν
παρ' Αἰγυπτίοις γραμμάτων, πρῶτον μὲν τὴν ἑτέ-
ρωθεν ἄφιξιν εἰς Αἴγυπτον, ἔπειτα δὲ τὴν ἐκεῖθεν
ἀπαλλαγὴν οὕτως ἀρχαίαν τοῖς χρόνοις, ὡς ἐγγύς
που προτερεῖν[2] αὐτὴν τῶν Ἰλιακῶν ἔτεσι χιλίοις.
105 ὑπὲρ ὧν δ' ὁ Μανεθὼς οὐκ ἐκ τῶν παρ' Αἰγυπτίοις
γραμμάτων,[3] ἀλλ', ὡς αὐτὸς ὡμολόγηκεν, ἐκ τῶν
ἀδεσπότως μυθολογουμένων προστέθεικεν, ὕστερον
ἐξελέγξω κατὰ μέρος ἀποδεικνὺς τὴν ἀπίθανον
αὐτοῦ ψευδολογίαν.

Fr. 51.   THEOPHILUS, *Ad Autolycum*, III, 20 (Otto).

Ὁ δὲ Μωσῆς ὁδηγήσας[4] τοὺς Ἰουδαίους, **ὡς**
ἔφθημεν εἰρηκέναι, ἐκβεβλημένους ἀπὸ γῆς Αἰγύπτου

---

[1] δὲ Eus. : om. L, Lat.
[2] που προτερεῖν Eus., Lat. : τοῦ πρότερον L.
[3] γραμμάτων ed. pr. (*litteris* Lat., *libris* Eus.) : πραγμάτων L.
[4] Sc. ἦν : ὡδήγησε Boeckh.

---

[1] This total is reckoned from Tethmôsis (Amôsis) to the
end of the reign of Sethôsis, the latter being taken as 60
years (*cf.* § 231, where Sethôs is said to have reigned for
59 years after driving out Hermaeus).

Such is Manetho's account; and, if the time is reckoned according to the years mentioned, it is clear that the so-called Shepherds, our ancestors, quitted Egypt and settled in our land 393 years [1] before the coming of Danaus to Argos. Yet the Argives regard Danaus as belonging to a remote antiquity.[2] Thus Manetho has given us evidence from Egyptian records upon two very important points: first, upon our coming to Egypt from elsewhere; and secondly, upon our departure from Egypt at a date so remote that it preceded the Trojan war [3] by wellnigh a thousand years.[4] As for the additions which Manetho has made, not from the Egyptian records, but, as he has himself admitted, from anonymous legendary tales,[5] I shall later refute them in detail, and show the improbability of his lying stories.

Fr. 51 [6] (*from* Theophilus, *Ad Autolyc.* iii. 19).

Moses was the leader of the Jews, as I have already said, when they had been expelled from Egypt by

[2] The mythical King Inachus was held to be still more ancient: *cf.* Fr. 4, 1 (p. 19 n. 4).

[3] The traditional date of the Trojan war is 1192-1183 B.C.

[4] This appears to be about four times too high a figure: 250 years would be a nearer estimate.

[5] *Cf.* Fr. 54, §§ 229, 287, for Manetho's use of popular traditions.

[6] This list of Dynasties XVIII., XIX. is obviously derived wholly from Josephus, any variations from the text of Josephus being merely corruptions. Theophilus, Bishop of Antioch, wrote his apologia for the Christian faith (three books addressed to a friend Autolycus) in the second half of ii. A.D.

ὑπὸ βασιλέως Φαραὼ οὗ τοὔνομα *Τέθμωσις*, ὅς,
φασίν, μετὰ τὴν ἐκβολὴν τοῦ λαοῦ ἐβασίλευσεν ἔτη
εἴκοσι πέντε καὶ μῆνας δ', ὡς ὑφῄρηται Μαναιθώς.

2. Καὶ μετὰ τοῦτον *Χεβρῶν*, ἔτη ιγ'.

3. Μετὰ δὲ τοῦτον *Ἀμένωφις*, ἔτη κ', μῆνας
ἑπτά.

4. Μετὰ δὲ τοῦτον ἡ ἀδελφὴ αὐτοῦ *Ἀμέσση*,
ἔτη κα', μῆνα α'.[1]

5. Μετὰ δὲ ταύτην *Μήφρης*, ἔτη ιβ', μῆνας θ'.

6. Μετὰ δὲ τοῦτον *Μηφραμμούθωσις*, ἔτη
κ',[2] μῆνας ι'.

7. Καὶ μετὰ τοῦτον *Τυθμώσης*, ἔτη θ', μῆνας
η'.

8. Καὶ μετὰ τοῦτον *Ἀμένωφις*,[3] ἔτη λ', μῆνας
ι'.

9. Μετὰ δὲ τοῦτον *Ὧρος*, ἔτη λς,' μῆνας ε'.

10. Τούτου δὲ θυγάτηρ,[4] ‹*Ἀκεγχερής*›, ἔτη
ι[β'], μῆνας α'.[4]

11. Μετὰ δὲ ταύτην ‹*Ῥαθῶτις*, ἔτη θ'›.

12. ‹Μετὰ δὲ τοῦτον *Ἀκεγχήρης*, ἔτη ιβ', μῆνας
ε'›.

13. ‹Μετὰ δὲ τοῦτον *Ἀκ*› ε[γ]χ[ή]ρης, ἔτη ιβ',
μῆνας γ'.

14. Τοῦ δὲ *Ἄρμαϊς*, ἔτη δ', μῆνα α'.

15. Καὶ μετὰ τοῦτον *Ῥαμέσσης* ἐνιαυτὸν, μῆνας
δ'.

16. Καὶ μετὰ τοῦτον *Ῥαμέσσης Μιαμμού*,
ἔτη ξς'[5] καὶ μῆνας β'.

King Pharaôh whose name was Tethmôsis. After the expulsion of the people, this king, it is said, reigned for 25 years 4 months, according to Manetho's reckoning.

2. After him, Chebrôn ruled for 13 years.

3. After him, Amenôphis, for 20 years 7 months.

4. After him, his sister Amessê, for 21 years 1 month [9 months in Josephus].

5. After her, Mêphrês, for 12 years 9 months.

6. After him, Mêphrammuthôsis, for 20 years [25 years in Josephus] 10 months.

7. After him, Tuthmôsês, for 9 years 8 months.

8. After him, Amenôphis, for 30 years 10 months.

9. After him, Ôrus, for 36 years 5 months.

10. Next, his daughter [Acenchĕrês] reigned for 12 years 1 month.

11. After her, [Rathôtis, for 9 years.

12. After him, Acenchêrês, for 12 years 5 months.

13. After him, Ac]enchêrês [II.], for 12 years 3 months.

14. His son Harmaïs, for 4 years 1 month.

15. After him, Ramessês for 1 year and 4 months.

16. After him, Ramessês Miammû(n), for 66 years 2 months.

---

¹ a' *i.e.* ἕνα, in error for ἐννέα, Josephus, Fr. 50, § 95 (Müller).

² For κε', as in Josephus, Fr. 50, § 95.

³ Δαμενόφις Otto.

⁴ Restored from Josephus (Boeckh): MSS. θυγάτηρ ἔτη ι', μῆνας γ'. μετὰ δὲ ταύτην Μερχερής, ἔτη ιβ', μῆνας γ'.

⁵ μετὰ δὲ τοῦτον Μέσσης Μιαμμού, ἔτη [ξ]ϛ' Otto.

17. Καὶ μετὰ τοῦτον Ἀμένωφις, ἔτη ιθ΄, μῆνας ϛ΄.

Τοῦ δὲ Σέθως, ὃς[1] καὶ Ῥαμέσσης, ἔτη ι΄, ὃν[2] φασιν ἐσχηκέναι πολλὴν δύναμιν ἱππικῆς καὶ παράταξιν ναυτικῆς.

Fr. 52. Syncellus, pp. 115, 130, 133.

ΚΑΤΑ ΑΦΡΙΚΑΝΟΝ.

Ὀκτωκαιδεκάτη δυναστεία Διοσπολιτῶν βασιλέων ιϛ΄.

Ὧν πρῶτος Ἀμώς, ἐφ᾽ οὗ Μωϋσῆς ἐξῆλθεν ἐξ Αἰγύπτου, ὡς ἡμεῖς ἀποδεικνύομεν, ὡς δὲ ἡ παροῦσα ψῆφος ἀναγκάζει, ἐπὶ τούτου τὸν Μωϋσέα συμβαίνει νέον ἔτι εἶναι.

Δεύτερος κατὰ Ἀφρικανὸν κατὰ τὴν ιη΄ δυναστείαν ἐβασίλευσε Χεβρώς, ἔτη ιγ΄.

Τρίτος, Ἀμενωφθίς, ἔτη κδ΄.[3]

Τέταρτος,[4] Ἀμενσίς,[5] ἔτη κβ΄.

---

[1] τοῦ δὲ Θοῖσσος Otto.
[2] οὓς Otto, adding after ναυτικῆς the words κατὰ τοὺς ἰδίους χρόνους.
[3] κα΄ m.   [4] τετάρτη Müller.   [5] Ἀμερσίς A.

---

[1] See p. 100 n. 1.
[2] See p. 101 n. 2.   On the basis of new evidence scholars now tend to conclude that the Exodus took place c. 1445 B.C. (see e.g. J. W. Jack, *The Date of the Exodus*, 1925): Jericho fell c. 1400 B.C. (J. Garstang, *The Heritage of Solomon*, 1934, p. 281).
[3] *I.e.* Africanus.

17. After him, Amenôphis, for 19 years 6 months.
18. Then, his son Sethôs, also called Ramessês,
for 10 years. He is said to have possessed
a large force of cavalry and an organized
fleet.

DYNASTY XVIII.

Fr. 52 (*from Syncellus*). ACCORDING TO AFRICANUS.

The Eighteenth Dynasty [1] consisted of 16 kings of
Diospolis.

The first of these was Amôs, in whose reign
Moses went forth from Egypt,[2] as I [3] here declare ;
but, according to the convincing evidence of the
present calculation [4] it follows that in this reign
Moses was still young.

The second king of the Eighteenth Dynasty, according to Africanus, was Chebrôs, who reigned for
13 years.

The third king, Amenôphthis,[5] reigned for 24 (21)
years.

The fourth king (queen), Amensis (Amersis), reigned
for 22 years.

[4] *I.e.* by Syncellus.
[5] This Greek transcription of " Amenhotpe," retaining
both the labial and the dental, is the fullest form
of the name, " Amenôthês " showing assimilation :
" Amenôphis," which is regularly used to represent
" Amenhotpe," actually comes from another name,
" Amen(em)ôpe " (B.G.). The month Phamenôth
(February-March) is named from the " feast of
Amenôthês ".

Πέμπτος, Μίσαφρις, ἔτη ιγ'.

Ἕκτος, Μισφραγμούθωσις, ἔτη κϛ', ἐφ οὗ ὁ
ἐπὶ Δευκαλίωνος κατακλυσμός.

Ὁμοῦ ἐπὶ Ἀμώσεως τοῦ καὶ Μισφραγμουθώσεως
ἀρχῆς κατὰ Ἀφρικανὸν γίνονται ἔτη ξθ'. Τοῦ γὰρ
Ἀμὼς οὐδ' ὅλως εἶπεν ἔτη.

ζ'   Τούθμωσις, ἔτη θ'.

η'   Ἀμενῶφις, ἔτη λα'   Οὗτός ἐστιν ὁ Μέμ-
        νων εἶναι νομιζόμενος καὶ φθεγγόμενος λίθος.

θ'   Ὧρος, ἔτη λζ'.

ι'   Ἀχερρῆς, ἔτη λβ'.

ια'   Ῥαθῶς, ἔτη ἕξ.

ιβ'   Χεβρής, ἔτη ιβ'.

ιγ'   Ἀχερρῆς, ἔτη ιβ'.

ιδ'   Ἀρμεσίς,[1] ἔτη ε'.

ιε'   Ῥαμεσσῆς, ἔτος α'

ιϛ'   Ἀμενωφάθ,[2] ἔτη ιθ

Ὁμοῦ, ἔτη σξγ'.

[1] B : Ἀμεσῆς A.   [2] B : Ἀμενώφ G.

---

[1] This note about Memnôn in both Africanus and Eusebius should be transferred to the ninth king of the dynasty,
Ôrus or Amenôphis III.

[Footnote continued on opposite page.

The fifth, Misaphris, for 13 years.

The sixth, Misphragmuthôsis, for 26 years : in his reign the flood of Deucalion's time occurred.

Total, according to Africanus, down to the reign of Amôsis, also called Misphragmuthôsis, 69 years. Of the length of the reign of Amôs he said nothing at all.

   7. Tuthmôsis, for 9 years.

   8. Amenôphis, for 31 years. This is the king who was reputed to be Memnôn and a speaking statue.[1]

   9. Ôrus, for 37 years.

  10. Acherrês,[2] for 32 years.

  11. Rathôs, for 6 years.

  12. Chebrês, for 12 years.

  13. Acherrês, for 12 years.

  14. Armesis, for 5 years.

  15. Ramessês, for 1 year.

  16. Amenôphath (Amenôph), for 19 years.

Total, 263 years.

The reference is to the two monolithic colossi of Amenôphis III. (Baedeker[8], pp. 345 f.) : see Pausanias, i. 42 (the Thebans say it was a statue not of Memnôn, but of Phamenôph, who dwelt in those parts) with J. G. Frazer's note (vol. ii. pp. 530 f.), and Tacitus, *Ann.* ii. 61. Amenôphis III. (Memnôn) is correctly named in Greek Amenôth and Phamenôth by the poetess Balbilla (time of Hadrian) : see Werner Peek in *Mitt. des Deutsch. Inst. für äg. Alt. in Kairo*, v. 1 (1934), pp. 96, 99 ; *Sammelbuch*, 8211, 8213.

  [2] For possible identifications of Nos. 10, 12, and 13 see p. 101 n. 1. Nos. 14, 15, and 16 should be transferred to Dynasty XIX. : see p. 148 n. 1. Armesis (Armaîs) is probably Haremhab : Ramessês, vizier of Haremhab and afterwards Ramessês I., was probably of Heliopolitan origin (P. E. Newberry).

Fr. 53 (a).　*Syncellus*, pp. 116, 129, 133, 135.

ΚΑΤΑ ΕΥΣΕΒΙΟΝ.

'Οκτωκαιδεκάτη δυναστεία Διοσπολιτῶν
βασιλέων ιδ'.

*Ὧν πρῶτος, Ἄμωσις, ἔτη κε'.
β' Χεβρὼν δεύτερος, ἔτη ιγ'.
γ' Ἀμμενῶφις, ἔτη κα'.
δ' Μίφρης, ἔτη ιβ'.
ε' Μισφραγμούθωσις, ἔτη κϛ'.

'Ομοῦ ἀπ' Ἀμώσεως τοῦ πρώτου τῆς προκειμένης
ιη' δυναστείας ἕως Μισφραγμουθώσεως ἀρχῆς κατὰ
Εὐσέβιον ἔτη γίνονται οα', βασιλεῖς πέντε ἀντὶ τῶν
ἕξ· τὸν γὰρ τέταρτον Ἀμένσην παραδραμών, οὗ ὁ
Ἀφρικανὸς καὶ οἱ λοιποὶ μέμηνται, ἔτη κβ' αὐτοῦ
ἐκολόβωσεν.

ϛ' Τούθμωσις, ἔτη θ'.
ζ' Ἀμένωφις, ἔτη λα'. Οὗτός ἐστιν ὁ Μέμνων
εἶναι νομιζόμενος καὶ φθεγγόμενος λίθος.
η' *Ὧρος, ἔτη λϛ' (ἐν ἄλλῳ λη').
θ' Ἀχενχέρσης, ⟨ἔτη ιβ'⟩.
⟨Ἄθωρις, ἔτη λθ'⟩ [1].
⟨Κενχέρης⟩, ἔτη ιϛ'. [2]

Κατὰ τοῦτον Μωϋσῆς τῆς ἐξ Αἰγύπτου πορείας
τῶν Ἰουδαίων ἡγήσατο. (Syncellus adds : *Μόνος
Εὐσέβιος ἐπὶ τούτου λέγει τὴν τοῦ Ἰσραὴλ διὰ
Μωϋσέως ἔξοδον, μηδενὸς αὐτῷ λόγου μαρτυροῦντος,
ἀλλὰ καὶ πάντων ἐναντιουμένων τῶν πρὸ αὐτοῦ, ὡς
μαρτυρεῖ.*)

114

Fr. 53 (a) (*from Syncellus*).   ACCORDING TO
EUSEBIUS.

The Eighteenth Dynasty consisted of fourteen
kings of Diospolis.

The first of these, Amôsis, reigned for 25 years.

2. The second, Chebrôn, for 13 years.

3. Ammenôphis, for 21 years.

4. Miphrês, for 12 years.

5. Misphragmuthôsis, for 26 years.

Total from Amôsis, the first king of this Eighteenth
Dynasty, down to the reign of Misphragmuthôsis
amounts, according to Eusebius, to 71 years ; and
there are five kings, not six. For he omitted the
fourth king, Amensês, mentioned by Africanus and
the others, and thus cut off the 22 years of his reign.

6. Tuthmôsis, for 9 years.

7. Amenôphis, for 31 years.   This is the king
   who was reputed to be Memnôn and a speaking statue.[1]

8. Ôrus, for 36 years (in another copy, 38 years).

9. Achenchersês [for 12 years].

[Athôris, for 39 years (? 9).]

[Cencherês] for 16 years.

About this time Moses led the Jews in their march
out of Egypt. (Syncellus adds : Eusebius alone
places in this reign the exodus of Israel under Moses,
although no argument supports him, but all his predecessors hold a contrary view, as he testifies.)

[1] See p. 113 n. 1.

---

[1] θ′ Müller.

[2] B omits Ἀθωρις and Κενχέρης, reading θ′ Ἀχενχέρσης,
ἔτη ιϛ′.

ι΄ Ἀχερρῆς, ἔτη η΄.

ια΄ Χερρῆς, ἔτη ιε΄.

ιβ΄ Ἀρμαῒς ὁ καὶ Δαναός, ἔτη ε΄, μεθ᾽ ἃ ἐκ τῆς
　　Αἰγύπτου ἐκπεσὼν καὶ φεύγων τὸν ἀδελφὸν
　　Αἴγυπτον εἰς τὴν Ἑλλάδα ἀφικνεῖται, κρα-
　　τήσας τε τοῦ Ἄργους βασιλεύει τῶν Ἀρ-
　　γείων.

ιγ΄ Ῥαμεσσῆς[1] ὁ καὶ Αἴγυπτος, ἔτη ξη΄.

ιδ΄ Ἀμμένωφις, ἔτη μ΄.

'Ομοῦ, ἔτη τμη΄.

Προσέθηκεν ὑπὲρ τὸν Ἀφρικανὸν ἔτη πε΄ Εὐσέβιος κατὰ τὴν ιη΄ δυναστείαν. (Syncellus, p. 116:
Εὐσέβιος δύο βασιλεῖς περιέκρυψεν, ἔτη δὲ προσέθηκε πε΄, τμη΄ παραθεὶς ἀντὶ σξγ΄ τῶν παρ᾽ Ἀφρι-
κανῷ.)

(b) Eusebius, *Chronica I.* (Armenian Version),
p. 99.

Octava decima dynastia Diospolitarum regum
XIV, quorum primus

Amoses, annis XXV.
Chebron, annis XIII.
Amophis, annis XXI.
Memphres, annis XII.
Mispharmuthosis, annis XXVI.
Tuthmosis, annis IX.
Amenophis, annis XXXI.　Hic est qui Memnon
　　　putabatur, petra loquens.
Orus, annis XXVIII.

---

[1] Dindorf : Ἀμεσσῆς B.

10. Acherrês, for 8 years.
11. Cherrês, for 15 years.
12. Armaïs, also called Danaus, for 5 years : thereafter, he was banished from Egypt and, fleeing from his brother Aegyptus, he arrived in Greece, and, seizing Argos, he ruled over the Argives.
13. Ramessês, also called Aegyptus, for 68 years.
14. Ammenôphis, for 40 years.
Total, 348 years.

Eusebius assigns 85 years more than Africanus to the Eighteenth Dynasty. (Syncellus elsewhere says : Eusebius leaves out two kings, but adds 85 years, setting down 348 years instead of the 263 years of the reckoning of Africanus.)

(b) ARMENIAN VERSION OF EUSEBIUS.

The Eighteenth Dynasty consisted of fourteen kings of Diospolis. The first of these, Amoses, reigned for 25 years.
2. Chebron, for 13 years.
3. Amophis, for 21 years.
4. Memphres, for 12 years.
5. Mispharmuthosis, for 26 years.
6. Tuthmosis, for 9 years.
7. Amenophis, for 31 years. This is the king who was reputed to be Memnon, a speaking stone.
8. Orus, for 28 years.

Achencheres¹ . . . , annis XVI.   Huius aetate
Moses ducem se praebuit Hebraeis ab Aegypto
excedentibus.
Acherres, annis VIII.
Cherres, annis XV.
Armaïs, qui et Danaus, annis V; quibus peractis,
Aegyptiorum regione pulsus Aegyptumque
fratrem suum fugiens, evasit in Graeciam,
Argisque captis, imperavit Argivis.
Ramesses, qui et Aegyptus, annis LXVIII.
Amenophis, annis XL.

Summa dominationis CCCXLVIII.

Fr. 54.   Josephus, *Contra Apionem*, I, 26–31,
§§ 227–287.

26
227   'Εφ' ἑνὸς δὲ πρώτου στήσω τὸν λόγον, ᾧ καὶ
μάρτυρι μικρὸν ἔμπροσθεν τῆς ἀρχαιότητος ἐχρη-
228 σάμην.   ὁ γὰρ Μανεθὼς οὗτος, ὁ τὴν Αἰγυπτιακὴν
ἱστορίαν ἐκ τῶν ἱερῶν γραμμάτων μεθερμηνεύειν
ὑπεσχημένος, προειπὼν τοὺς ἡμετέρους προγόνους
πολλαῖς μυριάσιν ἐπὶ τὴν Αἴγυπτον ἐλθόντας
κρατῆσαι τῶν ἐνοικούντων, εἶτ' αὐτὸς ὁμολογῶν
χρόνῳ πάλιν ὕστερον ἐκπεσόντας τὴν νῦν 'Ιου-
δαίαν κατασχεῖν καὶ κτίσαντας 'Ιεροσόλυμα τὸν
νεὼν κατασκευάσασθαι, μέχρι μὲν τούτων ἠκολού-
229 θησε ταῖς ἀναγραφαῖς.   ἔπειτα δὲ δοὺς ἐξουσίαν

¹ A lacuna here, as in the Greek version.

---

¹ According to *O.T. 1 Kings* vi. 1, the building of
Solomon's Temple was begun 480 years after the Exodus :

9. Achencheres . . . , for 16 years.   In his time
   Moses became leader of the Hebrews in their
   exodus from Egypt.
10. Acherres, for 8 years.
11. Cherres, for 15 years.
12. Armaïs, also called Danaus, for 5 years : at the
    end of this time he was banished from the
    land of Egypt.   Fleeing from his brother
    Aegyptus, he escaped to Greece, and after
    capturing Argos, he held sway over the
    Argives.
13. Ramesses, also called Aegyptus, for 68 years.
14. Amenophis, for 40 years.

Total for the dynasty, 348 years.

Fr. 54 (*from* Josephus, *Contra Apionem*, I. 26-31,
§§ 227-287).

(Josephus discusses the calumnies of the Egyptians
against the Jews, whom they hate.)
   The first writer upon whom I shall dwell is one
whom I used a little earlier as a witness to our antiquity.   I refer to Manetho.   This writer, who had
undertaken to translate the history of Egypt from
the sacred books, began by stating that our ancestors
came against Egypt with many tens of thousands and
gained the mastery over the inhabitants ; and then
he himself admitted that at a later date again they
were driven out of the country, occupied what is now
Judaea, founded Jerusalem, and built the temple.[1]
Up to this point he followed the chronicles : there-

if the Exodus is dated *c.* 1445 B.C. (see p. 110 n. 2), the
Temple was founded *c.* 965 B.C.

119

αὐτῷ διὰ τοῦ φάναι γράψειν τὰ μυθευόμενα καὶ
λεγόμενα περὶ τῶν Ἰουδαίων λόγους ἀπιθάνους
παρενέβαλεν, ἀναμῖξαι βουλόμενος ἡμῖν πλῆθος
Αἰγυπτίων λεπρῶν καὶ ἐπὶ ἄλλοις ἀρρωστήμασιν,
ὥς φησι, φυγεῖν ἐκ τῆς Αἰγύπτου καταγνωσθέντων.
230 Ἀμένωφιν γὰρ βασιλέα προθείς,[1] ψευδὲς ὄνομα,
καὶ διὰ τοῦτο χρόνον αὐτοῦ τῆς βασιλείας ὁρίσαι
μὴ τολμήσας, καίτοι γε ἐπὶ τῶν ἄλλων βασιλέων
ἀκριβῶς τὰ ἔτη προστιθείς, τούτῳ προσάπτει
τινὰς μυθολογίας, ἐπιλαθόμενος σχεδὸν ὅτι πεντακοσίοις ἔτεσι καὶ δεκαοκτὼ πρότερον ἱστόρηκε
γενέσθαι τὴν τῶν Ποιμένων ἔξοδον εἰς Ἱεροσόλυμα.
231 Τέθμωσις γὰρ ἦν βασιλεὺς ὅτε ἐξῆεσαν, ἀπὸ δὲ
τούτου τῶν μεταξὺ[2] βασιλέων κατ’ αὐτόν ἐστι
τριακόσια ἐνενηκοντατρία ἔτη μέχρι τῶν δύο
ἀδελφῶν Σέθω καὶ Ἑρμαίου, ὧν τὸν μὲν Σέθων
Αἴγυπτον, τὸν δὲ Ἕρμαιον Δαναὸν μετονομα-
σθῆναί φησιν, ὃν ἐκβαλὼν ὁ Σέθως ἐβασίλευσεν
ἔτη νθ′ καὶ μετ’ αὐτὸν ὁ πρεσβύτερος τῶν υἱῶν
232 αὐτοῦ Ῥάμψης ξϚ′. τοσούτοις οὖν πρότερον ἔτεσιν
ἀπελθεῖν ἐξ Αἰγύπτου τοὺς πατέρας ἡμῶν ὡμο-
λογηκώς, εἶτα τὸν Ἀμένωφιν εἰσποιήσας ἐμβόλιμον
βασιλέα, φησὶν τοῦτον ἐπιθυμῆσαι θεῶν γενέσθαι
θεατήν, ὥσπερ Ὧρ εἷς τῶν πρὸ αὐτοῦ βεβασιλευ-

---

[1] προθείς Cobet : προσθείς L.
[2] τούτου τῶν μεταξὺ conj. Niese (et ab hoc tempore regum
qui postea fuerunt Lat.) : τούτων μεταξὺ τῶν L.

---

[1] Cf. " the botch (or boil) of Egypt " (perhaps elephan-
tiasis), Deuteronomy xxviii. 27.

120

after, by offering to record the legends and current
talk about the Jews, he took the liberty of inter-
polating improbable tales in his desire to confuse
with us a crowd of Egyptians, who for leprosy
and other maladies [1] had been condemned, he says,
to banishment from Egypt. After citing a king
Amenôphis, a fictitious person,—for which reason he
did not venture to define the length of his reign,
although in the case of the other kings he adds
their years precisely,—Manetho attaches to him certain legends, having doubtless forgotten that according to his own chronicle the exodus of the
Shepherds to Jerusalem took place 518 years [2]
earlier. For Tethmôsis was king when they set out ;
and, according to Manetho, the intervening reigns
thereafter occupied 393 years down to the two
brothers Sethôs and Hermaeus, the former of whom,
he says, took the new name of Aegyptus, the latter
that of Danaus. Sethôs drove out Hermaeus and
reigned for 59 years ; then Rampsês, the elder of his
sons, for 66 years. Thus, after admitting that so
many years had elapsed since our forefathers left
Egypt, Manetho now interpolates this intruding
Amenôphis. This king, he states, conceived a desire
to behold the gods, as Ôr,[3] one of his predecessors on

[2] This number seems to be obtained by adding 393 +
59 + 66 : in that case the reign of Sethôsis is counted
twice, (1) as 60, (2) as 59 years (cf. Fr. 50, § 103).

[3] Ôr, or Hôrus, is the ninth king in Manetho's list of
Dynasty XVIII. (Frs. 51, 52), in reality Amenôphis III.
Reinach points out that Herodotus (ii. 42) tells the same
story of the Egyptian Heracles, and conjectures that there
is perhaps confusion with the god Hôrus.

κότων, ἀνενεγκεῖν δὲ τὴν ἐπιθυμίαν ὁμωνύμῳ
μὲν αὐτῷ Ἀμενώφει, πατρὸς δὲ Παάπιος [1] ὄντι,
233 θείας δὲ δοκοῦντι μετεσχηκέναι φύσεως κατά τε
σοφίαν καὶ πρόγνωσιν τῶν ἐσομένων. εἰπεῖν οὖν
αὐτῷ τοῦτον τὸν ὁμώνυμον ὅτι δυνήσεται θεοὺς
ἰδεῖν, εἰ καθαρὰν ἀπό τε λεπρῶν καὶ τῶν ἄλλων
μιαρῶν ἀνθρώπων τὴν χώραν ἅπασαν ποιήσειεν.
234 ἡσθέντα δὲ τὸν βασιλέα πάντας τοὺς τὰ σώματα
λελωβημένους ἐκ τῆς Αἰγύπτου συναγαγεῖν· γενέ-
235 σθαι δὲ τὸ πλῆθος [2] μυριάδας ὀκτώ· καὶ τούτους

---

[1] *Ed. pr.* (*cf.* § 243): Πάπιος L
[2] Conj. Niese (after Lat.): τοῦ πλήθους L.

---

[1] For this Amenôphis, a historical personage, later
deified (*cf.* the deification of Imhotep, Fr. 11), Amenhotpe,
son of Hapu, and minister of Amenôphis III., see G.
Maspero, *New Light on Ancient Egypt* (1909), pp. 189-195 :
Sethe, in *Aegyptiaca* (Ebers, *Festschrift*), 1897, pp. 107-116 :
Breasted, *Anc. Rec.* ii. §§ 911 ff. ; Warren R. Dawson,
The Bridle of Pegasus, 1930, pp. 49-79.   In 1934-35
excavations by the French Institute, Cairo, revealed
all that remains of the splendour of the funerary temple
of Amenhotpe, son of Hapu, among a series of such temples
to the N. of Medinet Habu : see Robichon and Varille,
Le Temple du Scribe Royal Amenhotep, Fils de Hapou, i.
Cairo, 1936.   An inscription of iii. B.C. (and therefore
contemporary with Manetho), headed Ἀμενώτου ὑποθῆκαι,
" Precepts of Amenôtes or Amenôphis," was published
by Wilcken in *Aegyptiaca*, 1897, pp. 142 ff.   It is inscribed upon a limestone ostracon of Deir el-Bahri ; and
the first three injunctions run : " Practise wisdom along
with justice," " Revere both the gods and your parents,"

the throne, had done ; and he communicated his
desire to his namesake Amenôphis,[1] Paapis' son, who,
in virtue of his wisdom and knowledge of the future,
was reputed to be a partaker in the divine nature.
This namesake, then, replied that he would be able
to see the gods if he cleansed the whole land of lepers
and other polluted persons.   The king was delighted,
and assembled [2] all those in Egypt whose bodies were
wasted by disease :   they numbered 80,000 persons.

" Take counsel at leisure, but accomplish speedily whatever
you do ".

An ostracon, found at Deir el-Bahri, and giving the
draft of an inscription concerning the deified Amenôphis,
was published by A. Bataille, *Études de Papyrologie*, IV.
(1938), pp. 125-131 : it celebrates the cure of a certain
Polyaratos. See O. Guéraud in *Bull. Inst. Fr. d'Arch. Or.*,
xxvii. (1927), pp. 121 ff., P. Jouguet, " Les Grands Dieux
de la Pierre Sainte à Thèbes," *Mélanges Glotz*, II. pp.
493-500.

For the historical interpretation of this whole passage,
§§ 232-251, see Meyer, *Geschichte* [2], ii. 1, pp. 421 ff.   King
Amenôphis is at one time Merneptah, son of Rameses II. ;
at another time, Amenôphis IV. (Akhnaten), some 200
years earlier.   The doings of the polluted, the persecution
of the gods, and the slaughter of the holy animals, clearly
portray the fury of Akhnaten and his followers against
Egyptian religion.   For a popular Egyptian parallel to
§§ 232 ff., see the Potter's Oracle, one of the Rainer Papyri
(iii. A.D.) edited by Wilcken in *Hermes*, xl. 1905, pp. 544 ff.
and by G. Manteuffel, *De Opusculis Graecis Aegypti e
papyris, ostracis, lapidibusque collectis*, 1930, No. 7 ; and
cf. the prophecy of the lamb, Manetho, Fr. 64.

For a theory about the identity of the polluted (they
are the troops of Sethôs I., sent to Tanis by his father
Ramessês I. during the ascendancy of Haremhab), see
P. Montet, " La Stèle de l'An 400 Retrouvée," in *Kêmi*,
iii. 1935, pp. 191-215.

[2] In an incredibly short time (§ 257).

εἰς τὰς λιθοτομίας τὰς ἐν τῷ πρὸς ἀνατολὴν μέρει
τοῦ Νείλου ἐμβαλεῖν αὐτόν, ὅπως ἐργάζοιντο καὶ
τῶν ἄλλων Αἰγυπτίων εἶεν κεχωρισμένοι.[1] εἶναι δέ
τινας ἐν αὐτοῖς καὶ τῶν λογίων ἱερέων φησὶ λέπρᾳ
236 συνεσχημένους.[2] τὸν δὲ Ἀμένωφιν ἐκεῖνον, τὸν
σοφὸν καὶ μαντικὸν ἄνδρα, ὑποδεῖσαι[3] πρὸς αὑτόν
τε καὶ τὸν βασιλέα χόλον τῶν θεῶν, εἰ βιασθέντες
ὀφθήσονται· καὶ προσθέμενον εἰπεῖν ὅτι συμμαχή-
σουσί τινες τοῖς μιαροῖς καὶ τῆς Αἰγύπτου κρα-
τήσουσιν ἐπ᾽ ἔτη δεκατρία, μὴ τολμῆσαι μὲν
αὐτὸν εἰπεῖν ταῦτα τῷ βασιλεῖ, γραφὴν δὲ κατα-
λιπόντα περὶ πάντων ἑαυτὸν ἀνελεῖν, ἐν ἀθυμίᾳ
237 δὲ εἶναι τὸν βασιλέα. κἄπειτα κατὰ λέξιν οὕτως
γέγραφεν· "τῶν δ᾽ ἐν[4] ταῖς λατομίαις ὡς χρόνος
ἱκανὸς διῆλθεν ταλαιπωρούντων, ἀξιωθεὶς ὁ βασιλεὺς ἵνα πρὸς[5] κατάλυσιν αὐτοῖς καὶ σκέπην ἀπο-
μερίσῃ τὴν τότε τῶν Ποιμένων ἐρημωθεῖσαν πόλιν
Αὔαριν συνεχώρησεν· ἔστι δ᾽ ἡ πόλις κατὰ τὴν
238 θεολογίαν ἄνωθεν Τυφώνιος. οἱ δὲ εἰς ταύτην
εἰσελθόντες καὶ τὸν τόπον τοῦτον εἰς[6] ἀπόστασιν
ἔχοντες, ἡγεμόνα αὐτῶν τινα τῶν Ἡλιοπολιτῶν
ἱερέων Ὀσάρσηφον[7] λεγόμενον[8] ἐστήσαντο καὶ

---

[1] εἶεν κεχωρισμένοι conj. Holwerda : οἱ ἐγκεχωρισμένοι L.

[2] συνεσχημένους conj. Niese : συνεχομένους Dindorf : συγ-
κεχυμένους L.

[3] ὑποδεῖσαι Dindorf : ὑποδεῖσθαι L.

[4] δ᾽ ἐν Bekker : δὲ L.　　[5] πρὸς bracketed by Niese.

[6] εἰς bracketed as apparently spurious by Niese : ⟨ὁρμη-
τήριον⟩ εἰς ἀπ. Holwerda.

[7] L : Ὀσάρσιφον conj. Hudson.

[8] Transp. Niese (a more natural place for the participle) :
λεγόμενόν τινα . . . Ὀσ. L.

These he cast into the stone-quarries [1] to the east of
the Nile, there to work segregated from the rest of the
Egyptians. Among them, Manetho adds, there were
some of the learned priests, who had been attacked by
leprosy. Then this wise seer Amenôphis was filled
with dread of divine wrath against himself and the
king if the outrage done to these persons should be
discovered ; and he added a prediction that certain
allies would join the polluted people and would take
possession of Egypt for 13 years. Not venturing to
make this prophecy himself to the king, he left a
full account of it in writing, and then took his own
life. The king was filled with despondency. Then
Manetho continues as follows (I quote his account
verbatim) : " When the men in the stone-quarries had
suffered hardships for a considerable time, they
begged the king to assign to them as a dwelling-place
and a refuge the deserted city of the Shepherds,
Auaris, and he consented. According to religious
tradition [2] this city was from earliest times dedicated to Typhôn. Occupying this city and using the
region as a base for revolt, they appointed as their
leader one of the priests of Hêliopolis called Osarsêph,[3]

---

[1] The quarries of Tura were known to Herodotus (ii. 8,
124) as the source of building-stone for the Pyramids.

On forced labour in quarries in Ptolemaic times,
Reinach refers to Bouché-Leclercq, *Histoire des Lagides*,
iii. 241 ; iv. 193, 337 f.

[2] *Cf.* Fr. 42, § 78.

[3] Osarsêph, the leader of the movement, is later (§ 250)
identified with Moses. The name Osarsêph is a possible
Egyptian name : *cf.* Ranke, *Personennamen* I. p. 85,
No. 3 *wsir-sp'*. Wilcken (*Chrestomathie*, i. 1, p. 106)
derives the name from a holy animal Sêph ; but the Jews
would naturally see in it a form of the name Joseph.

τούτῳ πειθαρχήσοντες [1] ἐν πᾶσιν ὠρκωμότησαν.
239 ὁ δὲ πρῶτον μὲν αὐτοῖς νόμον ἔθετο μήτε προσκυνεῖν θεοὺς μήτε τῶν μάλιστα ἐν Αἰγύπτῳ
θεμιστευομένων ἱερῶν ζῴων ἀπέχεσθαι μηδενός,
πάντα δὲ θύειν καὶ ἀναλοῦν, συνάπτεσθαι δὲ
240 μηδενὶ πλὴν τῶν συνομωμοσμένων.[2] τοιαῦτα δὲ
νομοθετήσας καὶ πλεῖστα ἄλλα μάλιστα τοῖς
Αἰγυπτίοις ἐθισμοῖς ἐναντιούμενα ἐκέλευσεν πολυ-
χειρίᾳ τὰ τῆς πόλεως ἐπισκευάζειν τείχη καὶ πρὸς
πόλεμον ἑτοίμους γίνεσθαι τὸν πρὸς Ἀμένωφιν τὸν
241 βασιλέα. αὐτὸς δέ, προσλαβόμενος μεθ' ἑαυτοῦ
καὶ τῶν ἄλλων ἱερέων καὶ συμμεμιαμμένων τινὰς [3]
ἔπεμψε πρέσβεις πρὸς τοὺς ὑπὸ Τεθμώσεως
ἀπελασθέντας Ποιμένας εἰς πόλιν τὴν καλουμένην
Ἱεροσόλυμα, καὶ τὰ καθ' ἑαυτὸν καὶ τοὺς ἄλλους
τοὺς συνατιμασθέντας δηλώσας ἠξίου συνεπιστρα-
242 τεύειν ὁμοθυμαδὸν ἐπ' Αἴγυπτον. ἐπάξειν [4] μὲν
οὖν αὐτοὺς ἐπηγγείλατο πρῶτον μὲν εἰς Αὔαριν τὴν
προγονικὴν αὐτῶν πατρίδα καὶ τὰ ἐπιτήδεια τοῖς
ὄχλοις παρέξειν ἀφθόνως, ὑπερμαχήσεσθαι δὲ ὅτε
δέοι καὶ ῥᾳδίως ὑποχείριον αὐτοῖς τὴν χώραν ποιή-
243 σειν. οἱ δὲ ὑπερχαρεῖς γενόμενοι πάντες προθύμως
εἰς κ' μυριάδας ἀνδρῶν συνεξώρμησαν καὶ μετ'

---

[1] Ed. pr.: -ήσαντες L.　　　　[2] Niese: συνωμοσμένων L.
[3] τινὰς add. Reinach (quosdam Lat.).
[4] ἐπανάξειν conj. Cobet.

---

[1] " Does the author know that the Decalogue begins
with an admonition to have no other god but Jehovah ?
Or does he recall Greek lists of duties (Xen., *Mem.* iv. 4,

and took an oath of obedience to him in everything.
First of all, he made it a law [1] that they should neither
worship the gods nor refrain from any of the animals [2]
prescribed as especially sacred in Egypt, but should
sacrifice and consume all alike, and that they should
have intercourse with none save those of their own
confederacy.   After framing a great number of laws
like these, completely opposed to Egyptian custom,
he ordered them with their multitude of hands, to
repair the walls of the city and make ready for war
against King Amenôphis.   Then, acting in concert
with certain other priests and polluted persons like
himself, he sent an embassy to the Shepherds who
had been expelled by Tethmôsis,[3] in the city called
Jerusalem ; and, setting forth the circumstances of
himself and his companions in distress, he begged
them to unite wholeheartedly in an attack upon
Egypt.   He offered to conduct them first to their
ancestral home at Auaris, to provide their hosts with
lavish supplies, to fight on their behalf whenever need
arose, and to bring Egypt without difficulty under
their sway.   Overjoyed at the proposal, all the
Shepherds, to the number of 200,000, eagerly set out,

19 ; *Carmen Aureum*, v. 1 ; *cf.* Dieterich, *Nekyia*, pp. 146
f.) which inculcate reverence for the gods as the first
precept ? " (Reinach).   Add Isocrates, *Ad Demonicum*,
§§ 13, 16, and the *Precepts of Sansnôs* (ii./iii. A.D.), as
inscribed in Nubia, *C.I.G.* iii. 5041 (Wilcken, *Chrestomathie*,
I. ii. p. 147, No. 116)—the first precept is " Revere the
divinity ".

[2] *Cf.* Tac., *Hist.* v. 4 : the Jews under Moses sacrificed
the ram as if to insult Ammôn, and the bull, because the
Egyptians worship Apis.   *Cf. O.T. Leviticus* xvi. 3.

[3] Tethmôsis for Amôsis, as in Fr. 50 (§ 94).

οὐ πολὺ ἦκον εἰς Αὔαριν. Ἀμένωφις δ' ὁ τῶν
Αἰγυπτίων βασιλεὺς ὡς ἐπύθετο τὰ κατὰ τὴν
ἐκείνων ἔφοδον, οὐ μετρίως συνεχύθη, τῆς παρὰ
Ἀμενώφεως τοῦ Παάπιος μνησθεὶς προδηλώσεως
244 καὶ πρότερον συναγαγὼν πλῆθος Αἰγυπτίων καὶ
βουλευσάμενος μετὰ τῶν ἐν τούτοις ἡγεμόνων, τά
τε ἱερὰ ζῷα τὰ [πρῶτα] [1] μάλιστα ἐν τοῖς ἱεροῖς
τιμώμενα ὡς ἑαυτὸν [2] μετεπέμψατο, καὶ τοῖς κατὰ
μέρος ἱερεῦσι παρήγγελλεν ὡς ἀσφαλέστατα τῶν
245 θεῶν συγκρύψαι τὰ ξόανα. τὸν δὲ υἱὸν Σέθων,
τὸν καὶ Ῥαμέσσην ἀπὸ Ῥαψηοῦς τοῦ πατρὸς
ὠνομασμένον, πενταέτη ὄντα ἐξέθετο πρὸς τὸν
ἑαυτοῦ φίλον. αὐτὸς δὲ διαβὰς ⟨σὺν⟩ [3] τοῖς
ἄλλοις Αἰγυπτίοις, οὖσιν εἰς τριάκοντα μυριάδας
ἀνδρῶν μαχιμωτάτων, καὶ τοῖς πολεμίοις ἀπ-
246 αντήσας [4] οὐ συνέβαλεν, ἀλλὰ μὴ δεῖν [5] θεομαχεῖν
νομίσας παλινδρομήσας ἧκεν εἰς Μέμφιν, ἀναλαβών
τε τόν τε Ἆπιν καὶ τὰ ἄλλα τὰ ἐκεῖσε μεταπεμ-
φθέντα ἱερὰ ζῷα, εὐθὺς εἰς Αἰθιοπίαν σὺν ἅπαντι τῷ
στόλῳ καὶ πλήθει τῶν Αἰγυπτίων ἀνήχθη· χάριτι
γὰρ ἦν αὐτῷ ὑποχείριος ὁ τῶν Αἰθιόπων βασιλεύς.
247 ὃς [6] ὑποδεξάμενος καὶ τοὺς ὄχλους πάντας ὑπολαβὼν
οἷς ἔσχεν ἡ χώρα τῶν πρὸς ἀνθρωπίνην τροφὴν
ἐπιτηδείων, καὶ πόλεις καὶ κώμας πρὸς τὴν τῶν

---

[1] Om. Lat.: bracketed by Bekker.
[2] Cobet: ὥς γε αὐτὸν L.
[3] Conj. Niese (cum aliis Lat.).
[4] Cobet (occurrens Lat.): ἀπαντήσασιν L.
[5] Herwerden (cf. § 263): μέλλειν L.
[6] Niese (after Lat.): ὅθεν L.

and before long arrived at Auaris. When Amenôphis.
king of Egypt, learned of their invasion, he was sorely
troubled, for he recalled the prediction of Amenôphis,
son of Paapis. First, he gathered a multitude of
Egyptians ; and having taken counsel with the leading men among them, he summoned to his presence
the sacred animals which were held in greatest reverence in the temples, and gave instructions to each
group of priests to conceal the images of the gods as
securely as possible. As for his five-year-old son
Sethôs, also called Ramessês after his grandfather
Rapsês,[1] he sent him safely away to his friend.[2]
He then crossed the Nile with as many as 300,000 of
the bravest warriors of Egypt, and met the enemy.
But, instead of joining battle, he decided that he
must not fight against the gods, and made a hasty
retreat to Memphis. There he took into his charge
Apis and the other sacred animals which he had
summoned to that place ; and forthwith he set off for
Ethiopia[3] with his whole army and the host of
Egyptians. The Ethiopian king, who, in gratitude
for a service, had become his subject, welcomed him,
maintained the whole multitude with such products
of the country as were fit for human consumption,

---

[1] Rapsês : doubtless an error for Rampsês. There is
confusion here : the grandfather is Ramessês II. See
Meyer (*Aeg. Chron.* p. 91), who considers the words
" Sethôs also called " an interpolation (*cf.* § 98), intended
to identify a Sethôs son of Amenôphis and a Ramessês
son of Amenôphis.

[2] A curious indefiniteness : the reference may be to the
king of Ethiopia, mentioned in the next section.

[3] The truth is that Ethiopia (Nubia, Cush) was at that
time a province of the kingdom of the Pharaohs.

πεπρωμένων τρισκαίδεκα ἐτῶν ἀπὸ τῆς ἀρχῆς
αὐτοῦ[1] ἔκπτωσιν αὐτάρκεις, οὐχ ἧττον δὲ καὶ
στρατόπεδον Αἰθιοπικὸν πρὸς φυλακὴν ἐπέταξε
τοῖς παρ' Ἀμενώφεως τοῦ βασιλέως ἐπὶ τῶν
248 ὁρίων τῆς Αἰγύπτου. καὶ τὰ μὲν κατὰ τὴν Αἰθιοπίαν τοιαῦτα· οἱ δὲ Σολυμῖται κατελθόντες σὺν
τοῖς μιαροῖς τῶν Αἰγυπτίων οὕτως ἀνοσίως καὶ
<ὠμῶς>[2] τοῖς ἀνθρώποις προσηνέχθησαν, ὥστε τὴν
τῶν προειρημένων <Ποιμένων>[3] κράτησιν χρυσὸν
φαίνεσθαι τοῖς τότε τὰ τούτων ἀσεβήματα θεω-
249 μένοις· καὶ γὰρ οὐ μόνον πόλεις καὶ κώμας ἐνέπρησαν, οὐδὲ ἱεροσυλοῦντες οὐδὲ λυμαινόμενοι
ξόανα θεῶν ἠρκοῦντο, ἀλλὰ καὶ τοῖς ἀδύτοις[4]
ὀπτανίοις τῶν σεβαστευομένων ἱερῶν ζῴων χρώ-
μενοι διετέλουν, καὶ θύτας καὶ σφαγεῖς τούτων
ἱερεῖς καὶ προφήτας ἠνάγκαζον γίνεσθαι καὶ γυμ-
250 νοὺς ἐξέβαλλον. λέγεται δὲ ὅτι <ὁ>[5] τὴν πολιτείαν
καὶ τοὺς νόμους αὐτοῖς καταβαλόμενος ἱερεύς, τὸ
γένος Ἡλιοπολίτης, ὄνομα Ὀσαρσὴφ[6] ἀπὸ τοῦ ἐν
Ἡλιουπόλει θεοῦ Ὀσίρεως, ὡς μετέβη εἰς τοῦτο
τὸ γένος, μετετέθη τοὔνομα καὶ προσηγορεύθη
27 Μωυσῆς.''
251   Ἃ μὲν οὖν Αἰγύπτιοι φέρουσι περὶ τῶν Ἰουδαίων ταῦτ' ἐστὶ καὶ ἕτερα πλείονα, ἃ παρίημι

---

[1] + εἰς τὴν L (repeating πρὸς τὴν above): a verb (e.g.
παρέσχεν) seems to have dropped out.
[2] Add. Reinach.   [3] Add. Reinach.
[4] Bekker: αὐτοῖς L.   [5] Cobet: om. L.
[6] Cf. § 238: Ὀσαρσὶφ edd.

---

[1] According to Meyer (Aeg. Chron. p. 77), this section
with its identification of Osarsôph and Moses is due to an

assigned to them cities and villages sufficient for the
destined period of 13 years' banishment from his
realm, and especially stationed an Ethiopian army
on the frontiers of Egypt to guard King Amenôphis
and his followers. Such was the situation in
Ethiopia. Meanwhile, the Solymites [or dwellers in
Jerusalem] made a descent along with the polluted
Egyptians, and treated the people so impiously and
savagely that the domination of the Shepherds
seemed like a golden age to those who witnessed the
present enormities. For not only did they set towns
and villages on fire, pillaging the temples and muti-
lating images of the gods without restraint, but they
also made a practice of using the sanctuaries as
kitchens to roast the sacred animals which the people
worshipped : and they would compel the priests and
prophets to sacrifice and butcher the beasts, afterwards casting the men forth naked. It is said that
the priest who framed their constitution and their
laws was a native of Hêliopolis, named Osarsêph
after the god Osiris, worshipped at Hêliopolis ;
but when he joined this people, he changed his
name and was called Moses." [1]

Such, then, are the Egyptian stories about the
Jews,[2] together with many other tales which I pass

anti-Semitic commentator on Manetho. It is interesting
that Osiris should be thus identified with the mysterious
god of the Jews, whose name must not be uttered.

[2] *Cf.* Hecataeus of Abdera (in Diodorus Siculus, xl. 3):
the Jews are foreigners expelled from Egypt because of a
plague. See Meyer, *Geschichte* [2], ii. 1, p. 424. Hecataeus
lived for some time at the court of Ptolemy I. (323-285 B.C.),
and used Egyptian sources for his *Aegyptiaca*. *Cf.* Intro.
pp. xxvi f.

συντομίας ἔνεκα. λέγει δὲ ὁ Μανεθὼς πάλιν ὅτι
μετὰ ταῦτα ἐπῆλθεν ὁ Ἀμένωφις ἀπὸ Αἰθιοπίας
μετὰ μεγάλης δυνάμεως καὶ ὁ υἱὸς αὐτοῦ Ῥάμψης,
καὶ αὐτὸς ἔχων δύναμιν, καὶ συμβαλόντες οἱ δύο
τοῖς Ποιμέσι καὶ τοῖς μιαροῖς ἐνίκησαν αὐτοὺς καὶ
πολλοὺς ἀποκτείναντες ἐδίωξαν αὐτοὺς ἄχρι τῶν
252 ὁρίων τῆς Συρίας. ταῦτα μὲν καὶ τὰ τοιαῦτα
Μανεθὼς συνέγραψεν· ὅτι δὲ ληρεῖ καὶ ψεύδεται
περιφανῶς ἐπιδείξω, προδιαστειλάμενος ἐκεῖνο, τῶν
ὕστερον πρὸς ἄλλους[1] λεχθησομένων ἕνεκα. δέδωκε
γὰρ οὗτος ἡμῖν καὶ ὡμολόγηκεν ἐξ ἀρχῆς τὸ[2] μὴ
εἶναι τὸ γένος Αἰγυπτίους, ἀλλ' αὐτοὺς ἔξωθεν
ἐπελθόντας κρατῆσαι τῆς Αἰγύπτου καὶ πάλιν ἐξ
253 αὐτῆς ἀπελθεῖν. ὅτι δ' οὐκ ἀνεμίχθησαν ἡμῖν
ὕστερον τῶν Αἰγυπτίων οἱ τὰ σώματα λελωβη-
μένοι, καὶ ὅτι ἐκ τούτων οὐκ ἦν Μωυσῆς ὁ τὸν
λαὸν ἀγαγών, ἀλλὰ πολλαῖς ἐγεγόνει γενεαῖς
πρότερον, ταῦτα πειράσομαι διὰ τῶν ὑπ' αὐτοῦ
82 λεγομένων ἐλέγχειν.
254   Πρώτην δὴ τὴν αἰτίαν τοῦ πλάσματος ὑπο-
τίθεται καταγέλαστον. ὁ βασιλεὺς γάρ, φησίν,
Ἀμένωφις ἐπεθύμησε τοὺς θεοὺς ἰδεῖν. ποίους;
εἰ μὲν τοὺς παρ' αὐτοῖς νενομοθετημένους, τὸν
βοῦν καὶ τράγον καὶ κροκοδείλους καὶ κυνοκεφά-
255 λους, ἑώρα. τοὺς οὐρανίους δὲ πῶς ἐδύνατο; καὶ
διὰ τί ταύτην ἔσχε τὴν ἐπιθυμίαν; ὅτι νὴ Δία

---

[1] Niese : ἀλλήλους L (*alterna gratia* Lat.).
[2] Conj. Niese : τε L.

by for brevity's sake.   Manetho adds, however, that,
at a later date, Amenôphis advanced from Ethiopia
with a large army, his son Rampsês also leading a
force, and that the two together joined battle with
the Shepherds and their polluted allies, and defeated
them, killing many and pursuing the others to the
frontiers of Syria.   This then, with other tales of a
like nature, is Manetho's account.   Before I give
proof that his words are manifest lies and nonsense,
I shall mention one particular point, which bears
upon my later refutation of other writers.   Manetho
has made one concession to us.   He has admitted
that our race was not Egyptian in origin, but came
into Egypt from elsewhere, took possession of the
land, and afterwards left it.   But that we were not,
at a later time, mixed up with disease-ravaged
Egyptians, and that, so far from being one of these,
Moses, the leader of our people, lived many generations earlier, I shall endeavour to prove from
Manetho's own statements.

To begin with, the reason which he suggests for
his fiction is ridiculous.   " King Amenôphis," he
says, " conceived a desire to see the gods."   Gods
indeed !   If he means the gods established by their
ordinances,—bull, goat, crocodiles, and dog-faced
baboons,—he had them before his eyes ; and as
for the gods of heaven, how could he see them ?
And why did he conceive this eager desire ?
Because, by Zeus,[1] before his time another king

---

[1] A strange expression which seems to belong to an
anti-Semitic polemic.   In Josephus, c. Apion. ii. 263 (a
passage about Socrates), νὴ Δία has been restored to the
text by Niese's conjecture.

καὶ πρότερος αὐτοῦ βασιλεὺς ἄλλος ἑωράκει.
παρ' ἐκείνου τοίνυν ἐπέπυστο ποταποί τινές εἰσι
καὶ τίνα πρόπον αὐτοὺς εἶδεν, ὥστε καινῆς αὐτῷ
256 τέχνης οὐκ ἔδει. ἀλλὰ σοφὸς ἦν ὁ μάντις, δι' οὗ
τοῦτο κατορθώσειν ὁ βασιλεὺς ὑπελάμβανε. καὶ
πῶς οὐ προέγνω τὸ ἀδύνατον αὐτοῦ τῆς ἐπιθυμίας;
οὐ γὰρ ἀπέβη. τίνα δὲ καὶ λόγον εἶχε διὰ τοὺς
ἠκρωτηριασμένους ἢ λεπρῶντας ἀφανεῖς εἶναι
τοὺς θεούς; ὀργίζονται γὰρ ἐπὶ τοῖς ἀσεβήμασιν,
257 οὐκ ἐπὶ τοῖς ἐλαττώμασι τῶν σωμάτων. ὀκτὼ
δὲ μυριάδας τῶν λεπρῶν καὶ κακῶς διακειμένων
πῶς οἷόν τε μιᾷ σχεδὸν ἡμέρᾳ συλλεγῆναι; πῶς
δὲ παρήκουσεν τοῦ μάντεως ὁ βασιλεύς; ὁ μὲν
γὰρ αὐτὸν ἐκέλευσεν ἐξορίσαι τῆς Αἰγύπτου τοὺς
λελωβημένους, ὁ δ' αὐτοὺς εἰς τὰς λιθοτομίας
ἐνέβαλεν, ὥσπερ τῶν ἐργασομένων δεόμενος, ἀλλ'
258 οὐχὶ καθᾶραι τὴν χώραν προαιρούμενος. φησὶ
δὲ τὸν μὲν μάντιν αὐτὸν ἀνελεῖν τὴν ὀργὴν τῶν
θεῶν προορώμενον καὶ τὰ συμβησόμενα περὶ τὴν
Αἴγυπτον, τῷ δὲ βασιλεῖ γεγραμμένην τὴν πρόρ-
259 ρησιν [1] καταλιπεῖν. εἶτα πῶς οὐκ ἐξ ἀρχῆς ὁ
μάντις τὸν αὐτοῦ θάνατον προηπίστατο; πῶς δὲ
οὐκ εὐθὺς ἀντεῖπεν τῷ βασιλεῖ βουλομένῳ τοὺς
θεοὺς ἰδεῖν; πῶς δ' εὔλογος ὁ φόβος τῶν μὴ παρ'
αὐτὸν συμβησομένων κακῶν; ἢ τί χεῖρον ἔδει
παθεῖν οὗ δρᾶν [2] ἑαυτὸν ἔσπευδεν;
260 Τὸ δὲ δὴ πάντων εὐηθέστατον ἴδωμεν. πυθό-

---

[1] Ed. pr.: πρόσρησιν L.
[2] Herwerden (quam quod se ipse perimere festinabat Lat.):
οὐδ' ἂν L.

had seen them ! From this predecessor, then, he
had learned their nature and the manner in which
he had seen them, and in consequence he had no need
of a new system. Moreover, the prophet by whose
aid the king expected to succeed in his endeavour,
was a sage. How, then, did he fail to foresee the im-
possibility of realizing this desire ? It did, in fact,
come to naught. And what reason had he for as-
cribing the invisibility of the gods to the presence of
cripples or lepers ? Divine wrath is due to impious
deeds, not to physical deformities. Next, how
could 80,000 lepers and invalids be gathered together in practically a single day ? And why did
the king turn a deaf ear to the prophet ? The prophet had bidden him expel the cripples from Egypt,
but the king cast them into stone-quarries, as if he
needed labourers, not as if his purpose was to purge
the land. Manetho says, moreover, that the prophet took his own life, because he foresaw the anger
of the gods and the fate in store for Egypt, but left
in writing his prediction to the king. Then how
was it that the prophet had not from the first fore-
knowledge of his own death ? Why did he not
forthwith oppose the king's desire to see the gods ?
Was it reasonable to be afraid of misfortunes which
were not to happen in his time ? Or what worse
fate could have been his than that which he hastened
to inflict upon himself ?

But let us now examine [1] the most ridiculous part

[1] The passage §§ 260-266 repeats unnecessarily the
substance of §§ 237-250 : possibly these are extracts from
two treatises utilizing the same material.

μενος γὰρ ταῦτα καὶ περὶ τῶν μελλόντων φοβηθείς,
τοὺς λελωβημένους ἐκείνους, ὧν αὐτῷ καθαρίσαι[1]
προείρητο τὴν Αἴγυπτον, οὐδὲ τότε τῆς χώρας
ἐξήλασεν, ἀλλὰ δεηθεῖσιν αὐτοῖς ἔδωκε πόλιν, ὥς
φησι, τὴν πάλαι μὲν οἰκηθεῖσαν ὑπὸ τῶν Ποιμένων,
261 Αὔαριν δὲ καλουμένην. εἰς ἣν ἀθροισθέντας αὐτοὺς
ἡγεμόνα φησὶν ἐξελέσθαι τῶν ἐξ Ἡλιουπόλεως
πάλαι γεγονότων ἱερέων, καὶ τοῦτον αὐτοῖς εἰσ-
ηγήσασθαι μήτε θεοὺς προσκυνεῖν μήτε τῶν ἐν[2]
Αἰγύπτῳ θρησκευομένων ζῴων ἀπέχεσθαι, πάντα
δὲ θύειν καὶ κατεσθίειν, συνάπτεσθαι δὲ μηδενὶ
πλὴν τῶν συνομωμοσμένων,[3] ὅρκοις τε τὸ πλῆθος
ἐνδησάμενον, ἦ μὴν τούτοις ἐμμενεῖν τοῖς νόμοις,
καὶ τειχίσαντα τὴν Αὔαριν πρὸς τὸν βασιλέα
262 πόλεμον ἐξενεγκεῖν. καὶ προστίθησιν ὅτι ἔπεμψεν
εἰς Ἱεροσόλυμα παρακαλῶν ἐκείνους αὐτοῖς συμ-
μαχεῖν καὶ δώσειν αὐτοῖς τὴν Αὔαριν ὑπισχνού-
μενος, εἶναι γὰρ αὐτὴν τοῖς ἐκ τῶν Ἱεροσολύμων
ἀφιξομένοις προγονικήν, ἀφ' ἧς ὁρμωμένους αὐτοὺς
263 πᾶσαν τὴν Αἴγυπτον καθέξειν. εἶτα τοὺς μὲν
ἐπελθεῖν εἴκοσι στρατοῦ μυριάσι λέγει, τὸν βασιλέα
δὲ τῶν Αἰγυπτίων Ἀμένωφιν οὐκ οἰόμενον δεῖν
θεομαχεῖν εἰς τὴν Αἰθιοπίαν εὐθὺς ἀποδρᾶναι, τὸν
δὲ Ἄπιν καί τινα τῶν ἄλλων ἱερῶν ζῴων παρα-
τεθεικέναι τοῖς ἱερεῦσι διαφυλάττεσθαι κελεύσαντα.
264 εἶτα τοὺς Ἱεροσολυμίτας ἐπελθόντας τάς τε πόλεις
ἀνιστάναι καὶ τὰ ἱερὰ κατακαίειν καὶ τοὺς ἱερέας[4]

136

of the whole story. Although he had learned these
facts, and had conceived a dread of the future, the
king did not, even then, expel from his land those
cripples of whose taint he had previously been bidden
to purge Egypt, but instead, at their request, he
gave them as their city (Manetho says) the former
habitation of the Shepherds, Auaris, as it was called.
Here, he adds, they assembled, and selected as their
leader a man who had formerly been a priest in
Heliopolis. This man (according to Manetho) in-
structed them not to worship the gods nor to refrain
from the animals revered in Egypt, but to sacrifice
and devour them all, and to have intercourse with
none save those of their own confederacy. Then
having bound his followers by oath to abide strictly
by these laws, he fortified Auaris and waged war
against the king. This leader, Manetho adds, sent
to Jerusalem, inviting the people to join in alliance
with him, and promising to give them Auaris, which,
he reminded them, was the ancestral home of those
who would come from Jerusalem, and would serve as
a base for their conquest of the whole of Egypt.
Then, continues Manetho, they advanced with an
army of 200,000 men; and Amenôphis, king of
Egypt, thinking he ought not to fight against the
gods, fled straightway into Ethiopia after enjoining
that Apis and some of the other sacred animals should
be entrusted to the custody of the priests. Thereafter, the men from Jerusalem came on, made deso-
late the cities, burned down the temples, massacred

---

[1] Cobet: καθαρεῦσαι L.   [2] Conj. Niese: ἐπ' L.
[3] Niese: συνωμοσμένων L.   [4] Bekker: ἱππέας L, Lat.

ἀποσφάττειν, ὅλως τε μηδεμιᾶς ἀπέχεσθαι παρα-
265 νομίας μηδὲ ὠμότητος. ὁ δὲ τὴν πολιτείαν καὶ
τοὺς νόμους αὐτοῖς καταβαλόμενος [1] ἱερεύς, φησίν,
ἦν τὸ γένος Ἡλιοπολίτης, ὄνομα δ' Ὀσαρσὴφ [2]
ἀπὸ τοῦ ἐν Ἡλιουπόλει θεοῦ Ὀσίρεως, μεταθέμενος
266 δὲ Μωυσῆν αὐτὸν προσηγόρευσε. τρισκαιδεκάτῳ
δέ φησιν ἔτει τὸν Ἀμένωφιν,—τοσοῦτον γὰρ αὐτῷ
χρόνον εἶναι τῆς ἐκπτώσεως πεπρωμένον,— ἐξ
Αἰθιοπίας ἐπελθόντα μετὰ πολλῆς στρατιᾶς καὶ
συμβαλόντα τοῖς Ποιμέσι καὶ τοῖς μιαροῖς νικῆσαί
τε τῇ μάχῃ καὶ κτεῖναι πολλοὺς ἐπιδιώξαντα
29 μέχρι τῶν τῆς Συρίας ὅρων.
267　　Ἐν τούτοις πάλιν οὐ συνίησιν ἀπιθάνως ψευ-
δόμενος. οἱ γὰρ λεπροὶ καὶ τὸ μετ' αὐτῶν πλῆθος,
εἰ καὶ πρότερον ὠργίζοντο τῷ βασιλεῖ καὶ τοῖς
τὰ περὶ αὐτοὺς πεποιηκόσι κατὰ [τε] [3] τὴν τοῦ
μάντεως προαγόρευσιν, ἀλλ' ὅτε τῶν λιθοτομιῶν
ἐξῆλθον καὶ πόλιν παρ' αὐτοῦ καὶ χώραν ἔλαβον,
πάντως [4] ἂν γεγόνεισαν πρᾳότεροι πρὸς αὐτόν.
268 εἰ δὲ δὴ [5] κἀκεῖνον ἐμίσουν, ἰδίᾳ μὲν ἂν αὐτῷ [6]
ἐπεβούλευον, οὐκ ἂν δὲ πρὸς ἅπαντας ἤραντο
πόλεμον, δῆλον ὅτι πλείστας ἔχοντες συγγενείας
269 τοσοῦτοί γε τὸ πλῆθος ὄντες. ὅμως δὲ καὶ τοῖς
ἀνθρώποις πολεμεῖν διεγνωκότες, οὐκ ἂν εἰς τοὺς
αὐτῶν θεοὺς πολεμεῖν ἐτόλμησαν οὐδ' ὑπεναν-
τιωτάτους ἔθεντο νόμους τοῖς πατρίοις αὐτῶν καὶ
270 οἷς ἐνετράφησαν. δεῖ δὲ ἡμᾶς τῷ Μανεθῷ [7] χάριν

---

[1] Ed. pr.: καταβαλλόμενος L.
[2] Ὀσαρσὶφ ed. pr.: Ἀρσὴφ L.
[3] Om. Lat., Bekker.　　　　[4] Ed. pr.: πάντες L, Lat.
[5] εἰ δ' ἔτι conj. Niese (porro si adhuc Lat.).

the priests, and, in short, committed every possible
kind of lawlessness and savagery. The priest who
framed their constitution and their laws was, according to Manetho, a native of Hêliopolis, Osarsêph
by name, after Osiris the god worshipped in Hêliopolis : but he changed his name and called himself
Moses. Thirteen years later—this being the destined period of his exile—Amenôphis, according to
Manetho, advanced from Ethiopia with a large army,
and joining battle with the Shepherds and the polluted people, he defeated them, killing many, after
pursuing them to the frontiers of Syria.

Here again Manetho fails to realize the improbability of his lying tale. Even if the lepers and their
accompanying horde were previously angry with the
king and the others who had treated them thus in
obedience to the seer's prediction, certainly when
they had left the stone-quarries and received from
him a city and land, they would have grown more
kindly disposed to him. If indeed they still hated
him, they would have plotted against him personally,
instead of declaring war against the whole people ;
for obviously so large a company must have had
numerous relatives in Egypt. Notwithstanding,
once they had resolved to make war on the Egyptians,
they would never have ventured to direct their war-
fare against their gods, nor would they have framed
laws completely opposed to the ancestral code under
which they had been brought up. We must, however, be grateful to Manetho for stating that the

---

⁶ ἃν αὐτῷ ed. pr.: ἄνῶ (= ἀνθρώπῳ) L: ἃν (alone) conj.
Niese : ἃν ἀνθρώπῳ Reinach.

⁷ Niese: Μανέθωνι L.

ἔχειν, ὅτι ταύτης τῆς παρανομίας οὐχὶ τοὺς ἐξ
Ἱεροσολύμων ἐλθόντας ἀρχηγοὺς γενέσθαι φησίν,
ἀλλ' αὐτοὺς ἐκείνους ὄντας Αἰγυπτίους καὶ τούτων μάλιστα τοὺς ἱερέας ἐπινοῆσαί τε ταῦτα καὶ
ὁρκωμοτῆσαι τὸ πλῆθος.

271 Ἐκεῖνο μέντοι πῶς οὐκ ἄλογον, τῶν μὲν οἰκείων
αὐτοῖς καὶ τῶν φίλων συναποστῆναι[1] οὐδένα μηδὲ
τοῦ πολέμου τὸν κίνδυνον συνάρασθαι, πέμψαι δὲ
τοὺς μιαροὺς εἰς Ἱεροσόλυμα καὶ τὴν παρ' ἐκείνων
272 ἐπάγεσθαι συμμαχίαν; ποίας αὐτοῖς φιλίας ἢ
τίνος αὐτοῖς οἰκειότητος προϋπηργμένης; τοὐναντίον γὰρ ἦσαν πολέμιοι καὶ τοῖς ἔθεσι[2] πλεῖστον
διέφερον. ὁ δέ φησιν εὐθὺς ὑπακοῦσαι τοῖς ὑπ-
ισχνουμένοις ὅτι τὴν Αἴγυπτον καθέξουσιν, ὥσπερ
αὐτῶν οὐ σφόδρα τῆς χώρας ἐμπείρως ἐχόντων,
273 ἧς βιασθέντες ἐκπεπτώκασιν. εἰ μὲν οὖν ἀπόρως
ἢ κακῶς ἔπραττον, ἴσως ἂν καὶ παρεβάλλοντο,
πόλιν δὲ κατοικοῦντες εὐδαίμονα καὶ χώραν
πολλὴν κρείττω τῆς Αἰγύπτου καρπούμενοι, διὰ
τί ποτ' ἂν ἐχθροῖς μὲν πάλαι τὰ δὲ σώματα λε-
λωβημένοις, οὓς μηδὲ τῶν οἰκείων οὐδεὶς ὑπέμενε,
τούτοις ἔμελλον παρακινδυνεύσειν βοηθοῦντες; οὐ
γὰρ δή γε τὸν γενησόμενον προῄδεσαν δρασμὸν
274 τοῦ βασιλέως· τοὐναντίον γὰρ αὐτὸς εἴρηκεν ὡς

---

[1] Bekker (consensit Lat.): συναποστῆσαι L.
[2] Hudson (moribus Lat.): ἤθεσι L.

---

[1] In § 245 we are told that Amenôphis himself led his
host in this useless march, and that his son was only
5 years old. Only here is Pêlusium mentioned as the
destination of the march.

[Footnote continued on opposite page.

authors of this lawlessness were not the newcomers
from Jerusalem, but that company of people who
were themselves Egyptians, and that it was, above
all, their priests who devised the scheme and bound
the multitude by oath.

Moreover, how absurd it is to imagine that, while
none of their relatives and friends joined in the revolt
and shared in the perils of war, these polluted persons
sent to Jerusalem and gained allies there ! What
alliance, what connexion had previously existed between them ? Why, on the contrary, they were
enemies, and differed widely in customs. Yet
Manetho says that they lent a ready ear to the
promise that they would occupy Egypt, just as if
they were not thoroughly acquainted with the
country from which they had been forcibly expelled !
Now, if they had been in straitened or unhappy circumstances, they would perhaps have taken the risk ;
but dwelling, as they did, in a prosperous city and
enjoying the fruits of an ample country, superior to
Egypt, why ever should they be likely to hazard
their lives by succouring their former foes, those
maimed cripples, whom none even of their own
kinsfolk could endure ? For of course they did not
foresee that the king would take flight. On the contrary, Manetho has himself stated that the son [1] of

Pêlusium, " the celebrated eastern seaport and key to
Egypt " (Baedeker [8], pp. 197 f.), the famous frontier
fortress, in Ancient Egyptian *Šnw*. A scarab of the late
Twelfth Dynasty or early Thirteenth, published by
Newberry in *J. Eg. Arch.* xviii. (1932), p. 141, shows the
place-name written within the fortress-sign. The name
Pêlusium is from πηλός " mud ": *cf.* Strabo, 17. 1, 21,
for the muddy pools or marshes around Pêlusium.

ὁ παῖς τοῦ Ἀμενώφιος τριάκοντα μυριάδας ἔχων
εἰς τὸ Πηλούσιον ὑπηντίαζεν. καὶ τοῦτο μὲν
ᾔδεισαν πάντως οἱ παραγινόμενοι, τὴν δὲ μετά-
νοιαν αὐτοῦ καὶ τὴν φυγὴν πόθεν εἰκάζειν ἔμελλον;
275 ἔπειτα [1] κρατήσαντάς φησι τῆς Αἰγύπτου πολλὰ
καὶ δεινὰ δρᾶν τοὺς ἐκ τῶν Ἱεροσολύμων ἐπι-
στρατεύσαντας, καὶ περὶ τούτων ὀνειδίζει καθάπερ
οὐ πολεμίους αὐτοὺς [2] ἐπαγαγὼν ἢ δέον τοῖς ἔξωθεν
ἐπικληθεῖσιν ἐγκαλεῖν, ὁπότε ταῦτα πρὸ τῆς
ἐκείνων ἀφίξεως ἔπραττον καὶ πράξειν ὠμωμό-
276 κεσαν οἱ τὸ γένος Αἰγύπτιοι. ἀλλὰ καὶ χρόνοις
ὕστερον Ἀμένωφις ἐπελθὼν ἐνίκησε μάχῃ καὶ
κτείνων τοὺς πολεμίους μέχρι τῆς Συρίας ἤλα-
σεν· οὕτω γὰρ παντάπασίν ἐστιν ἡ Αἴγυπτος τοῖς
277 ὁποθενδηποτοῦν ἐπιοῦσιν εὐάλωτος. καίτοι [3] οἱ
τότε πολέμῳ κρατοῦντες αὐτήν, ζῆν πυνθανόμενοι
τὸν Ἀμένωφιν, οὔτε τὰς ἐκ τῆς Αἰθιοπίας ἐμβολὰς
ὠχύρωσαν, πολλὴν εἰς τοῦτο παρασκευὴν ἔχοντες,
οὔτε τὴν ἄλλην ἡτοίμασαν δύναμιν. ὁ δὲ καὶ μέχρι
τῆς Συρίας ἀναιρῶν, φησίν, αὐτοὺς ἠκολούθησε
διὰ τῆς ψάμμου τῆς ἀνύδρου, δῆλον ὅτι οὐ ῥάδιον
30 οὐδὲ ἀμαχεὶ στρατοπέδῳ διελθεῖν.
278   Κατὰ μὲν οὖν τὸν Μανεθὼν οὔτε ἐκ τῆς Αἰγύπτου τὸ γένος ἡμῶν ἐστιν οὔτε τῶν ἐκεῖθέν
τινες ἀνεμίχθησαν· τῶν γὰρ λεπρῶν καὶ νοσούντων
πολλοὺς μὲν εἰκὸς ἐν ταῖς λιθοτομίαις ἀποθανεῖν
πολὺν χρόνον ἐκεῖ γενομένους καὶ κακοπαθοῦντας,
πολλοὺς δ᾽ ἐν ταῖς μετὰ ταῦτα μάχαις, πλείστους
δ᾽ ἐν τῇ τελευταίᾳ καὶ τῇ φυγῇ.

[1] Hudson : εἶτα Niese : deinde Lat. : τὰ σιτία L.

Amenôphis marched with 300,000 men to confront them at Pêlusium. This was certainly known to those already present; but how could they possibly guess that he would change his mind and flee? Manetho next says that, after conquering Egypt, the invaders from Jerusalem committed many heinous crimes; and for these he reproaches them, just as if he had not brought them in as enemies, or as if he was bound to accuse allies from abroad of actions which before their arrival native Egyptians were performing and had sworn to perform. But, years later, Amenôphis returned to the attack, conquered the enemy in battle, and drove them, with slaughter, right to Syria. So perfectly easy a prey is Egypt to invaders, no matter whence they come! And yet those who at that time conquered the land, on learning that Amenôphis was alive, neither fortified the passes between it and Ethiopia, although their resources were amply sufficient, nor did they keep the rest of their forces in readiness! Amenôphis, according to Manetho, pursued them with carnage over the sandy desert right to Syria. But obviously it is no easy matter for an army to cross the desert even without fighting.

Thus, according to Manetho, our race is not of Egyptian origin, nor did it receive any admixture of Egyptians. For, naturally, many of the lepers and invalids died in the stone-quarries during their long term of hardship, many others in the subsequent battles, and most of all in the final engagement and the rout.

---

² Reinach: αὐτοῖς L.   ³ Conj. Thackeray: καὶ L.

31
279
　　Λοιπόν μοι πρὸς αὐτὸν εἰπεῖν περὶ Μωυσέως
τοῦτον δὲ τὸν ἄνδρα θαυμαστὸν μὲν Αἰγύπτιοι
καὶ θεῖον νομίζουσι, βούλονται δὲ προσποιεῖν αὐτοῖς μετὰ βλασφημίας ἀπιθάνου, λέγοντες Ἡλιο-
πολίτην εἶναι τῶν ἐκεῖθεν ἱερέων ἕνα διὰ τὴν
280 λέπραν συνεξεληλασμένον. δείκνυται δ' ἐν ταῖς
ἀναγραφαῖς ὀκτωκαίδεκα σὺν τοῖς πεντακοσίοις
πρότερον ἔτεσι γεγονὼς καὶ τοὺς ἡμετέρους
ἐξαγαγὼν ἐκ τῆς Αἰγύπτου πατέρας εἰς τὴν
281 χώραν τὴν νῦν οἰκουμένην ὑφ' ἡμῶν. ὅτι δ' οὐδὲ
συμφορᾷ τινι τοιαύτῃ περὶ τὸ σῶμα κεχρημένος
ἦν, ἐκ τῶν λεγομένων ὑπ' αὐτοῦ δῆλός ἐστι· τοῖς
γὰρ λεπρῶσιν ἀπείρηκε μήτε μένειν ἐν πόλει μήτ'
ἐν κώμῃ κατοικεῖν, ἀλλὰ μόνους περιπατεῖν κατ-
εσχισμένους τὰ ἱμάτια, καὶ τὸν ἁψάμενον αὐτῶν
282 ἢ ὁμωρόφιον γενόμενον οὐ καθαρὸν ἡγεῖται. καὶ
μὴν κἂν θεραπευθῇ τὸ νόσημα καὶ τὴν αὐτοῦ
φύσιν ἀπολάβῃ, προείρηκέν τινας ἁγνείας,[1] καθαρ-
μοὺς πηγαίων ὑδάτων λουτροῖς καὶ ξυρήσεις
πάσης τῆς τριχός, πολλάς τε κελεύει καὶ παν-
τοίας ἐπιτελέσαντα θυσίας τότε παρελθεῖν εἰς τὴν
283 ἱερὰν πόλιν. καίτοι[2] τοὐναντίον εἰκὸς ἦν προνοίᾳ
τινὶ καὶ φιλανθρωπίᾳ χρήσασθαι τὸν ἐν τῇ συμφορᾷ ταύτῃ γεγονότα πρὸς τοὺς ὁμοίως[3] αὐτῷ
δυστυχήσαντας. οὐ μόνον δὲ περὶ τῶν λεπρῶν
οὕτως ἐνομοθέτησεν, ἀλλ' οὐδὲ τοῖς καὶ τὸ βραχύ-
τατόν τι τοῦ σώματος ἠκρωτηριασμένοις ἱερᾶσθαι
284 συγκεχώρηκεν, ἀλλ' εἰ καὶ μεταξύ τις ἱερώμενος

---

[1] + καὶ Lat., Reinach.　　　[2] Ed. pr.: καὶ L.
[3] Ed. pr.: ὁμοίους L, Lat.

144

It remains for me to reply to Manetho's statements about Moses. The Egyptians regard him as a wonderful, even a divine being, but wish to claim him as their own by an incredible calumny, alleging that he belonged to Hêliopolis and was dismissed from his priesthood there owing to leprosy. The records, however, show that he lived 518 years [1] earlier, and led our forefathers up out of Egypt to the land which we inhabit at the present time. And that he suffered from no such physical affliction is clear from his own words. He has, in fact, forbidden lepers [2] either to stay in a town or to make their abode in a village ; they must go about in solitude, with their garments rent. Anyone who touches them or lives under the same roof with them he considers unclean. Moreover, even if the malady is cured and the leper resumes normal health, Moses has prescribed certain rites of purification—to cleanse himself in a bath of spring-water and to shave off all his hair,—and enjoins the performance of a number of different sacrifices before entrance into the holy city. Yet it would have been natural, on the contrary, for a victim of this scourge to show some consideration and kindly feeling for those who shared the same misfortune. It was not only about lepers that he framed such laws : those who had even the slightest mutilation of the body were disqualified for the priesthood ; [3] and if a priest in the course of his ministry met with an

---

[1] 518 years. See n. on § 230.

[2] For the laws of leprosy, here summarized, see *O.T. Leviticus* xiii. (especially 45 f.) and xiv.

[3] *Cf. Leviticus* xxi. 17-23 (exclusion from the priesthood of anyone " that hath a blemish ").

τοιαύτῃ χρήσαιτο συμφορᾷ, τὴν τιμὴν αὐτὸν
285 ἀφείλετο. πῶς οὖν εἰκὸς ἐκεῖνον[1] ταῦτα νομο-
θετεῖν ἀνοήτως <ἢ τοὺς>[2] ἀπὸ τοιούτων συμ-
φορῶν συνειλεγμένους προσέσθαι[3] καθ᾽ ἑαυτῶν εἰς
286 ὄνειδός τε καὶ βλάβην νόμους συντιθεμένους; ἀλλὰ
μὴν καὶ τοὔνομα λίαν ἀπιθάνως μετατέθεικεν·
Ὀσαρσὴφ[4] γάρ, φησίν, ἐκαλεῖτο. τοῦτο μὲν οὖν
εἰς τὴν μετάθεσιν οὐκ ἐναρμόζει, τὸ δ᾽ ἀληθὲς
ὄνομα δηλοῖ τὸν ἐκ τοῦ ὕδατος σωθέντα [Μωσῆν]·[5]
τὸ γὰρ ὕδωρ οἱ Αἰγύπτιοι μῶϋ καλοῦσιν.
287 Ἱκανῶς οὖν γεγονέναι νομίζω κατάδηλον[6] ὅτι
Μανεθώς, ἕως μὲν ἠκολούθει ταῖς ἀρχαίαις ἀναγραφαῖς, οὐ πολὺ τῆς ἀληθείας διημάρτανεν, ἐπὶ
δὲ τοὺς ἀδεσπότους μύθους τραπόμενος ἢ συνέθη-
κεν αὐτοὺς ἀπιθάνως ἤ τισι τῶν πρὸς ἀπέχθειαν
εἰρηκότων ἐπίστευσεν.

[1] ἢ 'κεῖνον Niese.   [2] Add. Niese.
[3] Niese: προέσθαι L.   [4] Ed. pr.: Ὀαρσὴφ L.
[5] Bracketed as a gloss (Niese).
[6] Bekker: καὶ δῆλον δ᾽ L (δ᾽ om. ed. pr.).

---

[1] The same etymology (with the necessary addition that
ὑσῆς means " saved ") recurs in Josephus, Antiq. ii. 228:
cf. Philo, De Vita Moysis, i. 4, § 17. There is a word in
Ancient Egyptian, mw, meaning " water," but the connexion with the name Moses is hypothetical. Similar
forms appear as personal names in Pharaonic times, e.g.

accident of this nature, he was deprived of his office. How improbable, then, that Moses should be so foolish as to frame these laws, or that men brought together by such misfortunes should approve of legislation against themselves, to their own shame and injury ! But, further, the name, too, has been transformed in an extremely improbable way. According to Manetho, Moses was called Osarsêph. These names, however, are not interchangeable : the true name means " one saved out of the water," for water is called " mō-y " by the Egyptians.[1]

It is now, therefore, sufficiently obvious, I think, that, so long as Manetho followed the ancient records, he did not stray far from the truth ; but when he turned to unauthorized legends, he either combined them in an improbable form or else gave credence to certain prejudiced informants.

Ms.i from the Old Kingdom, *Ms* (very common) from the New Kingdom. In *Exodus* ii. 10 " Moses " is " drawn out " (Hebr. *mashah*) of the water—a derivation " hardly meant to be taken seriously " (T. H. Robinson, in Oesterley and Robinson, *History of Israel*, I. p. 81).

See further Alan H. Gardiner, " The Egyptian Origin of some English Personal Names," in *Journ. of Amer. Orient. Soc.* 56 (1936), pp. 192-4. Gardiner points out (p. 195, n. 28) that ὑσῆς (mentioned above) is clearly a perversion of ασιης [or ἐσιῆς, = Egyptian *ḥsy*, " praised," LS⁹], the Greek equivalent of the Coptic *hasie*, " favoured " ; but an Egyptian became " favoured " by the fact of being drowned, not by being saved from drowning.

Fr. 55.   *Syncellus, p. 134.   ΚΑΤΑ ΑΦΡΙΚΑΝΟΝ.*

'Εννεακαιδεκάτη δυναστεία βασιλέων ζ'[1] Διοσπολιτῶν.

α' Σέθως, ἔτη να'.

β' 'Ραψάκης, ἔτη ξα'.[2]

γ' 'Αμμενέφθης, ἔτη κ'.

δ' 'Ραμεσσῆς, ἔτη ξ'.

ε' 'Αμμενεμνῆς, ἔτη ε'.

ϛ' Θούωρις, ὁ παρ' 'Ομήρῳ[3] καλούμενος Πόλυβος, 'Αλκάνδρας ἀνήρ, ἐφ' οὗ[4] τὸ "Ιλιον ἑάλω, ἔτη ζ'.

'Ομοῦ, ἔτη σθ'.

[1] MSS. : ϛ' Müller, who explains the error as due to someone who thought that 'Αλκάνδρας ἀνήρ denoted a seventh king.

[2] ξϛ' Müller.   [3] *Odyssey*, iv. 126.

[4] m. : ζ' 'Αλκάνδρος ἀνήρ, ἐφ' οὗ MSS.

---

[1] Dynasty XIX. : *c.* 1310-1200 B.C.   The lists given by Africanus and Eusebius for Dynasty XIX. are in very bad confusion.   Armaïs (Haremhab) should begin the line, which Meyer gives as follows :—

Haremhab : Ramessês I. : Sethôs I. : Ramessês II. (the Louis Quatorze of Egyptian history : 67 years, see Breasted, *Anc. Rec.* iv. § 471 ; *C.A.H.* ii. pp. 139 ff.) : Mernepath : Amenmesês : Mernepath II. Siptah : Sethôs II. : Ramessês Siptah : <Arsu the Syrian>.

W. Struve (*Die Ära ἀπὸ Μενόφρεως und die XIX. Dynastie Manethos*, in *Zeitschr. für äg. Sprache*, Bd. 63 (1928), pp. 45-50) gives a revised sequence with additional identifications : (1) Harmaïs (Haremhab), (2) Ramessês I., (3) Amenôphath (Seti I. Mernepath), (4) Sesôs (Struve's emendation for Sethôs), also called Ramessês Miamoun

DYNASTY XIX.

Fr. 55 (*from Syncellus*). ACCORDING TO AFRICANUS.

The Nineteenth Dynasty [1] consisted of seven (six) kings of Diospolis.

1. Sethôs, for 51 years.
2. Rapsacês, for 61 (66) years.
3. Ammenephthês, for 20 years.
4. Ramessês, for 60 years.
5. Ammenemnês, for 5 years.
6. Thuôris, who in Homer is called Polybus, husband of Alcandra, and in whose time Troy was taken,[2] reigned for 7 years.

Total, 209 years.

(Ramessês II. Seso), (5) Amenephthês (Merneptah), (6) [Amenophthês or Menophthês, emended from the form Menophrês in Theon of Alexandria], (Seti II. Merneptah), (7) Ramessês III. Siptah, (8) Ammenemes (Amenmeses), (9) Thuôris or Thuôsris, also called Siphthas. *Cf.* Petrie, *History of Egypt*, iii. pp. 120 ff. Struve points also to a new Sôthis date, 1318 B.C., in the reign of Seti I. (according to Petrie's chronology, 1326-1300 B.C.).

[2] The Fall of Troy was traditionally dated 1183 B.C.: *cf.* p. 107 n. 3.

In Homer, *Odyssey*, iv. 126, a golden distaff and a silver work-basket with wheels beneath and golden rims,—treasures in the palace of Menelaus at Sparta,—are described as gifts to Helen from " Alcandrê, the wife of Polybus who dwelt in Egyptian Thebes where the amplest store of wealth is laid up in men's houses " ; while to Menelaus himself Polybus had given two silver baths, two tripods, and ten talents of gold. See W. H. D. Rouse, *The Story of Odysseus*, 1937, p. 56 : " Polybos was a great nobleman in the Egyptian Thebes, with a palace full of treasures ".

149

'Επὶ τὸ αὐτὸ δευτέρου τόμου Μανεθῶ βασιλεῖς
Ϛϛ', ἔτη ‚βρκα'.

Fr. 56 (a).   *Syncellus*, p. 136.   ΚΑΤΑ ΕΥΣΕΒΙΟΝ

'Εννεακαιδεκάτη δυναστεία βασιλέων ε' Διοσπολιτῶν.

α' Σέθως, ἔτη νε'.
β' 'Ραμψής, ἔτη ξϛ'.
γ' 'Αμμενεφθίς, ἔτη μ'.
δ' 'Αμμενέμης, ἔτη κϛ'.
ε' Θούωρις, ὁ παρ' 'Ομήρῳ καλούμενος Πό-
    λυβος, 'Αλκάνδρας ἀνήρ, ἐφ' οὗ τὸ "Ιλιον
    ἑάλω, ἔτη ζ'.

'Ομοῦ, ἔτη ρϛδ'.
'Επὶ τὸ αὐτὸ β' τόμου Μανεθῶ βασιλέων Ϛβ'
ἔτη ‚αρκα'.[1]

(b) EUSEBIUS, *Chronica* I. (Armenian Version).
p. 102.

Nona decima dynastia Diospolitarum regum V.

Sethos, annis LV.
Rampses, annis LXVI.
Amenephthis, annis VIII.
Ammenemes, annis XXVI.

---

[1] ‚βρκα' corr. Müller.

Sum total in the Second Book of Manetho, ninety-six kings, for 2121 years.[1]

Fr. 56 (a) (*from Syncellus*). ACCORDING TO EUSEBIUS.

The Nineteenth Dynasty consisted of five kings of Diospolis.

1. Sethôs, for 55 years.
2. Rampsês, for 66 years.
3. Ammenephthis, for 40 years.
4. Ammenemês, for 26 years.
5. Thuôris, who in Homer is called Polybus, husband of Alcandra, and in whose reign Troy was taken, reigned for 7 years.

Total, 194 years.
Sum total in the Second Book of Manetho, for ninety-two kings, 1121 (2121) years.

(b) ARMENIAN VERSION OF EUSEBIUS.

The Nineteenth Dynasty consisted of five kings of Diospolis.

1. Sethos, for 55 years.
2. Rampses, for 66 years.
3. Amenephthis, for 8 years.
4. Ammenemes, for 26 years.

---

[1] For the corrected total of Book II., see Fr. 4, n. 4 (246 or 289 kings for 2221 years). The wide difference between the number of kings (96 or 92 as compared with 246 or 289) is puzzling : Meyer conjectures that about 150 or 193 of the larger numbers were ephemeral or co-regents.

Thuoris, ab Homero dictus Polybus, vir strenuus
et fortissimus,[1] cuius aetate Ilium captum
est, annis VII.

Summa annorum CLXXXXIV.

Manethonis libro secundo conflatur summa
LXXXXII regum, annorum MMCXXI.

ΤΟΜΟΣ ΤΡΙΤΟΣ

Fr. 57 (a).   *Syncellus*, p. 137.

ΚΑΤΑ ΑΦΡΙΚΑΝΟΝ.

Τρίτου τόμου Μανεθῶ.

Εἰκοστὴ δυναστεία βασιλέων Διοσπολιτῶν ιβ΄, οἱ
ἐβασίλευσαν ἔτη ρλε΄.

(b) *Syncellus*, p. 139.   *ΚΑΤΑ ΕΥΣΕΒΙΟΝ.*

Τρίτου τόμου Μανεθῶ.

Εἰκοστὴ δυναστεία βασιλέων Διοσπολιτῶν ιβ΄,
οἱ ἐβασίλευσαν ἔτη ροη΄.

[1] *I.e.* ἀνὴρ ᾿Αλκάνδρας Müller.

---

[1] Dynasty XX. c. 1200-1090 B.C.
    Setnakht : Ramessês III. c. 1200-1168 : Ramessês IV.-
XI. c. 1168-1090. Manetho's 12 kings probably included

5. Thuoris, by Homer called the active and
   gallant Polybus, in whose time Troy was
   taken, reigned for 7 years.

Total, 194 years.

In the Second Book of Manetho there is a total of
ninety-two kings, reigning for 2121 years.

BOOK III.

DYNASTY XX.

Fr. 57 (a) (*from Syncellus*). ACCORDING TO AFRICANUS.

From the Third Book of Manetho.

The Twentieth Dynasty [1] consisted of twelve kings
of Diospolis, who reigned for 135 years.

(b) ACCORDING TO EUSEBIUS.

From the Third Book of Manetho.

The Twentieth Dynasty consisted of twelve kings
of Diospolis, who reigned for 178 years.

Ramessês XII. and Herihor. The Great Papyrus Harris
(time of Ramessês III.) describes the anarchy between
Dynasties XIX. and XX.: see Breasted, *Anc. Rec.* iv.
§ 398.

A revised list of Dynasty XX. is given by Newberry in
Elliot Smith and Warren Dawson, *Egyptian Mummies,*
1924: see also T. E. Peet in *J. of Eg. Arch.* xiv. (1928),
pp. 52 f.

(c) Eusebius, *Chronica* I. (Armenian Version),
p. 103.

E Manethonis tertio libro.
Vicesima dynastia Diospolitanorum regum XII,
qui imperaverunt annis CLXXII.

Fr. 58.   *Syncellus*, p. 137.   *ΚΑΤΑ ΑΦΡΙΚΑΝΟΝ.*

Πρώτη καὶ εἰκοστὴ δυναστεία βασιλέων Τανιτῶν
ζ'.

α' Σμενδῆς, ἔτη κϛ'.
β' Ψουσέννης,[1] ἔτη μϛ'.
γ' Νεφερχερής,[2] ἔτη δ'.
δ' Ἀμενωφθίς, ἔτη θ'.
ε' Ὀσοχώρ, ἔτη ϛ'.
ϛ' Ψιναχῆς, ἔτη θ'.
ζ' Ψουσέννης,[3] ἔτη ιδ'.

Ὁμοῦ, ἔτη ρλ'.

[1] Ψουσένης Α.   [2] Νεφελχερής MSS.   [3] Σουσέννης Α.

---

[1] Dynasty XXI., resident at Tanis, c. 1090-c. 950 b.c.
(a dark period in Egyptian history). For identifications
with monumental and other evidence see Meyer, *Geschichte*[2],
ii. 2, p. 20 n. This Tanite Dynasty overlapped with the
Theban Dynasty XX.: see the Report of Wenamon,
Breasted, *Anc. Rec.* iv. §§ 557-591; *C.A.H.* ii. pp. 192 ff.

154

(c) Armenian Version of Eusebius.

From the Third Book of Manetho.
The Twentieth Dynasty consisted of twelve kings
of Diospolis, who reigned for 172 years.

Dynasty XXI.

Fr. 58 (*from Syncellus*). According to Africanus.

The Twenty-first Dynasty [1] consisted of seven kings
of Tanis.

1. Smendês,[2] for 26 years.
2. Psusen(n)ês [I.],[3] for 46 years.
3. Nephercherês (Nephelcherês), for 4 years.
4. Amenôphthis, for 9 years.
5. Osochôr, for 6 years.
6. Psinachês, for 9 years.
7. Psusennês [II.] (Susennês), for 14 years.

Total, 130 years.[4]

[2] For Smendês or Nesbenebded, a local noble of Tanis,
who seized the whole Delta and made himself king of
Lower Egypt, see *C.A.H.* ii. p. 191; iii. pp. 253 f.

[3] In Egyptian, Psusennês is Psukhe'mnê, " the star
appearing in Thebes ". In 1939-40 tombs of certain kings
of Dynasties XXI. and XXII. were excavated by P.
Montet at Tanis, the most valuable being the intact tomb
of Psusennês I., with its rich funerary equipment: in
several chambers sarcophagi, vases of many kinds, and
jewels were found, including the funerary outfit of Amenôphthis (Amon-em-apt, son of Psusennês I.) and the silver
sarcophagus of a certain Sesonchôsis (not the first king of
Dynasty XXII.), (*Ann. Serv. Antiq.*, tt. xxxix. f., 1939-40).

[4] Actual total of items, 114 years. Eusebius is probably correct with 41 years for 2nd king and 35 years for
7th (Meyer).

155

Fr. 59 (a).   *Syncellus*, p. 139.   ΚΑΤΑ ΕΥΣΕΒΙΟΝ.

Εἰκοστὴ πρώτη δυναστεία βασιλέων Τανιτῶν
ἑπτά.

α΄ Σμένδις, ἔτη κϛ΄.
β΄ Ψουσέννης, ἔτη μα΄.
γ΄ Νεφερχερής, ἔτη δ΄.
δ΄ Ἀμενωφθίς, ἔτη θ΄.
ε΄ Ὀσοχώρ, ἔτη ϛ΄.
ϛ΄ Ψιναχῆς, ἔτη θ΄.
ζ΄ Ψουσέννης, ἔτη λε΄.

Ὁμοῦ, ἔτη ρλ΄.

(b) EUSEBIUS, *Chronica* I. (Armenian Version),
p. 103.

Vicesima prima dynastia Tanitarum regum VII.

Smendis, annis XXVI.
Psusennes, annis XLI.
Nephercheres, annis IV.
Amenophthis, annis IX.
Osochor, annis VI.
Psinnaches, annis IX.
Psusennes, annis XXXV.

Summa annorum est CXXX.

Fr. 59 (a) (*from Syncellus*). ACCORDING TO
EUSEBIUS.

The Twenty-first Dynasty consisted of seven kings
of Tanis.

1. Smendis, for 26 years.
2. Psusennês, for 41 years.
3. Nephercherês, for 4 years.
4. Amenôphthis, for 9 years.
5. Osochôr, for 6 years.
6. Psinachês, for 9 years.
7. Psusennês, for 35 years.

Total, 130 years.

(b) ARMENIAN VERSION OF EUSEBIUS.

The Twenty-first Dynasty consisted of seven kings
of Tanis.

1. Smendis, for 26 years.
2. Psusennês, for 41 years.
3. Nephercherês, for 4 years.
4. Amenôphthis, for 9 years.
5. Osochôr, for 6 years.
6. Psinnaches, for 9 years.
7. Psusennes, for 35 years.

Total, 130 years.

Fr. 60. *Syncellus*, p. 137. *ΚΑΤΑ ΑΦΡΙΚΑΝΟΝ*

Εἰκοστὴ δευτέρα δυναστεία Βουβαστιτῶν βασιλέων θ'.

α' Σέσωγχις,[1] ἔτη κα'.
β' 'Οσορθών,[2] ἔτη ιε'.
γ' δ' ε' Ἄλλοι τρεῖς, ἔτη κε'.[3]
ς' Τακέλωθις, ἔτη ιγ'.
ζ' η' θ' Ἄλλοι τρεῖς, ἔτη μβ'.
Ὁμοῦ, ἔτη ρκ'.

Fr. 61 (a). *Syncellus*, p. 139. *ΚΑΤΑ ΕΥΣΕΒΙΟΝ.*

Εἰκοστὴ δευτέρα δυναστεία Βουβαστιτῶν βασιλέων τριῶν.

α' Σεσώγχωσις,[4] ἔτη κα'.
β' 'Οσορθών, ἔτη ιε'.
γ' Τακέλωθις, ἔτη ιγ'.
Ὁμοῦ, ἔτη μθ'.

[1] B : Σέσογχις A.   [2] B : 'Οσωρθών A.
[3] κθ' Boeckh.   [4] Σεσόγχωσις A.

---

[1] Dynasty XXII. *c.* 950–*c.* 730 B.C., kings of Libyan origin resident at Bubastis. For identifications with the monumental and other evidence see Meyer, *Geschichte*[2], ii. 2,

DYNASTY XXII.

Fr. 60 *(from Syncellus)*.   ACCORDING TO AFRICANUS.

The Twenty-second Dynasty [1] consisted of nine kings of Bubastus.

1. Sesônchis, for 21 years.
2. Osorthôn, [2] for 15 years.
3, 4, 5. Three other kings, for 25 [29] years.
6. Takelôthis, for 13 years.
7, 8, 9. Three other kings, for 42 years.

Total, 120 years. [3]

Fr. 61 (a) *(from Syncellus)*.   ACCORDING TO EUSEBIUS.

The Twenty-second Dynasty consisted of three kings of Bubastus.

1. Sesônchôsis, for 21 years.
2. Osorthôn, for 15 years.
3. Takelôthis, for 13 years.

Total, 49 years.

p. 58.   The first king, Sesonchôsis (Shishak, *O.T. 1 Kings* xiv. 25, *2 Chron.* xii.) overthrew the Tanites *c.* 940 B.C.   About 930 B.C. he captured Jerusalem and plundered the Temple of Solomon : see Peet, *Egypt and the Old Testament*, 1922. pp. 158 ff.   Albright (*The Archaeology of Palestine and the Bible* [2], 1932-3, p. 199), dates the conquest of Judah by Shishak between 924 and 917 B.C.

[2] The name Osorthôn is another form of Osorchô (Dynasty XXIII. No. 2—Africanus), the Egyptian Osorkon.

[3] Actual total of items, 116 years.

159

(b) Eusebius, *Chronica* I. (Armenian Version),
p. 103.

Vicesima secunda dynastia Bubastitarum regum
III.

Sesonchosis, annis XXI.
Osorthon, annis XV.
Tacelothis, annis XIII.
Summa annorum XLIX.

Fr. 62.   *Syncellus*, p. 138.   *ΚΑΤΑ ΑΦΡΙΚΑΝΟΝ.*

Τρίτη καὶ εἰκοστὴ δυναστεία Τανιτῶν βασιλέων
δ'.

α' Πετουβάτης, ἔτη μ', ἐφ' οὗ 'Ολυμπιὰς
ἤχθη πρώτη.
β' 'Οσορχώ, ἔτη η', ὃν 'Ηρακλέα Αἰγύπτιοι
καλοῦσι.
γ' Ψαμμοῦς, ἔτη ι'.
δ' Ζήτ, ἔτη λα'.[1]
'Ομοῦ, ἔτη πθ'.

[1] λδ' B.

---

[1] Osorthôs (Aucher, Karst).
[2] Dynasty XXIII., resident at Tanis : the records of
these kings (dated by Breasted 745-718 B.C.) are much
confused. The name Petubatês (see Fr. 63 for the usual
Grecized form Petubastis) represents the Egyptian
Pedibaste. For King Osorcho (Osorkon III.) see the
stele of Piankhi, king of Ethiopia, whose vassal Osorkon
became (Breasted, *Anc. Rec.* iv. §§ 807, 811, 872, 878).
Psammûs has not been identified.

(b) Armenian Version of Eusebius.

The Twenty-second Dynasty consisted of three kings of Bubastus.

1. Sesônchôsis, for 21 years.
2. Osorthôn,[1] for 15 years.
3. Tacelôthis, for 13 years.

Total, 49 years.

Dynasty XXIII.

Fr. 62 (*from Syncellus*). According to Africanus.

The Twenty-third Dynasty[2] consisted of four kings of Tanis.

1. Petubatês, for 40 years: in his reign the Olympic festival[3] was first celebrated.
2. Osorchô, for 8 years: the Egyptians call him Hêraclês.*
3. Psammûs, for 10 years.
4. Zêt,[4] for 31 years (34).

Total, 89 years.

[3] The date of the first Olympic festival was conventionally fixed at 776-775 B.C.

* See G. A. Wainwright, *Sky-Religion*, pp. 35 f.

[4] The fact that the name Zêt, occurring in Africanus alone, is wrapped in obscurity, has led Flinders Petrie to suggest ("The Mysterious Zêt" in *Ancient Egypt*, 1914, p. 32) that the three Greek letters are a contraction for ζητεῖται or other word connected with ζητέω, meaning "A question (remains)," or "Query, about 31 years": for 31 years at this time no single ruler seemed to be predominant, and further search was needed to settle who should be entered as the king of Egypt. "Zêt." is found in wall-inscriptions at Pompeii: see Diehl, *Pompeianische Wandinschriften*, No. 682. The next inscription, No. 683, gives "Zêtêma" in full: a riddle follows.

Fr. 63 (a).   *Syncellus*, p. 140.   ΚΑΤΑ ΕΥΣΕΒΙΟΝ.

Εἰκοστὴ τρίτη δυναστεία Τανιτῶν βασιλέων
τριῶν.

α´ Πετουβάστις, ἔτη κε´.
β´ Ὀσορθών, ἔτη θ´, ὃν Ἡρακλέα Αἰγύπτιοι
    ἐκάλεσαν.
γ´ Ψαμμοῦς, ἔτη ι´.
Ὁμοῦ, ἔτη μδ´.

(b) Eusebius, *Chronica* I. (Armenian Version),
                    p. 103.

Vicesima tertia dynastia Tanitarum regum III.

Petubastis, annis XXV.

Deinde Osorthon, quem Aegyptii Herculem nun-
    cupaverunt, annis IX.[1]

Psammus,[2] annis X.

Summa annorum XLIV.

---

[1] annis IX. (Aucher).
[2] Phramus (Petermann): Psamus (Aucher, Karst).

Fr. 63 (a) (*from Syncellus*). ACCORDING TO
EUSEBIUS.

The Twenty-third Dynasty consisted of three kings
of Tanis.

1. Petubastis,[1] for 25 years.
2. Osorthôn, for 9 years : the Egyptians called
   him Hêraclês.
3. Psammûs, for 10 years.

Total, 44 years.

(b) ARMENIAN VERSION OF EUSEBIUS.

The Twenty-third Dynasty consisted of three kings
of Tanis.

1. Petubastis, for 25 years.
2. Osorthon, whom the Egyptians named Her-
   cules : for 9 years.
3. Psammus, for 10 years.

Total, 44 years.

[1] For a demotic romance of the time of Petubastis in
one of the Rainer Papyri, see Krall in *Vienna Oriental
Journal*, xvii. (1903), 1 : it is also found in papyri of
Paris and Strassburg. Parallels may be drawn between
this romance and Manetho ; *cf.* Spiegelberg, *Der Sagenkreis
des Königs Petubastis* (Leipzig, 1910), pp. 8 f.

Fr. 64.   *Syncellus*, p. 138.   ΚΑΤΑ ΑΦΡΙΚΑΝΟΝ.

Τετάρτη καὶ εἰκοστὴ δυναστεία.

Βόχχωρις Σαΐτης, ἔτη ϛʹ, ἐφ᾽ οὗ ἀρνίον ἐφθέγξατο . . . ἔτη πϙʹ.

Fr. 65 (a).   *Syncellus*, p. 140.   ΚΑΤΑ ΕΥΣΕΒΙΟΝ.

Εἰκοστὴ τετάρτη δυναστεία.

Βόχχωρις Σαΐτης, ἔτη μδʹ, ἐφ᾽ οὗ ἀρνίον
ἐφθέγξατο. Ὁμοῦ, ἔτη μδʹ.

---

[1] Dynasty XXIV., c. 720–c. 715 B.C. Before Bocchoris,
his father Tefnachte of Saïs (Tnephachthus in Diodorus
Siculus, i. 45, 2) became the most powerful among the
chiefs of the Delta (c. 730–720 B.C.).

For King Bocchoris see Alexandre Moret, *De Bocchori
Rege*, 1903. *Cf.* Diodorus Siculus, i. 65, 79, 1 (law of
contract : Bocchoris legislated for commerce), and 94, 5.
See Breasted, *Anc. Rec.* iv. § 884 : the only extant monuments of King Bocchoris are a few Serapeum *stelae* and a
wall inscription, which record the burial of an Apis in the
sixth year of his reign.

[2] See especially the demotic story (8 B.C.) of the pro-
phetic lamb, quoted by Krall in *Festgaben für Büdinger*,
pp. 3-11 (Innsbruck, 1898) : the lamb prophesied the conquest and enslavement of Egypt by Assyria, and the
removal of her gods to Nineveh. *Cf.* Aelian, *De Nat.
Anim.* xii. 3, and Manetho, Fr. 54, §§ 232 ff. A reference to
Manetho's description of the oracular lamb is preserved in
Pseudo-Plutarch, *De proverbiis Alexandrinorum* (Crusius,
1887), No. 21, τὸ ἀρνίον σοι λελάληκεν. Αἰγύπτιοι τοῦτο
ἀνέγραψαν ὡς ἀνθρωπείᾳ φωνῇ λαλῆσαν (or, as in Suidas, ἐν
Αἰγύπτῳ, ὥς φασιν, ἀνθρωπείᾳ φωνῇ ἐλάλησεν). εὑρέθη δὲ ἔχον

DYNASTY XXIV.

Fr. 64 (*from Syncellus*). ACCORDING TO AFRICANUS.

The Twenty-fourth Dynasty.[1]
Bochchôris of Saïs, for 6 years : in his reign a
lamb [2] spoke [3] . . . 990 years.

Fr. 65 (a) (*from Syncellus*). ACCORDING TO
EUSEBIUS.

The Twenty-fourth Dynasty.

Bochchôris of Saïs, for 44 years : in his reign a
lamb spoke. Total, 44 years.[4]

βασίλειον δράκοντα ἐπὶ τῆς κεφαλῆς αὐτοῦ πτερωτόν, (Suidas
adds, ἔχοντα μῆκος πήχεων δ′), καὶ τῶν βασιλέων τινὶ λελάληκε
τὰ μέλλοντα. ("The lamb has spoken to you. Egyptians
have recorded a lamb speaking with a human voice
[or, in Egypt, they say, a lamb spoke with a human
voice]. It was found to have upon its head a royal
winged serpent [4 cubits in length] ; and it foretold the
future to one of the kings.") See Meyer, *Ein neues
Bruchstück Manethos über das Lamm des Bokchoris* in
Zeitschr. für Ägypt. Sprache, xlvi. (1910), pp. 135 f. : he
points out the Egyptian character of the description—the
royal *uraeus*, four cubits long, with ostrich feathers on both
sides. *Cf.* Weill, *La fin du moyen empire égyptien*, pp.
116, 622.

[3] Here some essential words have been omitted from the
text.

[4] Contrast the " 6 years " assigned to Bocchoris by
Africanus (Fr. 64) : it is suspicious that Eusebius should
give 44 years for each of Dynasties XXIII., XXIV., and
XXV.

(b) Eusebius, *Chronica* I. (Armenian Version),
p. 104.

Vicesima quarta dynastia.
Bocchoris Saïtes, annis XLIV, sub quo agnus
locutus est.

Fr. 66. *Syncellus*, p. 138. *ΚΑΤΑ ΑΦΡΙΚΑΝΟΝ*.

Πέμπτη καὶ εἰκοστὴ δυναστεία Αἰθιόπων βασιλέων τριῶν.

α΄ Σαβάκων, ὃς αἰχμάλωτον Βόχχωριν ἑλὼν
ἔκαυσε ζῶντα, καὶ ἐβασίλευσεν ἔτη η΄.
β΄ Σεβιχὼς υἱός, ἔτη ιδ΄.
γ΄ Τάρκος, ἔτη ιη΄.
'Ομοῦ, ἔτη μ΄.

Fr. 67 (a). *Syncellus*, p. 140. *ΚΑΤΑ ΕΥΣΕΒΙΟΝ*.

Εἰκοστὴ πέμπτη δυναστεία Αἰθιόπων βασιλέων
τριῶν.

α΄ Σαβάκων, ὃς αἰχμάλωτον Βόχχωριν ἑλὼν
ἔκαυσε ζῶντα, καὶ ἐβασίλευσεν ἔτη ιβ΄.
β΄ Σεβιχὼς υἱός, ἔτη ιβ΄.
γ΄ Ταρακός, ἔτη κ΄.
'Ομοῦ, ἔτη μδ΄.

---

[1] Dynasty XXV. (Ethiopian), c. 715-663 B.C. :   the
three kings are Shabaka, Shabataka, and Taharka.
[2] *Cf.* Herodotus, ii. 137 (Sabacôs).

Shabaka had a great reputation for mildness and kind
rule: Petrie (*Religious Life*, 1924, pp. 193 f.) explains that

(b) Armenian Version of Eusebius.

The Twenty-fourth Dynasty.
Bocchoris of Saïs, for 44 years : in his reign a lamb spoke.

Dynasty XXV.

Fr. 66 *(from Syncellus)*. According to Africanus.

The Twenty-fifth Dynasty [1] consisted of three Ethiopian kings.
1. Sabacôn,[2] who, taking Bochchôris captive, burned him alive, and reigned for 8 years.
2. Sebichôs, his son, for 14 years.
3. Tarcus, for 18 years.

Total, 40 years.

Fr. 67 (a) *(from Syncellus)*. According to Eusebius.

The Twenty-fifth Dynasty consisted of three Ethiopian kings.
1. Sabacôn, who, taking Bochchôris captive, burned him alive, and reigned for 12 years.
2. Sebichôs. his son, for 12 years.
3. Taracus, for 20 years.

Total, 44 years.

Bochchoris was treated like a mock king in the ancient festival, the burning ceremonially destroying his kingly character. See Wainwright, *Sky-Religion*, pp. 38 ff.

[2] Taharka : in *O.T. 2 Kings* xix. 9, Tirhakah, King of Ethiopia. See Peet, *Egypt and the Old Testament*, 1922, pp. 175 ff.

(b) Eusebius, *Chronica* I. (Armenian Version),
p. 104.

Vicesima quinta dynastia Aethiopum regum III.

Sabacon, qui captum Bocchorim vivum combussit,
regnavitque annis XII.
Sebichos eius filius, annis XII.
Saracus,[1] annis XX.

Summa annorum XLIV.

Fr. 68.   *Syncellus*, p. 141.   *ΚΑΤΑ ΑΦΡΙΚΑΝΟΝ.*

Ἕκτη καὶ εἰκοστὴ δυναστεία Σαϊτῶν βασιλέων
ἐννέα.

α´ Στεφινάτης, ἔτη ζ´.
β´ Νεχεψώς, ἔτη ς´.
γ´ Νεχαώ, ἔτη η´.
δ´ Ψαμμήτιχος, ἔτη νδ´.
ε´ Νεχαὼ δεύτερος, ἔτη ς´. οὗτος εἷλε τὴν
    Ἱερουσαλήμ, καὶ Ἰωάχαζ τὸν βασιλέα
    αἰχμάλωτον εἰς Αἴγυπτον ἀπήγαγε.
ς´ Ψάμμουθις ἕτερος, ἔτη ἕξ.

---

[1] Taracus, Aucher, m.: Tarakos, Karst.

---

[1] Dynasty XXVI., 663-525 B.C.
Saïs (see p. 91 n. 4), now grown in power, with foreign
aid asserts independence, and rules over Egypt.   Herodotus, ii. 151 ff., supports the version of Africanus
but differs in (5) Necôs 16 years (Ch. 159), and (7) Apries
25 years (Ch. 161) (22 years in Diod. Sic. i. 68).   Eusebius
(Fr. 69) has preserved the Ethiopian Ammeris (*i.e.*
Tanutamûn) at the beginning of Dynasty XXVI.: so in
the *Book of Sothis* (App. IV.), No. 78, Amaês, 38 years.

(b) Armenian Version of Eusebius.

The Twenty-fifth Dynasty consisted of three Ethiopian kings.

1. Sabacon, who, taking Bocchoris captive, burned him alive, and reigned for 12 years.
2. Sebichos, his son, for 12 years.
3. Saracus (Taracus), for 20 years.

Total, 44 years.

DYNASTY XXVI.

Fr. 68 (*from Syncellus*). ACCORDING TO AFRICANUS.

The Twenty-sixth Dynasty [1] consisted of nine kings of Saïs.

1. Stephinatês, for 7 years.
2. Nechepsôs, for 6 years.
3. Nechaô, for 8 years.
4. Psammêtichus,[2] for 54 years.
5. Nechaô [3] the Second, for 6 years: he took Jerusalem, and led King Iôachaz captive into Egypt.
6. Psammuthis the Second, for 6 years.

---

[2] Psammêtichus I. (Psametik) = Psammêtk, " man, or vendor, of mixed wine," *cf.* Herodotus, ii. 151 (Griffith in *Catalogue of Demotic Papyri in the Rylands Library*, iii. pp. 44, 201). See Diod. Sic. i. 66, 67.

[3] Nechaô is an old name, an Egyptian plural form, " belonging to the *kas* " or bulls (Ápis and Mnevis), *O.T. 2 Chron.* xxxvi. 2-4. Battle of Megiddo, 609 B.C.: defeat and death of King Josiah by Necho (*2 Kings* xxiii. 29, xxiv. 1, xxv. 26). Johoahaz, son of Josiah, was led captive into Egypt. For these events, see Peet, *Egypt and the Old Testament*, 1922, p. 181 ff.

ζ′ Οὔαφρις, ἔτη ιθ′, ᾧ προσέφυγον ἁλούσης
    ὑπὸ Ἀσσυρίων Ἱερουσαλὴμ οἱ τῶν Ἰουδαίων
    ὑπόλοιποι.

η′ Ἄμωσις, ἔτη μδ′.

θ′ Ψαμμεχερίτης, μῆνας ϛ′.

Ὁμοῦ, ἔτη ρν′ καὶ μῆνας ϛ′.

Fr. 69 (a).   *Syncellus*, p. 143.   ΚΑΤΑ ΕΥΣΕΒΙΟΝ.

Ἕκτη καὶ εἰκοστὴ δυναστεία Σαϊτῶν βασιλέων θ′.

α′ Ἀμμέρις Αἰθίοψ, ἔτη ιβ′.

β′ Στεφινάθις, ἔτη ζ′.

γ′ Νεχεψώς, ἔτη ϛ′.

δ′ Νεχαώ, ἔτη η′.

ε′ Ψαμμήτιχος, ἔτη με′.[1]

ϛ′ Νεχαὼ δεύτερος, ἔτη ϛ′. οὗτος εἷλε τὴν
    Ἱερουσαλήμ, καὶ Ἰωάχαζ τὸν βασιλέα
    αἰχμάλωτον εἰς Αἴγυπτον ἀπήγαγε.

ζ′ Ψάμμουθις ἕτερος, ὁ καὶ Ψαμμήτιχος, ἔτη
    ιζ′.

[1] μδ′ Müller.

___

[1] Uaphris or Apries, in Egyptian Waḥibprē', the Hophra
of the *O.T.* Capture of Jerusalem by Nebuchadnezzar,
king of Babylon, 587 B.C. See Peet, *op. cit.* pp. 185 ff.

7. Uaphris,[1] for 19 years : the remnant of the
   Jews fled to him, when Jerusalem was
   captured by the Assyrians.
8. Amôsis,[2] for 44 years.
9. Psammecheritês,[3] for 6 months.

Total, 150 years 6 months.

Fr. 69 (a) (*from Syncellus*). ACCORDING TO
EUSEBIUS.

The Twenty-sixth Dynasty consisted of nine kings
of Saïs.

1. Ammeris the Ethiopian, for 12 years.
2. Stephinathis, for 7 years.
3. Nechepsôs, for 6 years.
4. Nechaô, for 8 years.
5. Psammêtichus, for 45 [44] years.
6. Nechaô the Second, for 6 years : he took
   Jerusalem, and led King Iôachaz captive
   into Egypt.
7. Psammuthis the Second, also called Psammêtichus, for 17 years.

---

[2] Amôsis should be Amasis (Ia'hmase), the general of
Uaphris or Apries : Amasis was first made co-regent with
Apries (569 B.C.), then two years later, after a battle, he
became sole monarch.

On the character of Amasis, " the darling of the people
and of popular legend," see the demotic papyrus translated
by Spiegelberg, *The Credibility of Herodotus' Account of
Egypt* (trans. Blackman), pp. 29 f.

[3] Psammêtichus III., defeated by Cambysês the Persian,
525 B.C. The three Psametiks are differentiated as
Psammêtichus, Psammuthis, and Psammecheritês (*cf.*
Fr. 20, n. 1).

η′ Οὔαφρις, ἔτη κε′, ᾧ προσέφυγον ἁλούσης
    ὑπὸ Ἀσσυρίων τῆς Ἱερουσαλὴμ οἱ τῶν
    Ἰουδαίων ὑπόλοιποι.
θ′ Ἄμωσις, ἔτη μβ′.

Ὁμοῦ, ἔτη ρξγ′.

(b) Eusebius, *Chronica* I. (Armenian Version),
        p. 104.

Vicesima sexta dynastia Saïtarum regum IX.

Ameres Aethiops, annis XVIII.
Stephinathes, annis VII.
Nechepsos, annis VI.
Nechao, annis VIII.
Psametichus, annis XLIV.
Nechao alter, annis VI.   Ab hoc Hierosolyma
    capta sunt, Iochasusque rex in Aegyptum
    captivus abductus.
Psamuthes alter, qui et Psammetichus, annis
    XVII.
Uaphres, annis XXV, ad quem reliquiae Iudae-
    orum, Hierosolymis in Assyriorum potestatem
    redactis, confugerunt.
Amosis, annis XLII.

Summa annorum CLXVII.

8. Uaphris, for 25 years : the remnant of the
   Jews fled to him, when Jerusalem was
   captured by the Assyrians.
9. Amôsis, for 42 years.

Total, 163 years.[1]

(b) ARMENIAN VERSION OF EUSEBIUS.

The Twenty-sixth Dynasty consisted of nine kings
of Saïs.

1. Ameres the Ethiopian, for 18 years.
2. Stephinathes, for 7 years.
3. Nechepsos, for 6 years.
4. Nechao, for 8 years.
5. Psametichus, for 44 years.
6. Nechao the Second, for 6 years : he took
   Jerusalem, and led King Ioachaz captive
   into Egypt.
7. Psamuthes the Second, also called Psammetichus, for 17 years.
8. Uaphres, for 25 years : the remnant of the
   Jews took refuge with him, when Jerusalem
   was subjugated by the Assyrians.
9. Amosis, for 42 years.

Total, 167 years.

---

[1] If 44 years are assigned to (5) Psammêtichus, the actual
total is 167, as in the Armenian Version.

Fr. 70. *Syncellus*, p. 141.   *ΚΑΤΑ ΑΦΡΙΚΑΝΟΝ.*

'Εβδόμη καὶ εἰκοστὴ δυναστεία Περσῶν βασιλέων
η'.

α' Καμβύσης ἔτει ε' τῆς ἑαυτοῦ βασιλείας
     Περσῶν ἐβασίλευσεν Αἰγύπτου ἔτη ϛ'.

β' Δαρεῖος 'Υστάσπου, ἔτη λϛ'.

γ' Ξέρξης ὁ μέγας, ἔτη κα'.

δ' 'Αρτάβανος, μῆνας ζ'.

ε' 'Αρταξέρξης, ἔτη μα'.

ϛ' Ξέρξης, μῆνας δύο.

ζ' Σογδιανός, μῆνας ζ'.

η' Δαρεῖος Ξέρξου, ἔτη ιθ'.

'Ομοῦ, ἔτη ρκδ', μῆνες δ'.

---

[1] Persian Domination, 525-332 B.C.

Dynasty XXVII., 525-404 B.C. After conquering
Egypt, Cambysês reigned three years, 525/4-523/2 B.C.
See *Cambridge Ancient History*, vi. pp. 137 ff.

An interesting papyrus fragment (P. Baden 4 No. 59:
v. / A.D.—see the facsimile in Plate III) contains this
Dynasty in a form which differs in some respects from
the versions given by Africanus and Eusebius. Like
Eusebius the papyrus inserts the Magi, and calls Artaxerxês
" the Long-handed " and his successor Xerxês " the
Second " : as in Africanus, Darius is " son of Hysta[spês] "
and Xerxês is " the Great ". To Cambysês the papyrus

DYNASTY XXVII.

Fr. 70 (*from Syncellus*).   ACCORDING TO AFRICANUS.

The Twenty-seventh Dynasty [1] consisted of eight Persian kings.

1. Cambysês in the fifth year of his kingship over the Persians became king of Egypt, and ruled for 6 years.
2. Darius, son of Hystaspês, for 36 years.
3. Xerxês the Great, for 21 years.
4. Artabanus,[2] for 7 months.
5. Artaxerxês,[3] for 41 years.
6. Xerxês,[4] for 2 months.
7. Sogdianus, for 7 months.
8. Darius, son of Xerxês, for 19 years.

Total, 124 years 4 months.

---

gives 6½ years : to the Magi, 7½ months. The conquest of Egypt is assigned to the fourth year of Cambysês' reign, and it was in that year that the campaign began. Artaxerxês is described as " the son " (*i.e.* of Xerxês); while Darius II. is correctly named " the Illegitimate ". See Bilabel's note on the papyrus (*l.c.*).

[2] Artabanus, vizier, and murderer of Xerxês I., 465 B.C.

[3] Artaxerxês I., " Long-hand " (" whether from a physical peculiarity or political capacity is uncertain," *C.A.H.* vi. p. 2), 465-424 B.C.

[4] Xerxês II. was murdered by his half-brother Sogdianus, who was in turn defeated and put to death in 423 B.C. by another half-brother Ochus (Darius II., nicknamed Nothos, " the Illegitimate,"), not " son of Xerxês ". Darius II. died in 404 B.C.

Fr. 71 (a).   *Syncellus*, p. 143.   *ΚΑΤΑ ΕΥΣΕΒΙΟΝ*.

Εἰκοστὴ ἑβδόμη δυναστεία Περσῶν βασιλέων η'.

α' Καμβύσης ἔτει πέμπτῳ τῆς αὐτοῦ βα-
    σιλείας ἐβασίλευσεν Αἰγύπτου ἔτη γ'.

β' Μάγοι, μῆνας ζ'.

γ' Δαρεῖος, ἔτη λς'.

δ' Ξέρξης ὁ Δαρείου, ἔτη κα'.

ε' Ἀρταξέρξης ὁ μακρόχειρ, ἔτη μ'.

ϛ' Ξέρξης ὁ δεύτερος, μῆνας β'.

ζ' Σογδιανός, μῆνας ζ'.

η' Δαρεῖος ὁ Ξέρξου, ἔτη ιθ'.

Ὁμοῦ, ἔτη ρκ' καὶ μῆνες δ'.

(b)   Eusebius,   *Chronica* I. (Armenian Version),
                p. 105.

Vicesima septima dynastia Persarum regum VIII.

Cambyses, qui regni sui quinto[1] anno Aegyptiorum
    potitus est, annis III.

Magi, mensibus septem.

Darius, annis XXXVI.

Xerxes Darii, annis XXI.

Artaxerxes, annis XL.

Xerxes alter, mensibus II.

Sogdianus, mensibus VII.

Darius Xerxis, annis XIX.

Summa annorum CXX, mensiumque IV.

[1] Aucher: XV. MSS.

Fr. 71 (a) (*from Syncellus*). ACCORDING TO
EUSEBIUS.

The Twenty-seventh Dynasty consisted of eight
Persian kings.

1. Cambysês in the fifth year of his kingship
    became king of Egypt, and ruled for 3 years.
2. Magi, for 7 months.
3. Darius, for 36 years.
4. Xerxês, son of Darius, for 21 years.
5. Artaxerxês of the long hand, for 40 years.
6. Xerxês the Second, for 2 months.
7. Sogdianus, for 7 months.
8. Darius, son of Xerxês, for 19 years.

Total, 120 years 4 months.

(b) ARMENIAN VERSION OF EUSEBIUS.

The Twenty-seventh Dynasty consisted of eight
Persian kings.

1. Cambyses in the fifth [1] year of his kingship
    became king of Egypt, and ruled for 3
    years.
2. Magi, for 7 months.
3. Darius, for 36 years.
4. Xerxes, son of Darius, for 21 years.
5. Artaxerxês, for 40 years.
6. Xerxês the Second, for 2 months.
7. Sogdianus, for 7 months.
8. Darius, son of Xerxes, for 19 years.

Total, 120 years 4 months.

[1] The Armenian text has " 15th ".

177

Fr. 72 (a). *Syncellus*, p. 142. *ΚΑΤΑ ΑΦΡΙΚΑΝΟΝ.*

Εἰκοστὴ ὀγδόη δυναστεία. Ἀμύρτεος Σαΐτης, ἔτη ϛ'.

(b) *Syncellus*, p. 144. *ΚΑΤΑ ΕΥΣΕΒΙΟΝ.*

Εἰκοστὴ ὀγδόη δυναστεία. Ἀμυρταῖος Σαΐτης, ἔτη ϛ'.

(c) EUSEBIUS, *Chronica* I. (Armenian Version), p. 105.

Vicesima octava dynastia. **Amyrtes Saïtes,** annis [1] VI.

Fr. 73 (a). *Syncellus*, p. 142. *ΚΑΤΑ ΑΦΡΙΚΑΝΟΝ.*

Ἐνάτη καὶ εἰκοστὴ δυναστεία. Μενδήσιοι βασιλεῖς δ'.

α' Νεφερίτης, ἔτη ϛ'.
β' Ἄχωρις, ἔτη ιγ'.
γ' Ψάμμουθις, ἔτος α'.
δ' Νεφερίτης, μῆνας δ'.

Ὁμοῦ, ἔτη κ', μῆνες δ'.

[1] Aucher, m.: mensibus MSS., according to Müller.

---

[1] Dynasty XXVIII.–XXX., Egyptian kings: 404-341 B.C.—a brief period of independence.
Dynasty XXVIII., Amyrtaeus of Saïs, 404-399 B.C.: no Egyptian king of this name is known on the monuments. See Werner Schur in *Klio*, **xx.** 1926, pp. 273 ff.

Dynasty XXVIII.

Fr. 72 (a) (*from Syncellus*). According to Africanus.

The Twenty-eighth Dynasty.[1] Amyrteos of Saïs, for 6 years.

(b) According to Eusebius.

The Twenty-eighth Dynasty. Amyrtaeus of Saïs, for 6 years.

(c) Armenian Version of Eusebius.

The Twenty-eighth Dynasty. Amyrtes of Saïs, for 6 years.[2]

Dynasty XXIX.

Fr. 73 (a) (*from Syncellus*). According to Africanus.

The Twenty-ninth Dynasty:[3] four kings of Mendês.

1. Nepheritês, for 6 years.
2. Achôris, for 13 years.
3. Psammuthis, for 1 year.
4. Nepheritês [II.], for 4 months.

Total, 20 years 4 months.

---

[2] 6 years (Aucher, Karst): 6 months (Müller). The Armenian words for " month " and " year " are so similar that corruption is likely (Margoliouth).

[3] Dynasty XXIX., resident at Mendês in E. Delta (Baedeker [8], p. 183), 398-381 B.C. On the sequence of these rulers see H. R. Hall in *C.A.H.* vi. p. 145 and n.

(b) *Syncellus*, p. 144.   *ΚΑΤΑ ΕΥΣΕΒΙΟΝ.*

Εἰκοστὴ ἐνάτη δυναστεία.   Μενδήσιοι βασιλεῖς δ'.

α' Νεφερίτης, ἔτη ς'.
β' Ἄχωρις, ἔτη ιγ'.
γ' Ψάμμουθις, ἔτος α'.
δ' Νεφερίτης, μῆνας δ'.
ε' Μοῦθις, ἔτος α'.

'Ομοῦ, ἔτη κα' καὶ μῆνες δ'.

(c) Eᴜsᴇʙɪᴜs, *Chronica* I. (Armenian Version),
p. 106.

Vicesima nona dynastia Mendesiorum regum
quattuor.

Nepherites, annis VI.
Achoris, annis XIII.
Psamuthes, anno I.
Muthes, anno I.
Nepherites mensibus IV.

Summa annorum XXI, mensiumque IV.

(b) ACCORDING TO EUSEBIUS.

The Twenty-ninth Dynasty: four kings [1] of Mendês.

1. Nepheritês, for 6 years.
2. Achôris, for 13 years.
3. Psammuthis, for 1 year.
4. Nepheritês [II.], for 4 months.
5. Muthis, for 1 year.

Total, 21 years 4 months.

(c) ARMENIAN VERSION OF EUSEBIUS.

The Twenty-ninth Dynasty consisted of four kings of Mendes.

1. Nepherites, for 6 years.
2. Achoris, for 13 years.
3. Psamuthes, for 1 year.
4. Muthes, for 1 year.
5. Nepherites [II.], for 4 months.

Total, 21 years and 4 months.

---

[1] Muthis or Muthês was a usurper, hence the number of kings is given as four. He is unknown to the Monuments. Aucher suggests that the name Muthis may be merely a repetition, curtailed, of the name Psammuthis.

Fr. 74 (a).　*Syncellus*, p. 144.　*ΚΑΤΑ ΑΦΡΙΚΑΝΟΝ.*

Τριακοστὴ δυναστεία Σεβεννυτῶν βασιλέων τριῶν.

　α΄ Νεκτανέβης, ἔτη ιη΄.
　β΄ Τεώς, ἔτη β΄.
　γ΄ Νεκτανεβός, ἔτη ιη΄.

'Ομοῦ, ἔτη λη΄.

(b) *Syncellus*, p. 145　*ΚΑΤΑ ΕΥΣΕΒΙΟΝ.*

Τριακοστὴ δυναστεία Σεβεννυτῶν βασιλέων τριῶν.

　α΄ Νεκτανέβης, ἔτη ι΄.
　β΄ Τεώς, ἔτη β΄.
　γ΄ Νεκτανεβός, ἔτη η΄.

'Ομοῦ, ἔτη κ΄.

---

[1] Dynasty XXX. resident at Sebennytus (see Intro.
p. xiii), 380-343 B.C.: Nectanebês I. (Nekhtenêbef), 380-363,
Teôs or Tachôs (Zedhôr), 362-361, Nectanebus II. (Nekht-
horehbe), 360-343. See E. Meyer, *Zur Geschichte der 30.
Dynastie* in *Zeitschrift für Ägyptische Sprache*, Bd. 67,
pp. 68-70.

It is certain that Manetho knew only 30 dynasties and
ended with the conquest of Egypt by Ôchus : see Unger,

DYNASTY XXX.

Fr. 74 (a) (*from Syncellus*). ACCORDING TO AFRICANUS.

The Thirtieth Dynasty [1] consisted of three kings of Sebennytus.

1. Nectanebês, for 18 years.
2. Teôs, for 2 years.
3. Nectanebus,[2] for 18 years.

Total, 38 years.

(b) ACCORDING TO EUSEBIUS.

The Thirtieth Dynasty consisted of three kings of Sebennytus.

1. Nectanebês, for 10 years.
2. Teôs, for 2 years.
3. Nectanebus, for 8 years.

Total, 20 years.

Chronol. des Manetho, pp. 334 f. Under Olymp. 107 (*i.e.* 352-348 B.C.) Jerome (*Chronicle*, p. 203 Fotheringham, p. 121 Helm) notes: Ochus Aegyptum tenuit, Nectanebo in Aethiopiam pulso, in quo Aegyptiorum regnum destructum est. Huc usque Manethos. (" Ochus possessed Egypt, when he had driven Nectanebô into Ethiopia : thereby the kingship of the Egyptians was destroyed. So far Manetho [or, Here ends the History of Manetho] ").

[2] For the later renown of this king as magician in popular legend, see the *Dream of Nectonabôs*, in Wilcken, *Urkunden der Ptolemäerzeit*, i. pp. 369 ff.

(c) Eusebius, *Chronica* I. (Armenian Version),
p. 106.

Tricesima dynastia Sebennytarum regum III.

Nectanebis, annis X.
Teos, annis II.
Nectanebus, annis VIII.
Summa annorum XX.

Fr. 75 (a). *Syncellus*, p. 145. *KATA AΦPIKANON*.

Πρώτη καὶ τριακοστὴ δυναστεία Περσῶν βασιλέων τριῶν.

α΄ Ὦχος[1] εἰκοστῷ ἔτει τῆς ἑαυτοῦ βασιλείας
  Περσῶν ἐβασίλευσεν Αἰγύπτου ἔτη β΄.[2]
β΄ Ἀρσῆς, ἔτη γ΄.
γ΄ Δαρεῖος, ἔτη δ΄.
Ὁμοῦ, ἔτη τρίτου τόμου ͵αν΄.[3]
Μέχρι τῶνδε Μανεθῶ.

[1] Syncellus (p. 486) thus describes the scope of Manetho's
History, wrongly putting λα΄ for λ΄ : ἕως Ὦχου καὶ Νεκτανεβὼ
ὁ Μανεθῶ τὰς λα΄ δυναστείας Αἰγύπτου περιέγραψε.
[2] This β΄ (instead of ϛ΄) is probably due to confusion
with the β΄ at the beginning of the next line (Aucher).
[3] ων΄ Boeckh, Unger.

---

[1] Dynasty XXXI. is not due to Manetho, but was added
later to preserve the continuity,—perhaps with the use of
material furnished by Manetho himself. No total is given
by Africanus and Eusebius,—a further proof that the whole
Dynasty is additional. In another passage (p. 486)
Syncellus states : " Manetho wrote an account of the 31

(c) Armenian Version of Eusebius.

The Thirtieth Dynasty consisted of 3 kings of Sebennytus.

1. Nectanebis, for 10 years.
2. Teos, for 2 years.
3. Nectanebus, for 8 years.

Total, 20 years.

Dynasty XXXI.

Fr. 75 (a) (*from Syncellus*). According to Africanus.

The Thirty-first Dynasty [1] consisted of three Persian kings.

1. Ôchus in the twentieth year [2] of his kingship over the Persians became king of Egypt, and ruled for 2 years.
2. Arsês, for 3 years.
3. Darius, for 4 years.

Total of years in Book III., 1050 years [3] [850].

Here ends the *History* of Manetho.

(an error for 30) Dynasties of Egypt down to the time of Ôchus and Nectanebô ": although mistaken about the number of the Dynasties, Syncellus is in the main correct.

[2] The 20th year of the kingship of Ôchus was 343 B.C. : the phrase is parallel to that used in Fr. 70, 1, and appears therefore to be Manetho's expression.

[3] The totals given by Africanus in Book III. are 135, 130, 120, 89, 6, 40, 150+, 124+, 6, 20+, 38, i.e. 858+ years. To reduce to 850, assign 116 years to Dynasty XXII. (as the items add), and 120 to Dynasty XXVII. (Meyer).

(b) *Syncellus*, p. 146.   *ΚΑΤΑ ΕΥΣΕΒΙΟΝ.*

Τριακοστὴ πρώτη δυναστεία Περσῶν βασιλέων
τριῶν.

α′ *Ὦχος* εἰκοστῷ ἔτει τῆς αὐτοῦ Περσῶν βασιλείας κρατεῖ τῆς Αἰγύπτου ἔτη ϛ′.
β′ *Μεθ*′ ὃν Ἀρσῆς Ὤχου, ἔτη δ′.
γ′ *Μεθ*′ ὃν Δαρεῖος, ἔτη ἕξ· ὃν Ἀλέξανδρος ὁ
Μακεδὼν καθεῖλε.

Ταῦτα τοῦ τρίτου ⟨τόμου⟩ Μανεθῶ.
Μέχρι τῶνδε Μανεθῶ.

(c) Eusebius, *Chronica* I. (Armenian Version),
p. 107.

Tricesima prima dynastia Persarum.

Ochus vicesimo iam anno Persis imperitans
    Aegyptum occupavit tenuitque annis VI.
Postea Arses Ochi, annis IV.
Tum Darius, annis VI, quem Macedo Alexander
    interfecit.   Atque haec e Manethonis tertio [1]
libro

    [1] Aucher, m. : secundo MSS., according to Müller.

---

    [1] Third Book (Aucher, Karst) : Second Book (Müller).
The Armenian words for " second " and " third " have
similar forms ; hence the corruption (Margoliouth).

(b) ACCORDING TO EUSEBIUS.

The Thirty-first Dynasty consisted of three Persian kings.

1. Ôchus in the twentieth year of his kingship over the Persians conquered Egypt, and ruled for 6 years.
2. His successor was Arsês, son of Ôchus, who reigned for 4 years.
3. Next, Darius reigned for 6 years : he was put to death by Alexander of Macedon.

These are the contents of the Third Book of Manetho.
Here ends the *History* of Manetho.

(c) ARMENIAN VERSION OF EUSEBIUS.

The Thirty-first Dynasty consisted of Persian kings.

1. Ochus in the twentieth year of his kingship over the Persians seized Egypt and held it for 6 years.
2. His successor was Arsês, son of Ochus, who reigned for 4 years.
3. Next, Darius reigned for 6 years : he was put to death by Alexander of Macedon.

These are the contents of the Third Book [1] of Manetho.

Η ΙΕΡΑ ΒΙΒΛΟΣ

Fr 76. EUSEBIUS, *Praeparatio Evangelica*,
II Prooem., p. 44 C (Gifford).

Πᾶσαν μὲν οὖν τὴν Αἰγυπτιακὴν ἱστορίαν εἰς
πλάτος τῇ Ἑλλήνων μετείληφε φωνῇ ἰδίως τε τὰ
περὶ τῆς κατ᾽ αὐτοὺς θεολογίας Μανεθὼς ὁ
Αἰγύπτιος, ἔν τε ᾗ ἔγραψεν Ἱερᾷ βίβλῳ καὶ
ἐν ἑτέροις αὐτοῦ συγγράμμασι.

Cf. Theodoretus, *Curatio*, II, p. 61 (Räder):

Μανεθὼς δὲ τὰ περὶ Ἴσιδος καὶ Ὀσίριδος καὶ
Ἄπιδος καὶ Σαράπιδος καὶ τῶν ἄλλων θεῶν τῶν
Αἰγυπτίων ἐμυθολόγησε.

Fr. 77. PLUTARCH, *De Is. et Osir.*, 9.

Ἔτι δὲ τῶν πολλῶν νομιζόντων ἴδιον παρ᾽
Αἰγυπτίοις ὄνομα τοῦ Διὸς εἶναι τὸν Ἀμοῦν (ὃ
παράγοντες ἡμεῖς Ἄμμωνα λέγομεν), Μανεθὼς
μὲν ὁ Σεβεννύτης τὸ κεκρυμμένον οἴεται καὶ τὴν
κρύψιν ὑπὸ ταύτης δηλοῦσθαι τῆς φωνῆς . . .

Fr. 78. PLUTARCH, *De Is. et Osir.*, 49.

Βέβωνα δὲ τινὲς μὲν ἕνα τῶν τοῦ Τυφῶνος
ἑταίρων γεγονέναι λέγουσιν, Μανεθὼς δ᾽ αὐτὸν

---

[1] Manetho's interpretation is from *imn*, "hidden,
secret": see Sethe, *Abhandl. Berl. Akad.*, 1929, p. 78,
§ 153. Herodotus, ii. 42, 3, tells a story which is probably
related to this meaning of Amûn.

THE SACRED BOOK.

Fr. 76 (*from* EUSEBIUS).

Now the whole history of Egypt and especially the details of Egyptian religion are expounded at length in Greek by Manetho the Egyptian, both in his *Sacred Book* and in other writings of his.

(*From* THEODORETUS.)

Manetho rehearsed the stories of Isis, Osiris, Apis, Serapis, and the other gods of Egypt.

Fr. 77 (*from* PLUTARCH, *Is. and Osir.*, ch. 9).

Further, the general belief is that the name Amûn,[1] which we transform into Ammôn, is an Egyptian proper noun, the title of Zeus[2]; but Manetho of Sebennytus is of opinion that this name has a meaning—" that which is concealed " and " concealment."

Fr. 78 (*from* PLUTARCH, *Is. and Osir.*, ch. 49).

Some say that Bebôn[3] was one of the comrades of Typhôn; but Manetho states that Typhôn himself

---

[2] The title Zeus Ammôn was already known to Pindar in the first half of the fifth century B.C. (*Pythians*, iv. 16, Fr. 36; see Pausanias, ix. 16, 1).

[3] The name " Bebôn," given to Typhôn, does not mean " prevention," but is the Egyptian *b'by*, an epithet of Sêth. In Greek, besides the form Βέβων, Βάβυς was used (Hellanicus in Athenaeus, xv. 680a). Typhôn, an unpopular deity, came into favour in Dynasty XIX., two kings of which were Sethôs I. and II.

τὸν Τυφῶνα καὶ Βέβωνα καλεῖσθαι· σημαίνει δὲ
τοὔνομα κάθεξιν ἢ κώλυσιν, ὡς τοῖς πράγμασιν
ὁδῷ βαδίζουσι καὶ πρὸς ὃ χρὴ φερομένοις ἐν-
ισταμένης τῆς τοῦ Τυφῶνος δυνάμεως.

Fr. 79.   PLUTARCH, De Is. et Osir., 62.

Ἔοικε δὲ τούτοις καὶ τὰ Αἰγύπτια. τὴν μὲν
γὰρ Ἶσιν πολλάκις τῷ τῆς Ἀθηνᾶς ὀνόματι καλοῦσι
φράζοντι τοιοῦτον λόγον " ἦλθον ἀπ᾽ ἐμαυτῆς,"
ὅπερ ἐστὶν αὐτοκινήτου φορᾶς δηλωτικόν· ὁ δὲ
Τυφών, ὥσπερ εἴρηται, Σὴθ καὶ Βέβων καὶ Σμὺ
ὀνομάζεται, βίαιόν τινα καὶ κωλυτικὴν ἐπίσχεσιν
⟨ἢ τιν᾽⟩[1] ὑπεναντίωσιν ἢ ἀναστροφὴν ἐμφαίνειν
βουλομένων τῶν ὀνομάτων. ἔτι τὴν σιδηρῖτιν
λίθον, ὀστέον Ὥρου, Τυφῶνος δὲ τὸν σίδηρον,
ὡς ἱστορεῖ Μανεθώς, καλοῦσιν. ὥσπερ γὰρ ὁ
σίδηρος πολλάκις μὲν ἑλκομένῳ καὶ ἑπομένῳ πρὸς
τὴν λίθον ὅμοιός ἐστι, πολλάκις δ᾽ ἀποστρέφεται
καὶ ἀποκρούεται πρὸς τοὐναντίον, οὕτως ἡ σωτήριος

[1] ⟨ἢ τιν᾽⟩ Pohlenz.

---

[1] Explanation is difficult. The name of the goddess
Neith with whom Athena is often identified has been
interpreted " that which is, ᴐr exists " (Mallet, Le Culte
de Neit à Saïs, p. 189). As a genuine etymology of the
name, this is impossible ; but it may be that in the late
period a connexion was imagined between Nt, " Neith,"
and nt(t), " that which is " (B.G.). It is suggestive that
the Coptic word meaning " come " is na (A. Rusch,
Pauly-Wissowa-Kroll, R.-E. xvi. 2 (1935), col. 2190).

was also called Bebôn. The name means " check-
ing " or " prevention," and implies that, when
actions are proceeding in due course and tending to
their required end, the power of Typhôn obstructs
them.

Fr. 79 (*from* PLUTARCH, *Is. and Osir.*, ch. 62).

The usage of the Egyptians is also similar. They
often call Isis by the name of Athena, which expresses
some such meaning as " I came from Myself," [1] and is
indicative of self-originated movement. But Typhôn,
as I have already mentioned, is called Sêth, Bebôn,
and Smy,[2] these names implying a certain violent
and obstructive force, or a certain opposition or overthrow. Further, as Manetho records, they call the
loadstone " the bone of Hôrus," but iron " the bone
of Typhôn." [3] Just as iron is often like to be attracted and led after the stone, but often again turns
away and is repelled in the opposite direction, so the

---

[2] Smy is not a name of Typhôn, but may mean " con-
federate " in Egyptian (from *sm*), to unite). In religious
texts the phrase Sêth and his *sm*)*yt*, i.e. " Sêth and his con-
federates," often occurs. See Kees on Sêth in Pauly-
Wissowa-Kroll, *R.-E.* ii. A. 2 (1923), cols. 1896 ff.

[3] Interesting confirmation of the correctness of Plutarch
and Manetho is given by G. A. Wainwright in his article
" Iron in Egypt " (*J. Eg. Arch.* xviii. 1932, p. 14). He
compares *Pyramid Texts*, § 14, " the *bi*) which came forth
out of Setesh," and refers to Petrie's discovery at Ḳâw (an
important centre of Sêth worship) of great quantities of
gigantic bones, collected in piles : they were chiefly of
hippopotami,—mineralized, heavy, black bones, of metallic
lustre and appearance. It is clear that they were considered sacred to Sêth, as they were wrapped in linen and
were found here and there in tombs at Ḳâw.

καὶ ἀγαθὴ καὶ λόγον ἔχουσα τοῦ κόσμου κίνησις
ἐπιστρέφεταί τε καὶ προσάγεται καὶ μαλακωτέραν
ποιεῖ, πείθουσα τὴν σκληρὰν ἐκείνην καὶ τυφώνειον,
εἶτ' αὖθις ἀνασχεθεῖσα εἰς ἑαυτὴν ἀνέστρεψε καὶ
κατέδυσεν εἰς τὴν ἀπορίαν.

Fr. 80.   PLUTARCH, *De Is. et Osir.*, 28.

Πτολεμαῖος δὲ ὁ Σωτὴρ ὄναρ εἶδε τὸν ἐν Σινώπῃ
τοῦ Πλούτωνος κολοσσόν, οὐκ ἐπιστάμενος οὐδὲ
ἑωρακὼς πρότερον οἷος ⟨ἦν⟩ τὴν μορφήν, κελεύοντα
κομίσαι τὴν ταχίστην αὐτὸν εἰς Ἀλεξάνδρειαν.
ἀγνοοῦντι δ' αὐτῷ καὶ ἀποροῦντι, ποῦ καθίδρυται,

---

[1] The story of the transport of the colossus of Serapis to
Alexandria is told with variants by Tacitus, *Hist.* iv. 83,
84, Clement of Alexandria, *Protrep.* iv. p. 37, Stahlin, and
Cyrillus *in Jul.* p. 13, Spanh.: *cf.* also Plutarch, *De
sollert. anim.* 36, Eustathius on Dionys. Perieg. 254
(Müller, *Geogr. gr. min.* ii. p. 262). Both Tacitus and
Plutarch agree in assigning the introduction of the statue
to Ptolemy I. : Clement and Cyril attribute it to Ptolemy
II. See Parthey, *Über Is. und Osir.* pp. 213 ff. Tacitus
gives (from Lysimachus) the more circumstantial account,
adding the name of the King of Pontus, Scydrothemis ;
but Plutarch mentions other names (*e.g.* Manetho) which
Tacitus omits. The new cult of Serapis was intended to
unite the Greek ruling class and their Egyptian subjects.
(See Intro. p. xiv.) Georg Lippold (*Festschrift Paul Arndt*,
1925, p. 126) holds the sculptor of the statue to be the
famous Bryaxis of Athens, *c.* 350 B.C. ; and thus the image
was worshipped at Sinôpe for about 70 years before it was
taken to Alexandria. The most trustworthy copy of the
statue is that in the Museum at Alexandria : see *Athen.
Mitt.* xxxi. (1906), Plates VI, VII (A. W. Lawrence in

salutary, good, and rational movement of the world
at one time attracts, conciliates, and by persuasion
mollifies that harsh Typhonian power ; then again,
when the latter has recovered itself, it overthrows
the other and reduces it to helplessness.

Fr. 80 (*from* PLUTARCH, *Is. and Osir.*, ch. 28).

Ptolemy Sôtêr dreamed that he saw the colossal
statue [1] of Pluto at Sinôpê,[2] although he did not
know what manner of shape it had, having never
previously seen it ; and that it bade him convey it
with all possible speed to Alexandria.   The king was
at a loss and did not know where the statue stood ;
but as he was describing the vision to his friends,

J. Eg. Arch. xi. (1925), p. 182).   Only the Greek statue by
Bryaxis was brought from Sinôpe : the cult was organized
in Egypt itself, and Serapis became the paramount deity
of Alexandria with a magnificent temple in Rhakôtis.
If there were forty-two temples of Serapis in Egypt
(Aristides, viii. 56, 1, p. 96 Dind.)—this number being
one for each nome, the majority have left no trace :
Parthey (*op. cit.* pp. 216 f.) identifies eleven.

See Wilamowitz, *Hell. Dichtung*, i. p. 154, Wilcken,
Urkunden der Ptolemäerzeit, Intro. pp. 77 ff. (a full discussion
of the origin of the cult of Serapis).   *Cf.* also Rostovtzeff in
C.A.H. vii. pp. 145 f.

For the dream as a vehicle of religious propaganda, *cf.*
P. Cairo Zenon 34 (258-257 B.C. : see Deissmann, *Light
from the Ancient East*, pp. 152 ff.), and *Inscr. Gr.* xi. 4, 1299
(*c.* 200 B.C.).

[2] In the districts by the Black Sea, a great god of the
underworld was worshipped ; and this deity, as Rostovtzeff
holds, must be set in close connexion with the Alexandrine
Serapis.   See Julius Kaerst, *Geschichte des Hellenismus* [2], ii.
(1926), pp. 246 f., and *cf.* the late Roman coins of Sinôpe
with the Serapis-type (Plate IV, No. 3).

καὶ διηγουμένῳ τοῖς φίλοις τὴν ὄψιν, εὑρέθη πολυ-
πλανὴς ἄνθρωπος, ὄνομα Σωσίβιος, ἐν Σινώπῃ
φάμενος ἑωρακέναι τοιοῦτον κολοσσόν, οἷον ὁ
βασιλεὺς ἰδεῖν ἔδοξεν. ἔπεμψεν οὖν Σωτέλη καὶ
Διονύσιον, οἳ χρόνῳ πολλῷ καὶ μόλις, οὐκ ἄνευ
μέντοι θείας προνοίας, ἤγαγον ἐκκλέψαντες. ἐπεὶ
δὲ κομισθεὶς ὤφθη, συμβαλόντες οἱ περὶ Τιμόθεον
τὸν ἐξηγητὴν καὶ Μανέθωνα τὸν Σεβεννύτην Πλούτωνος ὂν ἄγαλμα, τῷ Κερβέρῳ τεκμαιρόμενοι καὶ
τῷ δράκοντι, πείθουσι τὸν Πτολεμαῖον, ὡς ἑτέρου
θεῶν οὐδενὸς ἀλλὰ Σαράπιδός ἐστιν. οὐ γὰρ ἐκεῖθεν οὕτως ὀνομαζόμενος ἧκεν, ἀλλ' εἰς Ἀλεξάνδρειαν
κομισθεὶς τὸ παρ' Αἰγυπτίοις ὄνομα τοῦ Πλούτωνος
ἐκτήσατο τὸν Σάραπιν.

Fr. 81.   Aelian, De Natura Animalium, X, 16 (Hercher).

Ἀκούω δὲ καὶ Μανέθωνα τὸν Αἰγύπτιον, σοφίας
ἐς ἄκρον ἐληλακότα ἄνδρα, εἰπεῖν ὅτι γάλακτος
ὑείου ὁ γευσάμενος ἀλφῶν ὑποπίμπλαται καὶ λέ-
πρας· μισοῦσι δὲ ἄρα οἱ Ἀσιανοὶ πάντες τάδε τὰ
πάθη. πεπιστεύκασι δὲ Αἰγύπτιοι τὴν ὗν καὶ ἡλίῳ
καὶ σελήνῃ ἐχθίστην εἶναι· ὅταν οὖν πανηγυρίζωσι
τῇ σελήνῃ, θύουσιν αὐτῇ ἅπαξ τοῦ ἔτους ὗς, ἄλλοτε
δὲ οὔτε ἐκείνῃ οὔτε ἄλλῳ τῳ τῶν θεῶν τόδε τὸ
ζῷον ἐθέλουσι θύειν.

---

[1] Timotheus (of Eleusis), the Eumolpid, is believed to
have introduced the Eleusinian Mysteries into Eleusis,
the suburb of Alexandria.

there came forward a far-travelled man, by name
Sôsibius, who declared that at Sinôpe he had seen
just such a colossus as the king had dreamt he saw.
He therefore despatched Sôtelês and Dionysius, who
after a long time and with difficulty, though not un-
aided by divine providence, stole away the statue.
When it was brought to Egypt and exhibited there,
Timotheus [1] the *exêgêtês* (expounder or interpreter),
Manetho [2] of Sebennytus, and their colleagues,
judging by the Cerberus and the serpent, came to the
conclusion that it was a statue of Pluto; and they
convinced Ptolemy that it represented no other god
than Serapis. For it had not come bearing this
name from its distant home, but after being conveyed
to Alexandria, it acquired the Egyptian name for
Pluto, namely Serapis.

Fr. 81 (*from* AELIAN).

I am told also that Manetho the Egyptian, who
attained the acme of wisdom, declared that one who
tastes sow's milk is infected with leprosy or scall.
All Asiatics, indeed, loathe these diseases. The
Egyptians hold that the sow is abhorred by both
Sun and Moon; so, when they celebrate the annual
festival in honour of the Moon, they sacrifice swine [3]
to the goddess, whereas at any other time they refuse
to sacrifice this animal to the Moon or to any other
deity.

[1] Manetho's connexion with the Serapis cult is vouched
for by a bust in the Serapeum at Carthage, *Corpus Inscr.
Lat.* viii. 1007: see Intro. p. xv.

[3] *Cf.* Herodotus, ii. 47, and see Newberry in *J. Eg.
Arch.* xiv. p. 213.

ΕΠΙΤΟΜΗ ΤΩΝ ΦΥΣΙΚΩΝ

**Fr. 82.　Diogenes Laertius, Prooem, § 10
(Hicks, L.C.L.).**

Θεοὺς δ' εἶναι ἥλιον καὶ σελήνην· τὸν μὲν Ὄσιριν,
τὴν δ' Ἶσιν καλουμένην. αἰνίττεσθαί τε αὐτοὺς διά
τε κανθάρου καὶ δράκοντος καὶ ἱέρακος καὶ ἄλλων,
ὥς φησι Μανεθὼς ἐν τῇ τῶν Φυσικῶν Ἐπιτομῇ.

**Fr. 83.　Eusebius, Praepar. Evang., III, 2,
p. 87 d (Gifford).**

Τὴν Ἶσίν φασι καὶ τὸν Ὄσιριν τὸν ἥλιον καὶ τὴν
σελήνην εἶναι, καὶ Δία μὲν τὸ διὰ πάντων χωροῦν
πνεῦμα, Ἥφαιστον δὲ τὸ πῦρ, τὴν δὲ γῆν Δήμητραν
ἐπονομάσαι· Ὠκεανόν τε τὸ ὑγρὸν ὀνομάζεσθαι παρ'
Αἰγυπτίοις καὶ τὸν παρ' αὐτοῖς ποταμὸν Νεῖλον, ᾧ
καὶ τὰς τῶν θεῶν ἀναθεῖναι γενέσεις· τὸν δὲ ἀέρα
φασὶν αὐτοὺς προσαγορεύειν Ἀθηνᾶν. τούτους δὲ
τοὺς πέντε θεούς, τὸν Ἀέρα λέγω καὶ τὸ Ὕδωρ τό
τε Πῦρ καὶ τὴν Γῆν καὶ τὸ Πνεῦμα, τὴν πᾶσαν
οἰκουμένην ἐπιπορεύεσθαι, ἄλλοτε ἄλλως εἰς μορφὰς
καὶ ἰδέας ἀνθρώπων τε καὶ παντοίων ζῴων σχημα-
τιζομένους· καὶ τούτων ὁμωνύμους παρ' αὐτοῖς
Αἰγυπτίοις γεγονέναι θνητοὺς ἀνθρώπους, Ἥλιον

---

[1] The Ancient Egyptian name Haʾpi is applied both to the
River Nile and to the god of the Nile.　Cf. Diod. Sic. i.
12. 6 (the same phrase, with πρὸς ᾧ for ᾧ, and ὑπάρξαι for
ἀναθεῖναι : τὰς γενέσεις—the same plural in Diod. Sic. i. 9, 6,

AN EPITOME OF PHYSICAL DOCTRINES.

Fr. 82 (from DIOGENES LAERTIUS).

The Egyptians hold the Sun and the Moon to be gods, the former being named Osiris, the latter Isis. They refer darkly to them under the symbols of beetle, serpent, hawk, and other creatures, as Manetho says in his *Epitome of Physical Doctrines*.

Fr. 83 (from EUSEBIUS).

The Egyptians say that Isis and Osiris are the Moon and the Sun ; that Zeus is the name which they gave to the all-pervading spirit, Hephaestus to fire, and Demeter to earth. Among the Egyptians the moist element is named Ocean and their own River Nile ; and to him they ascribed the origin of the Gods.[1] To Air, again, they give, it is said, the name of Athena. Now these five deities,—I mean Air, Water, Fire, Earth, and Spirit,—traverse the whole world, transforming themselves at different times into different shapes and semblances of men and creatures of all kinds. In Egypt itself there have also been born mortal men of the same names as these deities :

θεῶν γενέσεις ὑπάρξαι). See also Plutarch, *Is. et Osir.* 66, p. 377 C. The name Νεῖλος appears first in Hesiod, *Theogony* 338, which may be dated to the eighth century B.C.

In a *Hymn to the Nile*, engraved upon the rocks at Gebel Silsileh in Upper Egypt by command of Ramessês II., the river is described as " the living and beautiful Nile, . . . father of all the gods " (Wiedemann, *Religion of the Ancient Egyptians*, pp. 146 f.).

καὶ Κρόνον καὶ ῾Ρέαν, ἔτι δὲ Δία καὶ ῞Ηραν καὶ
῞Ηφαιστον καὶ ῾Εστίαν ἐπονομασθέντας. γράφει
δὲ καὶ τὰ περὶ τούτων πλατύτερον μὲν ὁ Μανεθώς,
ἐπιτετμημένως δὲ ὁ Διόδωρος . . .

Cf. Theodoretus, *Curatio*, III, p. 80 (Räder).

ΠΕΡΙ ΕΟΡΤΩΝ

Fr. 84.   Joannes Lydus, *De Mensibus*, IV, 87
(Wünsch).

᾽Ιστέον δέ, ὡς ὁ Μανέθων ἐν τῷ περὶ ἑορτῶν
λέγει τὴν ἡλιακὴν ἔκλειψιν πονηρὰν ἐπίρροιαν ἀνθρώποις ἐπιφέρειν περί τε τὴν κεφαλὴν καὶ τὸν
στόμαχον.

ΠΕΡΙ ΑΡΧΑΪΣΜΟΥ ΚΑΙ ΕΥΣΕΒΕΙΑΣ

Fr. 85.   Porphyrius, *De Abstinentia*, II, 55
(Nauck).

Κατέλυσε δὲ καὶ ἐν ῾Ηλίου πόλει [1] τῆς Αἰγύπτου
τὸν τῆς ἀνθρωποκτονίας νόμον ῎Αμωσις, ὡς μαρ-

[1] Εἰλειθυίας πόλει conj. Fruin.

---

[1] If the reference is not to a separate treatise, but to a
passage in the *Sacred Book*, translate : " in his account of
festivals ".

[2] On human sacrifice in Egypt, see Meyer, *Geschichte* [5],
I. ii. pp. 98 f. Herodotus, ii. 45, denies that men were
sacrificed in Egypt in his time ; but Seleucus, under

they were called Hêlios, Cronos, Rhea, as well as
Zeus, Hêra, Hêphaestus, and Hestia. Manetho
writes on this subject at considerable length, while
Diodorus gives a concise account. . . .

ON FESTIVALS.

Fr. 84 (*from* JOANNES LYDUS).

It must be understood that Manetho in his book
On Festivals [1] states that a solar eclipse exerts a
baneful influence upon men in their head and
stomach.

ON ANCIENT RITUAL AND RELIGION.

Fr. 85 (*from* PORPHYRIUS).

The rite of human sacrifice [2] at Hêliopolis (Eileithyiaspolis) [3] in Egypt was suppressed by Amôsis,[4]

Tiberius, wrote an account of human sacrifice in Egypt
(Athen. iv. p. 172d), and there is evidence for the sacrifice
of captives in Dynasties XVIII. and XIX. See Diod.
Sic. i. 88, 5, and *cf.* Frazer, *Golden Bough*, ii. pp. 254 ff.

Some writers have suggested that the contracted human
figure (the *tekenu*), wrapped in a skin and drawn on a
sledge, who is a regular feature of funeral processions in
the New Kingdom, may have been a remnant of human
sacrifice. This, however, is very doubtful: *cf.* N. de G.
Davies, *Five Theban Tombs*, pp. 9, 14. See further
G. A. Wainwright, *Sky-Religion*, pp. 33 f.

[3] See Fr. 86. The mention of Hêra (see *infra*) makes
it very probable that " Eileithyiaspolis " is the correct
reading here.

[4] Amôsis, *c.* 1570 B.C.

τυρεῖ Μανεθὼς ἐν τῷ περὶ ἀρχαϊσμοῦ καὶ εὐσεβείας.
ἐθύοντο δὲ τῇ "Ηρᾳ, καὶ ἐδοκιμάζοντο καθάπερ οἱ
ζητούμενοι καθαροὶ μόσχοι καὶ συσφραγιζόμενοι·
ἐθύοντο δὲ τῆς ἡμέρας τρεῖς, ἀνθ' ὧν κηρίνους
ἐκέλευσεν ὁ "Αμωσις τοὺς ἴσους ἐπιτίθεσθαι.

See also Eusebius, *Praepar. Evang.*, IV, 16, p. 155d
(Gifford) : Theodoretus, *Curatio*, VII, p. 192 (Räder).

Fr. 86.   PLUTARCH, *De Is. et Osir.*, 73.

Πολλῶν δὲ λεγόντων εἰς ταῦτα τὰ ζῷα τὴν
Τυφῶνος αὐτοῦ διῃρῆσθαι [1] ψυχήν, αἰνίττεσθαι
δόξειεν ἂν ὁ μῦθος, ὅτι πᾶσα φύσις ἄλογος καὶ
θηριώδης τῆς τοῦ κακοῦ δαίμονος γέγονε μοίρας,
κἀκεῖνον ἐκμειλισσόμενοι καὶ παρηγοροῦντες περιέπουσι ταῦτα καὶ θεραπεύουσιν· ἂν δὲ πολὺς ἐμ-
πίπτῃ καὶ χαλεπὸς αὐχμὸς ἐπάγων ὑπερβαλλόντως
ἢ νόσους ὀλεθρίους ἢ συμφορὰς ἄλλας παραλόγους
καὶ ἀλλοκότους, ἔνια τῶν τιμωμένων οἱ ἱερεῖς
ἀπάγοντες ὑπὸ σκότῳ μετὰ σιωπῆς καὶ ἡσυχίας

[1] Wyttenbach : διάρασθαι MSS.

---

[1] or " . . . . in discussing ancient ritual and religion.

[2] Drought is said to be a particular manifestation of
Typhôn ; see Plutarch, *Is. et Osir.*, 45, 51 *fin.* In reference to Egypt, drought naturally means, not absence of
rain, but insufficient inundation.

[3] For this striking trait in Egyptian religion see Erman-
Ranke, *Ägypten*, 1923, p. 184 n. 2, with the reference to
Lacau, *Recueil de travaux*, 26 (1904), p. 72 (sarcophagi of
Dynasty XII.) ; and *cf.* Alan H. Gardiner, *Hieratic
Papyri in the British Museum*, iii. (1935), No. V. C (a spell
of *c.* 1200 B.C. in which the reciter threatens the gods that
he will cut off the head of a cow taken from the forecourt

as Manetho testifies in his book *On Ancient Ritual and Religion*.[1] Men were sacrificed to Hêra : they were examined, like the pure calves which are sought out and marked with a seal. Three men used to be sacrificed each day ; but in their stead Amôsis ordered that the same number of waxen images should be offered.

Fr. 86 (*from* PLUTARCH, *Is. and Osir.*, ch. 73).

Now many say that the soul of Typhôn himself is diffused among these animals ; and this fable would seem to hint that every irrational and bestial nature is partaker of the evil spirit, and that, while seeking to conciliate and appease him, men tend and worship these animals. Should a long and severe drought [2] occur, bringing with it an excess of deadly diseases or other strange and unaccountable calamities, the priests lead off some of the sacred animals quietly and in silence under cover of darkness, threatening them at first and trying to frighten [3] them ; but, should

of the temple of Hathor, and will cause the sky to split in the middle), No. VIII. B (the Book of Banishing an Enemy, also dated *c.* 1200 B.C., containing threats to tear out the soul and annihilate the corpse of Osiris, and set fire to every tomb of his), and *The Attitude of the Ancient Egyptians to Death and the Dead*, 1935, pp. 12, 16 f., 39, note 17.

Threats to the gods also appear later in the Greek papyri : see L.C.L., *Select Papyri*, i. (Hunt and Edgar), pp. 309, 345, Th. Hopfner, *Griechisch-Ägyptischer Offenbarungszauber* (= *Stud. zur Pal. und Pap.*, Wessely, xxiii. 1924), §§ 187, 210 *et al.*, and *cf.* Porphyrius, *Epistula ad Anebonem*, 27, who remarks that this is peculiarly Egyptian. See Wilcken, *Chrestomathie*, i. 1, pp. 124 f. (" perhaps a remnant of ancient fetishism ").

ἀπειλοῦσι καὶ δεδίττονται τὸ πρῶτον, ἂν δ' ἐπιμένῃ,
καθιερεύουσι καὶ σφάττουσιν. ὡς δή τινα κολασμὸν
ὄντα τοῦ δαίμονος τοῦτον ἢ καθαρμὸν ἄλλως μέγαν
ἐπὶ μεγίστοις· καὶ γὰρ ἐν Εἰλειθυίας πόλει ζῶντας
ἀνθρώπους κατεπίμπρασαν, ὡς Μανεθὼς ἱστόρηκε,
Τυφωνείους καλοῦντες, καὶ τὴν τέφραν αὐτῶν λικ-
μῶντες ἠφάνιζον καὶ διέσπειρον. ἀλλὰ τοῦτο μὲν
ἐδρᾶτο φανερῶς καὶ καθ' ἕνα καιρὸν ἐν ταῖς κυνάσιν
ἡμέραις· αἱ δὲ τῶν τιμωμένων ζῴων καθιερεύσεις
ἀπόρρητοι καὶ χρόνοις ἀτάκτοις πρὸς τὰ συμπίπ-
τοντα γινόμεναι, τοὺς πολλοὺς λανθάνουσι, πλὴν
ὅταν <Ἄπιδος [1]> ταφὰς ἔχωσι, καὶ τῶν ἄλλων ἀνα-
δεικνύντες ἔνια πάντων παρόντων συνεμβάλλωσιν,
οἰόμενοι τοῦ Τυφῶνος ἀντιλυπεῖν καὶ κολούειν τὸ
ἡδόμενον.

ΠΕΡΙ ΚΑΤΑΣΚΕΥΗΣ ΚΥΦΙΩΝ

Fr. 87.   PLUTARCH, De Is. et Osir., 80.

Τὸ δὲ κῦφι μῖγμα μὲν ἑκκαίδεκα μερῶν συν-
τιθεμένων ἐστί, μέλιτος καὶ οἴνου καὶ σταφίδος καὶ

[1] ⟨Ἄπιδος⟩ add. Xylander.

---

[1] El Kab on the right bank of the Nile, 53 miles S. of
Luxor (Baedeker [3], p. 365 ff.), the seat of Nekhebyt, the
goddess of childbirth, and in prehistoric times the capital
of the southern kingdom.

[2] Kyphi (Anc. Egyptian k)pt, from k)p, to burn) is
mentioned in the Ebers Papyrus (Wreszinski, 98, 12 f.),
where ten ingredients (without honey and wine) are given.

the visitation continue, they consecrate the animals
and slaughter them, intending thus to inflict a kind
of chastisement upon the spirit, or at least to offer
a great atonement for heinous offences.   Moreover,
in Eileithyiaspolis,[1] as Manetho has related, they used
to burn men alive, calling them " Typhôn's followers " ; and their ashes they would winnow and
scatter broadcast until they were seen no more.
But this was done openly and at a set time, namely
in the dog-days ; whereas the consecrations of sacred
animals are secret ceremonies, taking place at ir-
regular intervals as occasion demands, unknown to
the common people except when the priests celebrate a funeral of Apis, and, displaying some of the
animals, cast them together into the tomb in the
presence of all, deeming that thus they are vexing
Typhôn in return and curtailing his delight.

ON THE MAKING OF KYPHI.

Fr. 87 (*from* PLUTARCH, *Is. and Osir.*, ch. 80).

Kyphi[2] is a mixture of sixteen ingredients—honey,
wine, raisins, cyperus [? galingale], resin, myrrh,

Recipes of a similar nature have been found at Edfu (two)
and at Philae (one) : they were inscribed in hieroglyphs
on temple-walls.   Kyphi had a double use—as incense and
as medicine.   See further Ganszyniec in Pauly-Wissowa-
Kroll, *R.-E.* (1924).   Parthey (*Isis und Osiris*, pp. 277 ff.)
describes the results of experiments with the recipes of
Plutarch, of Galen (also sixteen ingredients), and of Dioscorides (ten ingredients) : he gives first place to the kyphi
prepared according to the prescription of Dioscorides.

κυπέρου, ῥητίνης τε καὶ σμύρνης καὶ ἀσπαλάθου
καὶ σεσέλεως, ἔτι δὲ σχίνου τε καὶ ἀσφάλτου καὶ
θρύου καὶ λαπάθου, πρὸς δὲ τούτοις ἀρκευθίδων
ἀμφοῖν (ὧν τὴν μὲν μείζονα, τὴν δ' ἐλάττονα
καλοῦσι) καὶ καρδαμώμου καὶ καλάμου.

[ΤΑ ΠΡΟΣ ΗΡΟΔΟΤΟΝ]

Fr. 88.[1]   Etymologicum Magnum (Gaisford), s.v.
Λεοντοκόμος.

Τὸ δὲ λέων παρὰ τὸ λάω, τὸ θεωρῶ· ὀξυδερκέστατον γὰρ τὸ θηρίον, ὥς φησι Μανέθων ἐν τῷ
πρὸς Ἡρόδοτον, ὅτι οὐδέποτε καθεύδει ὁ λέων,
τοῦτο δὲ ἀπίθανον . . .

[1] Cf. also Fr. from Choeroboscus, Orthogr., in Cramer,
Anecd. Graeca Ox., ii. 235, 32 (= Etym. genuinum): . . . ἀπὸ
τούτου τοῦ λάω γέγονε λέων· ὀξυδερκέστατον γὰρ τὸ θηρίον· φασὶ
γὰρ ὅτι οὐδέποτε καθεύδει ὁ λέων. τοῦτο δὲ ἀπίθανον . . . See
Aelian, De Nat. Anim., v. 39: Αἰγυπτίους ὑπὲρ αὐτοῦ κομπάζειν
φασὶ λέγοντας ὅτι κρείττων ὕπνου λέων ἐστὶν ἀγρυπνῶν ἀεί.

---

[1] Aspalathus = Calycotome villosa.
[2] Cardamom = Elettaria cardamomum.   See L.C.L.,
Theophrastus, ix. 7, 3 (Hort).
[3] Manetho's note may refer to such passages in Herodotus
as ii. 65 ff. and iii. 108.

[Footnote continued on opposite page.

aspalathus,[1] seselis [hartwort]; mastic, bitumen, thryon [a kind of reed or rush], dock [monk's rhubarb], as well as of both junipers (arceuthids—one called the greater, the other the less), cardamom,[2] and reed [orris-root, or root of sweet flag].

[CRITICISMS OF HERODOTUS]

Fr. 88 [3] (from the *Etymologicum Magnum*).

The word λέων ("lion") comes from λάω, "I see": the animal has indeed the keenest of sight, as Manetho says in his *Criticism of Herodotus* that the lion never sleeps.[4] But this is hard to believe.

Choeroboscus, in his work *On Orthography* (iv./v. A.D.), gives the derivation of λέων according to Orus or Hôrus in almost the same words as those quoted above from the *Etymologicum Magnum*; but he omits the clause "as Manetho says in his *Criticism of Herodotus*" (Cramer, *Anecdota Graeca e codd. manuscriptis bibliothecarum Oxoniensium*, ii. p. 235, ll. 32 ff. = *Etymologicum Genuinum*).

Cf. Aelian, *On the Nature of Animals*, v. 39: "the Egyptians, they say, boast about this, adding that the lion is superior to sleep, being always awake." Aelian quotes from Apion (see p. 19 n. 3), who may well have taken his statement from Manetho.

[4] By a curious coincidence, in Egyptian also the words for "lion" (*m꜄i*) and "to see" (*m꜄)*) are very similar, and the word for "lion" is sometimes written as though it came from the verb "to see". Manetho possibly had this fact in mind when he stated that the lion never sleeps (Battiscombe Gunn).

Eustathius on Homer, *Iliad*, XI, 480:

(Τινὲς λέγουσιν) ὅτι ἐκ τοῦ λάω, τὸ βλέπω,
γίνεται ὥσπερ ὁ λέων, οὕτω καὶ ὁ λίς, κατὰ τὸν
γραμματικὸν Ὧρον, ὡς ὀξυδερκής, καὶ ὅτι, ὡς
φησι Μανέθων ἐν τοῖς πρὸς Ἡρόδοτον, οὐ καθεύδει
ὁ λέων ὅπερ ἀπίθανον . . .

(From Eustathius.)

(Some say) that from λάω, " I see," comes not only λέων, but also λίς (a lion), according to Ôrus the grammarian,[1] because of its keen sight ; and they add, as Manetho states in his *Criticisms of Herodotus*, that the lion never sleeps.   This is hard to believe.

---

[1] Ôrus or Hôrus (ᴠ. ᴀ.ᴅ.) was, according to Suidas, an Alexandrian grammarian who taught at Constantinople : none of his numerous works is extant.

APPENDIX I

PSEUDO–MANETHO

Syncellus, p. 72.

Πρόκειται δὲ λοιπὸν καὶ περὶ τῆς τῶν Αἰγυπτίων
δυναστείας μικρὰ διαλαβεῖν ἐκ τῶν Μανεθῶ τοῦ
Σεβεννύτου, ὃς ἐπὶ Πτολεμαίου τοῦ Φιλαδέλφου
4 ἀρχιερεὺς τῶν ἐν Αἰγύπτῳ εἰδωλείων χρηματίσας
ἐκ τῶν ἐν τῇ Σηριαδικῇ γῇ κειμένων στηλῶν ἱερά,
φησι, διαλέκτῳ καὶ ἱερογραφικοῖς γράμμασι κε-
χαρακτηρισμένων ὑπὸ Θὼθ τοῦ πρώτου Ἑρμοῦ, καὶ
ἑρμηνευθεισῶν μετὰ τὸν κατακλυσμὸν [ἐκ τῆς ἱερᾶς
διαλέκτου εἰς τὴν Ἑλληνίδα φωνὴν] [1] γράμμασιν
ἱερογλυφικοῖς, καὶ ἀποτεθέντων [2] ἐν βίβλοις ὑπὸ τοῦ
Ἀγαθοδαίμονος, υἱοῦ τοῦ δευτέρου Ἑρμοῦ, πατρὸς
12 δὲ τοῦ Τάτ, ἐν τοῖς ἀδύτοις τῶν ἱερῶν Αἰγύπτου,
προσεφώνησε τῷ αὐτῷ Φιλαδέλφῳ βασιλεῖ δευτέρῳ
Πτολεμαίῳ ἐν τῇ Βίβλῳ τῆς Σώθεος γράφων
ἐπὶ λέξεως οὕτως ·

---

[1] The words bracketed are probably a later interpolation.
[2] ἀποτεθεισῶν conj. Scaliger, Müller.

---

[1] Sêriadic land, *i.e.* Egypt, *cf.* Josephus, *Ant.* i. 71. In
an inscription the home of Isis is Σειρὰς γῆ, and Isis herself
is Νειλῶτις or Σειρίας, the Nile is Σείριος : see Reitzenstein,
Poimandres, p. 183.
[2] For the god Thôth inscribing records, see p. xiv n. 1.

208

APPENDIX I.

PSEUDO-MANETHO.

(*From* SYNCELLUS).

It remains now to make brief extracts concerning the dynasties of Egypt from the works of Manetho of Sebennytus. In the time of Ptolemy Philadelphus he was styled high-priest of the pagan temples of Egypt, and wrote from inscriptions in the Sêriadic land,[1] traced, he says, in sacred language and holy characters by Thôth,[2] the first Hermês, and translated after the Flood . . . in hieroglyphic characters. When the work had been arranged in books by Agathodaemôn, son of the second Hermês[3] and father of Tat, in the temple-shrines of Egypt, Manetho dedicated it to the above King Ptolemy II. Philadelphus in his *Book of Sôthis*, using the following words :

---

[3] The second Hermês is Hermês Trismegistus, the teacher. For a discussion of the whole passage, see W. Scott, *Hermetica*, iii. pp. 492 f. He pointed out manifest breaches of continuity after χρηματίσας (end of l. 4) and after Αἰγύπτου (end of l. 12). If the intervening 8 lines are cut out (ἐκ τῶν . . . Αἰγύπτου), the sentence runs smoothly; and Scott suggested that these 8 lines originally stood in Manetho's letter after ἃ ἔμαθον. Even with this insertion there still remains a gap before ἱερὰ βιβλία, but apart from that lacuna, the whole becomes intelligible.

'Επιστολὴ Μανεθῶ τοῦ Σεβεννύτου πρὸς Πτολεμαῖον τὸν Φιλάδελφον.

"Βασιλεῖ μεγάλῳ Πτολεμαίῳ Φιλαδέλφῳ σεβαστῷ Μανεθῶ ἀρχιερεὺς καὶ γραμματεὺς τῶν κατ' Αἴγυπτον ἱερῶν ἀδύτων, γένει Σεβεννύτης ὑπάρχων Ἡλιουπολίτης, τῷ δεσπότῃ μου Πτολεμαίῳ χαίρειν.

Ἡμᾶς δεῖ λογίζεσθαι, μέγιστε βασιλεῦ, περὶ πάντων ὧν ἐὰν βούλῃ ἡμᾶς ἐξετάσαι πραγμάτων. ἐπιζητοῦντι οὖν[1] σοι περὶ τῶν μελλόντων τῷ κόσμῳ γίγνεσθαι, καθὼς ἐκέλευσάς μοι, παραφανήσεταί σοι ἃ ἔμαθον ἱερὰ βιβλία γραφέντα ὑπὸ τοῦ προπάτορος, τρισμεγίστου Ἑρμοῦ. ἔρρωσό μοι, δέσποτά μου βασιλεῦ."

Ταῦτα περὶ τῆς ἑρμηνείας τῶν ὑπὸ τοῦ δευτέρου Ἑρμοῦ γραφέντων βιβλίων λέγει.   μετὰ δὲ ταῦτα καὶ περὶ ἐθνῶν Αἰγυπτιακῶν πέντε ἐν τριάκοντα δυναστείαις ἱστορεῖ[2] . . .

---

[1] οὖν add. Boeckh.
[2] For the continuation of this, see Fr. 2, p. 10.

---

[1] Augustus, a title of the Roman emperor, was not used in Ptolemaic times.

[2] For a curious juxtaposition of Manetho and Hermês Trismegistus, see Wellmann in *Hermes*, xxxv. p. 367.

Letter of Manetho of Sebennytus to Ptolemy Philadelphus.

"To the great King Ptolemy Philadelphus Augustus.[1] Greeting to my lord Ptolemy from Manetho, high-priest and scribe of the sacred shrines of Egypt, born at Sebennytus and dwelling at Hêliopolis. It is my duty, almighty king, to reflect upon all such matters as you may desire me to investigate. So, as you are making researches concerning the future of the universe, in obedience to your command I shall place before you the Sacred Books which I have studied, written by your forefather, Hermês Trismegistus.[2] Farewell, I pray, my lord King."

Such is his account of the translation of the books written by the second Hermês. Thereafter Manetho tells also of five Egyptian tribes which formed thirty dynasties . . .

(Fr. 2, p. 11, follows directly after this.)

A MS. of Celsus gives a list of medical writers, Egyptian or Greek and Latin : they include (col. 1, ll. 9-13) Hermês Trismegistus, Manetho (MS. emmanetos), Nechepsô, Cleopatra regina. Here Manetho is followed by Nechepsô, to whom, along with Petosiris (perhaps another name of Nechepsô), works on astrology were attributed in the Second Century B.C. : see W. Kroll and M. Pieper in *R.-E.* xvi. 2 (1935), *s.v.* Nechepsô.

APPENDIX II

ERATOSTHENES (?)

Fr. 7 (a). *Syncellus*, p. 171.

Θηβαίων βασιλεῖς.

Ἀπολλόδωρος χρονικὸς ἄλλην Αἰγυπτίων τῶν Θηβαίων λεγομένων βασιλείαν ἀνεγράψατο βασιλέων λη', ἐτῶν ,αος'. ἥτις ἤρξατο μὲν τῷ 'βπ' ἔτει τοῦ κόσμου, ἔληξε δὲ εἰς τὸ ,γμε'[1] ἔτος τοῦ κόσμου, ὧν τὴν γνῶσιν, φησὶν, ὁ Ἐρατοσθένης λαβὼν Αἰγυπτιακοῖς ὑπομνήμασι καὶ ὀνόμασι κατὰ πρόσταξιν βασιλικὴν τῇ Ἑλλάδι φωνῇ παρέφρασεν οὕτως·

Θηβαίων βασιλέων τῶν μετὰ ,αρκδ' ἔτη τῆς διασπορᾶς λη' βασιλειῶν,

[1] ,γπος' m.

---

[1] This list of kings was said to have been taken by Apollodorus (ii. B.C.) from Eratosthenes of Cyrene (iii. B.C.) whom Apollodorus often followed as an authority; but according to Jacoby (*Apollodors Chronik*, pp. 399 ff., Fr. 117—Pseudo-Apollodorus) the list of " Theban " kings owes nothing either to Apollodorus or to Eratosthenes, but is the work of one who sought to recommend his compilation under two distinguished names. The list,

212

APPENDIX II.

ERATOSTHENES (?) (*From Syncellus*).

Fr. 7 (a).

Kings of Thebes.[1]

Apollodorus, the chronographer, recorded another dynasty of Egyptian kings,—the Thebans, as they are called,—thirty-eight kings ruling for 1076 years. This dynasty began in Anno Mundi 2900, and came to an end in Anno Mundi 3045 [3976]. The knowledge of these kings, he says, Eratosthenes took from Egyptian records and lists, and at the king's command he translated them into the Greek language, as follows :

Of the Theban kings in thirty-eight dynasties ruling 1124 years after the Dispersion,

containing thirty-eight kings, who ruled for 1076 years, is of Theban origin, derived from a Royal List such as that of Karnak : the explanations of the names are interesting, and the variations in Nos. 11 and 15 may be due to the priests themselves. Historically the list is of no great worth : several of the names are not proper names, but Throne-names, such as are found in the Royal Lists and the Turin Papyrus (Meyer, *Aeg. Chron.* pp. 99 ff.).

Kings 1-5 correspond to Dynasty I., 13-17 to Dynasty IV., 18-22 to Dynasty VI.

α' ‹πρῶτος›¹ ἐβασίλευσε Μήνης Θηβαῖος,² ὃ
ἑρμηνεύεται αἰώνιος³· ἐβασίλευσεν ἔτη ξβ'.
τοῦ δὲ κόσμου ἦν ἔτος ͵βπ'.

β' Θηβαίων δεύτερος ἐβασίλευσεν Ἀθώθης,
υἱὸς Μήνεως, ἔτη νθ'. οὗτος ἑρμηνεύεται
Ἑρμογένης. ἔτος τοῦ κόσμου ͵βπξβ'.

γ' Θηβαίων Αἰγυπτίων τρίτος ἐβασίλευσεν
Ἀθώθης ὁμώνυμος, ἔτη λβ'. τοῦ δὲ
κόσμου ἦν ἔτος ͵γκα'.

Syncellus, p. 180.

δ' Θηβαίων ἐβασίλευσε δ' Μιαβαῆς,⁴ υἱὸς
Ἀθώθεως, ἔτη ιθ'. οὗτος ἑρμηνεύεται
φιλόταυρος.⁵ τοῦ δὲ κόσμου ἦν ἔτος
͵γνγ'.

ε' Θηβαίων ἐβασίλευσε ε' Πεμφῶς,⁶ υἱὸς
Ἀθώθους, ὅ ἐστιν Ἡρακλείδης, ἔτη ιη'.
τοῦ δὲ κόσμου ἦν ἔτος ͵γοβ'.

Fr. 13.   Syncellus, p. 180.

ϛ' Θηβαίων Αἰγυπτίων ἐβασίλευσεν ϛ' Μομ-
χειρὶ Μεμφίτης, ἔτη οθ'. οὗτος ἑρ-

---

¹ πρῶτος add. Goar.
² Θηβαῖος conj. Meyer : Θηνίτης B : Θηβινίτης Θηβαῖος Dindorf.
³ αἰώνιος corr. Jablonski : διώνιος B, Διόνιος A.
⁴ Διαβιῆς B.
⁵ φιλόταυρος Bunsen : φιλέτ*οος codd. : φιλέταιρος Scaliger.
⁶ Σεμφῶς Bunsen.

214

1. The first was Mênês of Thebes, whose name, being interpreted, means "everlasting".[1] He reigned for 62 years.   Anno mundi 2900.

2. The second king of Thebes was Athôthês, son of Mênês, for 59 years.   His name, being interpreted, means "Born of Hermês".[2] Anno mundi 2962.

3. The third king of Thebes in Egypt was Athôthês II., for 32 years.   Anno mundi 3021.

4. The fourth king of Thebes was Miabaês, son of Athôthis, for 19 years.   His name, being interpreted, means "Bull-lover".[3]   Anno mundi 3053.

5. The fifth king of Thebes was Pemphôs (? Sempsôs, Semempsês), son of Athôthis. His name is "descendant of Hêraclês," and he reigned for 18 years.   Anno mundi 3072.

Fr. 13.

6. The sixth king of Thebes in Egypt was Momcheiri of Memphis, reigning for 79 years.   His name, being interpreted, means

[1] The Egyptian form of the name Mênês may quite well be interpreted as "the abiding one," from *mn*, "to endure".

[2] This etymology obviously assumes the presence of the divine name Thôth in the name Athôthês.

[3] The first element of the name Miabaês is clearly some form of the verb *mr*, "to love".

215

μηνεύεται ἡγήσανδρος[1]· περισσομελής,
[τοιγὰρ ἄμαχος].[2]   τοῦ δὲ κόσμου ἦν ,γϟ̅ʹ.

ζʹ Θηβαίων Αἰγυπτίων ἐβασίλευσεν ζʹ Στοῖχος,
υἱὸς αὐτοῦ· ὅ ἐστιν Ἄρης ἀναίσθητος, ἔτη
ϛʹ. τοῦ δὲ κόσμου ἦν ἔτος ,γρξθ̅ʹ.

ηʹ Θηβαίων Αἰγυπτίων ἐβασίλευσεν ὄγδοος Γο-
σορμίης, ὅ ἐστιν αἰτησιπαντός,[3] ἔτη λʹ.
τοῦ δὲ κόσμου ἦν ἔτος ,γροε̅ʹ.

θʹ Θηβαίων Αἰγυπτίων ἐβασίλευσεν θʹ Μάρης,
υἱὸς αὐτοῦ, ὅ ἐστιν Ἡλιόδωρος, ἔτη κϛʹ.
τοῦ δὲ κόσμου ἦν ἔτος ,γσε̅ʹ.

Syncellus, p. 190.

ιʹ Θηβαίων Αἰγυπτίων ιʹ ἐβασίλευσεν Ἀνωῦ-
φίς, ὅ ἐστιν ἐπίκωμος,[4] ἔτη κʹ. τοῦ δὲ
κόσμου ἦν ἔτος ,γσλα̅ʹ.

ιαʹ Θηβαίων Αἰγυπτίων ιαʹ ἐβασίλευσε Σίριος,
ὅ ἐστιν υἱὸς κόρης, ὡς δὲ ἕτεροι ἀβάσκαν-
τος, ἔτη ιη̅ʹ.   τοῦ δὲ κόσμου ἦν ἔτος ,γσνα̅ʹ.

ιβʹ Θηβαίων Αἰγυπτίων ιβʹ ἐβασίλευσε Χνοῦβος
ἢ Γνεῦρος, ὅ ἐστι Χρυσὸς ἢ Χρυσοῦς

---

[1] Conj. Bunsen : τῆς ἀνδρὸς codd. : ἔτης ἀνδρὸς Gutschmid.
[2] A gloss, which the codd. have before Μομχειρί.
[3] ἐτησιπαντός A : ἔτης παντος Gutschmid.
[4] B : ἐπίκομος A.

---

[1] With this interpretation of the name Marês (which
may correctly explain the second element as Rê, " the
Sun "), cf. ἥλιος εὐφεγγής, " a brilliant Sun," in *Hymn IV.*,

" leader of men ". He had exceeding
large limbs (and was therefore irresistible).
Anno mundi 3090.

7. The seventh king of Thebes in Egypt was his
son, Stoichos. The name means " unfeeling
Arês ". He reigned for 6 years. Anno
mundi 3169.

8. The eighth king of Thebes in Egypt was
Gosormiês, whose name means " all-demand-
ing ". He reigned for 30 years. Anno
mundi 3175.

9. The ninth king of Thebes in Egypt was his
son, Marês, whose name means " gift of the
Sun ".[1] He reigned for 26 years. Anno
mundi 3205.

10. The tenth king of Thebes in Egypt was
Anôÿphis, whose name means " revelling ".[2]
He reigned for 20 years. Anno mundi
3231.

11. The eleventh king of Thebes in Egypt was
Sirius, whose name means " son of the iris of
the eye," [3] or, as others say, " unharmed by
the evil eye ". He reigned for 18 years.
Anno mundi 3251.

12. The twelfth king of Thebes in Egypt was
Chnubos or Gneuros, which means " gold " [4]

---

line 32, A. Vogliano, *Madinet Madi, Primo Rapporto* (1936):
see note on No. 35 *infra*, p. 224.

[2] Possibly this explanation is based upon the Egyptian
word *unóf*, " to rejoice " (B.G.).

[3] In Egyptian *si-îri* means " son of the eye ".

[4] *Nûb* is Egyptian for " gold ".

υἱός,[1] ἔτη κβ'. τοῦ δὲ κόσμου ἦν ἔτος
,γσξθ'.
ιγ' Θηβαίων Αἰγυπτίων ιγ' ἐβασίλευσε Ῥαϑ-
ωσις, ὅ ἐστιν ἀρχικράτωρ, ἔτη ιγ'. τοῦ
δὲ κόσμου ἦν ἔτος ,γσηα'.
ιδ' Θηβαίων Αἰγυπτίων ιδ' ἐβασίλευσε Βιύρης,
ἔτη ι'. τοῦ δὲ κόσμου ἦν ἔτος ,γτδ'.

Fr. 17. Syncellus, p. 190.

ιε' Θηβαίων Αἰγυπτίων ιε' ἐβασίλευσε Σαῶφις,
κωμαστής, κατὰ δὲ ἐνίους χρηματιστής,
ἔτη κθ'. τοῦ δὲ κόσμου ἦν ἔτος ,γτιδ'.

Syncellus, p. 195.

ις' Θηβαίων ις' ἐβασίλευσε Σαῶφις β', ἔτη κζ'.
τοῦ δὲ κόσμου ἦν ἔτος ,γτμγ'.
ιζ' Θηβαίων ιζ' ἐβασίλευσε Μοσχερῆς,[2] ἡλιό-
δοτος, ἔτη λα'. τοῦ δὲ κόσμου ἦν ἔτος
,γτο'.
ιη' Θηβαίων ιη' ἐβασίλευσε Μοσθῆς,[3] ἔτη λγ'.
τοῦ δὲ κόσμου ἦν ἔτος ,γυα'.
ιθ' Θηβαίων ιθ' ἐβασίλευσε Παμμῆς, ἀρχοειδής,[4]
ἔτη λε'. τοῦ δὲ κόσμου ἦν ἔτος ,γυλδ'.

[1] Corr. Bunsen : Χνοῦβος Γνευρός, ὅ ἐστι Χρύσης Χρύσου υἱός
codd.
[2] Μεγχερῆς conj. Bunsen.
[3] Μεγχερῆς β' conj. Bunsen.
[4] Conj. Gutschmid : ἀρχονδής codd.

or " golden son " (or his son).   He reigned
for 22 years.   Anno mundi 3269.

13. The thirteenth king of Thebes in Egypt was
Raÿôsis, which means " the arch-master-
ful ".[1]   He reigned for 13 years   Anno
mundi 3291.

14. The fourteenth king of Thebes in Egypt was
Biÿrês, who reigned for 10 years.   Anno
mundi 3304.

Fr. 17.

15. The fifteenth king of Thebes in Egypt was
Saôphis, " reveller," or, according to some,
" money-getter, trafficker ".   He reigned for
29 years.   Anno mundi 3314.

16. The sixteenth king of Thebes was Saôphis II ,
who reigned for 27 years.   Anno mundi
3343.

17. The seventeenth king of Thebes was Moscherês
(? Mencherês), " gift of the Sun," who
reigned for 31 years.   Anno mundi 3370.

18. The eighteenth king of Thebes was Mosthês
(? Mencherês II.), who reigned for 33 years.
Anno mundi 3401.

19. The nineteenth king of Thebes was Pammês,
" leader-like," who reigned for 35 years.
Anno mundi 3434.

---

[1] Possibly, according to this explanation, Ra- (or Rha-)
is the Egyptian *ḥry*, " master," and the rest of the name
wôse(r), " powerful " (B.G.).

Fr. 22. Syncellus, p. 195.

κ΄ Θηβαίων κ΄ ἐβασίλευσεν Ἀπάππους, μέγιστος. οὗτος, ὥς φασι, παρὰ ὥραν μίαν ἐβασίλευσεν ἔτη ρ΄. τοῦ δὲ κόσμου ἦν ἔτος ,γυξθ΄.

κα΄ Θηβαίων κα΄ ἐβασίλευσεν Ἐχεσκοσοκάρας,[1] ἔτος α΄. τοῦ δὲ κόσμου ἦν ἔτος ,γφξθ΄.

κβ΄ Θηβαίων κβ΄ ἐβασίλευσε Νίτωκρις, γυνὴ ἀντὶ ἀνδρός, ὅ ἐστιν Ἀθηνᾶ νικηφόρος, ἔτη ς΄. τοῦ δὲ κόσμου ἦν ἔτος ,γφο΄.

Fr. 33. Syncellus, p. 196.

κγ΄ Θηβαίων κγ΄ ἐβασίλευσε Μυρταῖος[2] Ἀμμωνόδοτος, ἔτη κβ΄. τοῦ δὲ κόσμου ἦν ἔτος ,γφος΄.[3]

Syncellus, p. 204.

κδ΄ Θηβαίων κδ΄ ἐβασίλευσεν Οὐωσιμάρης,[4] κραταιός ἐστιν[5] ἥλιος, ἔτη ιβ΄. τοῦ δὲ κόσμου ἦν ἔτος ,γφςη΄.

κε΄ Θηβαίων κε΄ ἐβασίλευσε Σεθίνιλος,[6] ὅ ἐστιν αὐξήσας τὸ πάτριον κράτος, ἔτη η΄. τοῦ δὲ κόσμου ἦν ἔτος ,γχι΄.

---

[1] B : ἐχεσκὸς ὀκάρας A   [2] Conj. Ἀμυρταῖος.
[3] m. : ,γφςη΄ codd.   [4] Jablonski : Θυωσιμάρης B.
[5] Bunsen : ὅ ἐστιν codd.
[6] B : Θίριλλος A : Θίνιλλος Dindorf.

220

Fr. 22.

20. The twentieth king of Thebes was Apappûs (Pepi),[1] "the very great". He, they say, ruled for 100 years all but one hour. Anno mundi 3469.

21. The twenty-first king of Thebes was Echeskosokaras, for 1 year. Anno mundi 3569.

22. The twenty-second ruler of Thebes was Nitôcris,[2] a queen, not a king. Her name means "Athêna the victorious," and she reigned for 6 years. Anno mundi 3570.

Fr. 33.

23. The twenty-third king of Thebes was Myrtaeus (Amyrtaeus), "gift of Ammôn," [3] for 22 years. Anno mundi 3576.

24. The twenty-fourth king of Thebes was Uôsimarês, "Mighty is the Sun," [4] for 12 years. Anno mundi 3598.

25. The twenty-fifth king of Thebes was Sethinilus (Thirillus), which means "having increased his ancestral power," for 8 years. Anno mundi 3610.

---

[1] Apappûs is the Phiôps of Fr. 20. 4, with a curious misunderstanding of his reign of 94 years.

[2] See p. 54 n. 2, and Wainwright, *Sky-Religion*, pp. 41, 45.

[3] This interpretation is based upon the common Egyptian name Amenerdais, "Amûn has given him ".

[4] The Egyptian *Wôse-mi-Rê* means "Mighty like the Sun ": Uôsimarês may however be intended for the first half of the *praenomen* of Ramessês II., *Wese-mê-Rê*, but this means "Rê is mighty in justice " (B.G.).

κϛ´ Θηβαίων κϛ´ ἐβασίλευσε Σεμφρουκράτης,
  ὅ ἐστιν Ἡρακλῆς Ἁρποκράτης, ἔτη ιη´.
  τοῦ δὲ κόσμου ἦν ἔτος ͵γχιη´.

κζ´ Θηβαίων κζ´ ἐβασίλευσε Χουθήρ, ταῦρος
  τύραννος, ἔτη ζ´. τοῦ δὲ κόσμου ἦν ἔτος
  ͵γχλϛ´.

κη´ Θηβαίων κη´ ἐβασίλευσε Μευρής,[1] φίλος
  κόρης,[2] ἔτη ιβ´. τοῦ δὲ κόσμου ἦν ἔτος
  ͵γχμγ´.

κθ´ Θηβαίων κθ´ ἐβασίλευσε Χωμαεφθά,[3] κόσ-
  μος φιλήφαιστος, ἔτη ια´. τοῦ δὲ κόσμου
  ἦν ἔτος ͵γχνε´.

λ´ Θηβαίων λ´ ἐβασίλευσε Σοικούνιος [4] ὁχοτύραν-
  νος,[5] ἔτη ξ´. τοῦ δὲ κόσμου ἦν ἔτος ͵γχξϛ´.

Syncellus, p. 233.

λα´ Θηβαίων λα´ ἐβασίλευσε Πετεαθυρῆς, ἔτη
  ιϛ´. τοῦ δὲ κόσμου ἦν ἔτος ͵γψκζ´.

Fr. 37.

λβ´ Θηβαίων λβ´ ἐβασίλευσε ⟨Σταμμενέμης α´,[6]
  ἔτη κϛ´. τοῦ δὲ κόσμου ἦν ἔτος ͵γψμβ´.

---

[1] Conj. Μιειρής.   [2] Gutschmid: φιλόσκορος codd.
[3] Τωμαεφθά Bunsen. [4] Σοικοῦνις Bunsen.
[5] ὡς Ὤχος τύραννος Bunsen: Σοῦχος τύραννος Gutschmid.
[6] Ἀμμενέμης Bunsen. A lacuna here in codd.

---

[1] The first syllable of the name Chuthêr may represent
the Egyptian kŏ, " bull ".
[2] In Egyptian, " loving the eye " is mai-îri.

26. The twenty-sixth king of Thebes was Semphrucratês, which means "Heraclês Harpocratês," for 18 years. Anno mundi 3618.

27. The twenty-seventh king of Thebes was Chuthêr, "bull-lord,"[1] for 7 years. Anno mundi 3636.

28. The twenty-eighth king of Thebes was Meurês (Mieirês), "loving the iris of the eye,"[2] for 12 years. Anno mundi 3643.

29. The twenty-ninth king of Thebes was Chômaephtha (Tômaephtha), "world, loving Hêphaestus,"[3] for 11 years. Anno mundi 3655.

30. The thirtieth king of Thebes was Soicunius (or Soicunis), † hochotyrannos, †[4] (or Soicuniosochus the lord), for 60 years. Anno mundi 3666.

31. The thirty-first king of Thebes was Peteathyrês,[5] for 16 years. Anno mundi 3726.

Fr. 37.

32. The thirty-second king of Thebes was ⟨Stammenemês I. (Ammenemês I.), for 26 years. Anno mundi 3742.

[3] As to the latter part of the name, "loving Hêphaestus" is in Egyptian *mai-Ptah*: the emended Tô- represents the Egyptian *tŏ*, "world" (B.G.).

[4] Bunsen emends this *vox nihili* to mean "a tyrant like Ôchus": Gutschmid, to mean "Suchus the lord". The latter description may refer to one of the Sebekḥotpes.

[5] Peteathyrês, a well-formed name Pede-hathor, which does not occur as a king's name.

223

λγ′ Θηβαίων λγ′ ἐβασίλευσε⟩ Σταμμενέμης β′,
    ἔτη κγ′. τοῦ δὲ κόσμου ἦν ἔτος γψξη′.
λδ′ Θηβαίων λδ′ ἐβασίλευσε Σιστοσιχερμῆς,
    Ἡρακλῆς κραταιός,[1] ἔτη νε′. τοῦ δὲ κόσμου
    ἦν ἔτος ,γψϙα′.
λε′ Θηβαίων λε′ ἐβασίλευσε Μάρης, ἔτη μγ′.
    τοῦ δὲ κόσμου ἦν ἔτος ,γωμϛ′.

Fr. 40.

λϛ′ Θηβαίων λϛ′ ἐβασίλευσε Σιφθὰς[2] ὁ καὶ
    Ἑρμῆς, υἱὸς Ἡφαίστου, ἔτη ε′. τοῦ δὲ
    κόσμου ἦν ἔτος ,γωπθ′.

Syncellus, p. 278.

λζ′ Θηβαίων λζ′ ἐβασίλευσε Φρουορῶ[3] ἤτοι
    Νεῖλος, ἔτη ε′.[4] τοῦ δὲ κόσμου ἦν ἔτος
    ,γωϙδ′.[5]
λη′ Θηβαίων λη′ ἐβασίλευσε Ἀμουθαρταῖος, ἔτη
    ξγ′. τοῦ δὲ κόσμου ἦν ἔτος ,γϡιγ′.

[1] Σεσόρτωσις, Ἑρμῆς ἢ Ἡρακλῆς κραταιός conj. Bunsen.
[2] Bunsen : Σιφόας codd.   [3] Φονορῶ Bunsen.
[4] ιθ′ corr. Müller.   [5] ,γωπθ′ codd.

[1] Besides Marês and derived forms (Marrês, Aelian,
De Nat. Anim. vi. 7 ; Marros and Mendês, Diod. Sic. i.
61, 1 ; Imandês, Strabo, 17. 1. 37, 42), there are two types
of variants on the name of Amenemhêt III.—(1) Lamarês
(Fr. 34), Lamaris (Fr. 35), Labarês, Labaris ; and (2)
Pramarrês, Premanrês (Pr- = Pharaoh) : cf. Poremanrês,
P. Mich. Zen. 84, lines 18, 21, Porramanrês in A. Vogliano,
Madinet Madi, Primo Rapporto (1936), Hymn IV., line
34, where the first two syllables must be eliminated if

33. The thirty-third king of Thebes was⟩ Stammenemês II. (Ammenemês II.), for 23 years. Anno mundi 3768.

34. The thirty-fourth king of Thebes was Sistosichermês, " valiant Hêraclês " (Sistosis or Sesortôsis, " valiant Hermês or Hêraclês "), for 55 years.   Anno mundi 3791.

35. The thirty-fifth king of Thebes was Marês,[1] for 43 years.   Anno mundi 3846.

Fr. 40.

36. The thirty-sixth king of Thebes was Siphthas,[2] also called Hermês, " son of Hêphaestus," for 5 years.   Anno mundi 3889.

37. The thirty-seventh king of Thebes was Phruorô [3] (Phuorô) or " the Nile," for 5 (? 19) years.   Anno mundi 3894.

38. The thirty-eighth king of Thebes was Amuthartaeus, for 63 years.   Anno mundi 3913.

[Syncellus then adds (p. 279) in much the same phrase as that quoted at the beginning of Appendix II. : " These names Eratosthenes took from the sacred scribes at Diospolis and translated from Egyptian into the Greek language."]

the pentameter is to scan.   [See note on p. 50.   The temple at the vestibule of which the Hymn was inscribed is dated 95 B.C.]

[2] Siphthas is King Siptah (" son of Ptah "), probably Thuôris (Thuôsris), of Dynasty XIX.

[3] The Egyptian name for the River Nile is *p-yeor-o*. For comparisons of the King of Egypt with the River Nile, see Grapow, *Die Bildlichen Ausdruckedes Aegyptischen*, p. 62.

APPENDIX III

Τὸ Παλαιον Χρονικον.

Syncellus, p. 95.

Φέρεται γὰρ παρ' Αἰγυπτίοις παλαιόν τι χρονο-
γραφεῖον, ἐξ οὗ καὶ τὸν Μανεθῶ πεπλανῆσθαι νομίζω,
περιέχον λ' δυναστειῶν ἐν γενεαῖς πάλιν ριγ' χρόνον
ἄπειρον [καὶ οὐ τὸν αὐτὸν τοῦ[1] Μανεθῶ] ἐν μυριάσι
τρισὶ καὶ ͵ϛφκε', πρῶτον μὲν τῶν Ἀεριτῶν,[2] δεύτερον
δὲ τῶν Μεστραίων, τρίτον δὲ Αἰγυπτίων, οὕτω πως
ἐπὶ λέξεως ἔχον·

Θεῶν βασιλεία κατὰ τὸ Παλαιὸν Χρονικόν.

Ἡφαίστου χρόνος οὐκ ἔστι διὰ τὸ νυκτὸς καὶ
ἡμέρας αὐτὸν φαίνειν.

[1] Hopfner : τὸν A : ὃν Boeckh, Bunsen.
[2] Ἀὐριτῶν codd.

---

[1] The Old Chronicle is dated by Gutschmid to the end
of the second century after Christ. Gelzer would refer its
statements to another source than Manetho, perhaps
Ptolemy of Mendês ; while Meyer regards it as the work of
Panodôrus, c. A.D. 400 (*cf.* Fr. 2).

[2] By the name Manetho Syncellus refers, as always, to
the *Book of Sôthis* (App. IV.).

[3] The actual total of years from the items given, if 6 years
be assigned to Dynasty XXVIII., is 36,347, *i.e.* 178 years

APPENDIX III.

The Old Chronicle.

(*From Syncellus*).

Now, among the Egyptians there is current an old chronography,[1] by which indeed. I believe, Manetho [2] has been led into error.

In 30 dynasties with 113 generations, it comprises an immense period of time [not the same as Manetho gives] in 36,525 years,[3] dealing first with the Aeritae,[4] next with the Mestraei, and thirdly with the Egyptians. Its contents are somewhat as follows:—

Dynasties of the Gods according to the Old Chronicle.

Hêphaestus has no period assigned, because he shines night and day. Hêlios [the Sun], son of

less than the total given in the text. The number of generations, 113, is obtained by counting 1 for Dynasty XXVIII. and 7 for XXIX. This vast world-period of 36,525 years is 25 times the Sôthic period of 1461 calendar years (or 1460 Sôthic years): see *infra*, and for the Sôthic period, Intro. pp. xxix f.

[4] Aeritae and Mestraei are really the same as the third race, the Egyptians, the three names apparently referring to Egypt at three different dates. Aeria is an old name of Egypt (Euseb., *Chron.* in Syncellus, p. 293, Armenian Version (Schöne, p. 30), Aegyptus quae prius Aeria dicebatur . . .). Mestraei (Josephus, *Antiq.* 1. 6. 2)—from Mestraïm (p. 7 n. 2).

Ἥλιος Ἡφαίστου ἐβασίλευσεν ἐτῶν μυριάδας τρεῖς.

Ἔπειτα Κρόνος, φησί, καὶ οἱ λοιποὶ πάντες θεοὶ δώδεκα ἐβασίλευσαν ἔτη ͵γπϙδ'.

Ἔπειτα ἡμίθεοι βασιλεῖς ὀκτὼ ἔτη σιζ'.

Καὶ μετ' αὐτοὺς γενεαὶ ιε' Κυνικοῦ κύκλου ἀνεγράφησαν ἐν ἔτεσιν υμγ'.

Εἶτα Τανιτῶν ιϛ' δυναστεία, γενεῶν η', ἐτῶν ρϟ'.

Πρὸς οἷς ιζ' δυναστεία Μεμφιτῶν, γενεῶν δ', ἐτῶν ργ'.

Μεθ' οὓς ιη' δυναστεία Μεμφιτῶν, γενεῶν ιδ', ἐτῶν τμη'.

Ἔπειτα ιθ' δυναστεία Διοσπολιτῶν, γενεῶν ε', ἐτῶν ρϟδ'.

Εἶτα κ' δυναστεία Διοσπολιτῶν, γενεῶν η', ἐτῶν σκη'.

Ἔπειτα κα' δυναστεία Τανιτῶν, γενεῶν ϛ', ἐτῶν ρκα'.

Εἶτα κβ' δυναστεία Τανιτῶν, γενεῶν γ', ἐτῶν μη'.

Ἔπειτα κγ' δυναστεία Διοσπολιτῶν, γενεῶν β', ἐτῶν ιθ'.

Εἶτα κδ' δυναστεία Σαϊτῶν, γενεῶν γ', ἐτῶν μδ'.

Πρὸς οἷς κε' δυναστεία Αἰθιόπων, γενεῶν γ', ἐτῶν μδ'.

Μεθ' οὓς κϛ' δυναστεία Μεμφιτῶν, γενεῶν ζ', ἐτῶν ροζ'.

Hêphaestus, ruled for 30,000 years. Then Cronos (it says) and the remaining gods, 12 in number, reigned altogether for 3984 years. Next, the eight demi-gods were kings for 217 years; and after them 15 generations of the Sôthic Cycle are recorded with 443 years.[1]

Then follow :

The Sixteenth Dynasty of Kings of Tanis, in 8 generations, for 190 years.

The Seventeenth Dynasty of Kings of Memphis, in 4 generations, for 103 years.

The Eighteenth Dynasty of Kings of Memphis, in 14 generations, for 348 years.

The Nineteenth Dynasty of Kings of Diospolis, in 5 generations, for 194 years.

The Twentieth Dynasty of Kings of Diospolis, in 8 generations, for 228 years.

The Twenty-first Dynasty of Kings of Tanis, in 6 generations, for 121 years.

The Twenty-second Dynasty of Kings of Tanis, in 3 generations, for 48 years.

The Twenty-third Dynasty of Kings of Diospolis, in 2 generations, for 19 years.

The Twenty-fourth Dynasty of Kings of Saïs, in 3 generations, for 44 years.

The Twenty-fifth Dynasty of Ethiopian Kings, in 3 generations, for 44 years.

The Twenty-sixth Dynasty of Kings of Memphis, in 7 generations, for 177 years.

---

[1] This total comes, not from the *Book of Sôthis* which gives 395 for the first 15, but from Eratosthenes (App. II.). A smaller total than Manetho's 3357 years was desired in order to shorten the duration of the historical age of Egypt.

Καὶ μετ' αὐτοὺς κζ' δυναστεία[1] Περσῶν, γενεῶν
  ε', ἐτῶν ρκδ'.

.   .   .   .

Ἔπειτα κθ' δυναστεία Τανιτῶν γενεῶν ‹ζ'›,
  ἐτῶν λθ'.
Καὶ ἐπὶ πάσαις λ' δυναστεία Τανίτου ἑνός, ἔτη
  ιη'.
Τὰ πάντα ὁμοῦ τῶν λ' δυναστειῶν ἔτη Μγ'
  καὶ ͵ϛφκε'.

Ταῦτα ἀναλυόμενα, εἴτουν μεριζόμενα, παρὰ τὰ
͵αυξα' ἔτη εἴκοσι πεντάκις, τὴν παρ' Αἰγυπτίοις καὶ
Ἕλλησιν ἀποκατάστασιν τοῦ ζῳδιακοῦ μυθολογου-
μένην δηλοῖ, τοῦτ' ἔστι τὴν ἀπὸ τοῦ αὐτοῦ σημείου
ἐπὶ τὸ αὐτὸ σημεῖον, ὅ ἐστι πρῶτον λεπτὸν τῆς
πρώτης μοίρας τοῦ ἰσημερινοῦ ζῳδίου, κριοῦ λεγομένου παρ' αὐτοῖς, ὥσπερ καὶ ἐν τοῖς Γενικοῖς
τοῦ Ἑρμοῦ καὶ ἐν Κυραννίσι βίβλοις εἴρηται.

Ἐντεῦθεν δὲ οἶμαι καὶ Πτολεμαῖον τὸν Κλαύδιον
τοὺς προχείρους κανόνας τῆς ἀστρονομίας διὰ κε'
ἐτηρίδων ψηφίζεσθαι θεσπίσαι . . .

Ἐντεῦθεν δέ ἐστι καὶ τὸ ἀσύμφωνον τῶν τοιούτων
ἐκδόσεων πρός τε τὰς θείας ἡμῶν γραφὰς καὶ πρὸς
ἄλληλα ἐπιγνῶναι, ὅτι αὕτη μὲν ἡ παλαιοτέρα νομι-
ζομένη Αἰγυπτίων συγγραφὴ Ἡφαίστου μὲν ἄπειρον
εἰσάγει χρόνον, τῶν δὲ λοιπῶν κθ' δυναστειῶν ἔτη
τρισμύρια ͵ϛφκε', καίτοι τοῦ Ἡφαίστου πολλοῖς
ἔτεσι μετὰ τὸν κατακλυσμὸν καὶ τὴν πυργοποιΐαν

---

[1] Scaliger: codd. μετὰ τὰς κζ' δυναστείας, omit. γενεῶν.

The Twenty-seventh Dynasty of Persian Kings, in 5 generations, for 124 years.

[The Twenty-eighth Dynasty is here omitted—one king of Saïs reigning for 6 years.]

Then comes the Twenty-ninth Dynasty of Kings of Tanis in ⟨7⟩ generations for 39 years ; and finally the Thirtieth Dynasty consists of one King of Tanis for 18 years. The sum total of all the 30 Dynasties comprises 36,525 years.

If this total is broken up, or divided, 25 times into periods of 1461 years, it reveals the periodic return of the Zodiac which is commonly referred to in Egyptian and Greek books, that is, its revolution from one point back to that same point again, namely, the first minute of the first degree of the equinoctial sign of the Zodiac, the Ram as it is called by them, according to the account given in *The General Discourses of Hermês* and in the *Cyranides*.

Hence it was, I suppose, that Claudius Ptolemaeus [1] announced that the ready astronomical tables should be calculated in periods of 25 years . . .

Hence, too, the lack of harmony between such systems and our Holy Scriptures, as well as between one system and another, may be explained by the fact that this Egyptian record, which is held to be of great antiquity, assigns an immense period to Hêphaestus, and to the remaining 29 [2] Dynasties 36,525 years, although Hêphaestus ruled over Egypt

[1] Claudius Ptolemaeus, the famous mathematician, astronomer, and geographer, *c.* A.D. 100-178 : for his *Ready Tables* see p. 5 in the other section of this volume.

[2] An obviously incorrect summary of the enumeration of Dynasties given above.

τῆς Αἰγύπτου βασιλεύσαντος, ὡς δειχθήσεται ἐν τῷ δέοντι τόπῳ.

Ὁ δὲ παρ᾽ Αἰγυπτίοις ἐπισημότατος Μανεθῶ περὶ τῶν αὐτῶν λ᾽ δυναστειῶν γράψας, ἐκ τούτων δηλαδὴ λαβὼν τὰς ἀφορμάς, κατὰ πολὺ διαφωνεῖ περὶ τοὺς χρόνους πρὸς ταῦτα, καθὼς ἔστι καὶ ἐκ τῶν προειρημένων ἡμῖν ἀνωτέρω μαθεῖν καὶ ἐκ τῶν ἑξῆς λεχθησομένων. τῶν γὰρ ἐν τοῖς τρισὶ τόμοις ριγ᾽ γενεῶν ἐν δυναστείαις λ᾽ ἀναγεγραμμένων, αὐτῷ[1] ὁ χρόνος τὰ πάντα συνῆξεν ἔτη ,γφνε᾽, ἀρξάμενα τῷ ,αφπς᾽ ἔτει τοῦ κόσμου καὶ λήξαντα εἰς τὸ ,ερμζ᾽[2] κοσμικὸν ἔτος, ἤτοι πρὸ τῆς Ἀλεξάνδρου τοῦ Μακεδόνος κοσμοκρατορίας ἔτη που ιε᾽.

Ἐκ τούτων οὖν ἀφελών τις τὰ πρὸ τοῦ κατακλυσμοῦ χνς᾽ πρὸς ἀναπλήρωσιν τῶν ,βσμβ᾽ ἐξ Ἀδὰμ ἕως τοῦ κατακλυσμοῦ, ὡς ψευδῆ καὶ ἀνύπαρκτα, καὶ τὰ ἀπὸ τοῦ κατακλυσμοῦ ἕως τῆς πυργοποιίας καὶ συγχύσεως τῶν γλωσσῶν καὶ διασπορᾶς τῶν ἐθνῶν φλδ᾽, ἕξει σαφῶς τὴν ἀρχὴν τῆς Αἰγυπτιακῆς βασιλείας ἐκ τοῦ πρώτου βασιλεύσαντος τῆς Αἰγύπτου Μεστραΐμ, τοῦ καὶ Μήνεος λεγομένου παρὰ τῷ Μανεθῶ, ἀπὸ τοῦ ,βψος᾽ ἔτους τοῦ ἐξ Ἀδὰμ ἕως Νεκταναβῶ τοῦ ἐσχάτου βασιλέως Αἰγύπτου, ὡς εἶναι τὰ πάντα ἀπὸ Μεστραΐμ ἕως τοῦ αὐτοῦ Νεκταναβῶ ἔτη ,βτξε᾽, ἃ καὶ ἔφθασεν, ὡς προείρηται, εἰς τὸ κοσμικὸν ,ερμζ᾽[3] ἔτος πρὸ τῆς Ἀλεξάνδρου τοῦ κτίστου ἀρχῆς ἔτεσι ιε᾽ ἐγγύς.

---

[1] Boeckh : αὐτῶν codd., probably corrupt.

many years after the Flood and the Building of the Tower, as will be shown in the appropriate place.

The illustrious Egyptian Manetho, writing of these same 30 Dynasties, and obviously taking this as his starting-point, is widely divergent thereafter in the dates he gives, as one may learn both from what I have already said above, and from the remarks that will follow immediately. For in his three books, 113 generations are recorded in 30 Dynasties, and the time which he assigns amounts in all to 3555 years, beginning with Anno mundi 1586 and ending with 5147 [5141], or some 15 years before the conquest of the world by Alexander of Macedon.

If therefore one subtracts from this total the 656 years before the Flood in order to make up [with 1586] the 2242 years from Adam to the Flood,— these 656 years being regarded as falsely assigned or non-existent,—and the 534 years from the Flood to the Building of the Tower, the Confusion of Tongues, and the Dispersion of the Peoples, one will clearly find the rise of the kingdom of Egypt under the first Egyptian king, Mestraïm, who is by Manetho called Mênês, which began in the year 2776, the year of Adam, and continued down to Nectanabô, the last king of Egypt. Thus the sum total from Mestraïm down to this Nectanabô is 2365 years, which takes us, as has already been stated, to Anno mundi 5147 [5141], approximately 15 years before the rule of Alexander the Founder.

---

² l. ‚ερμα΄.   ³ ‚ερμα΄, marginal note in Goar.

APPENDIX IV.

Ἡ ΒΙΒΛΟΣ ΤΗΣ ΣΩΘΕΩΣ Ἡ Ὁ ΚΥΝΙΚΟΣ ΚΥΚΛΟΣ.

Syncellus, p. 170.

Αἰγύπτου τῆς πάλαι Μεστραίας βασιλέων
ἔτη.

α′ Μεστραῒμ ὁ καὶ Μήνης, ἔτη λε′.
β′ Κουρώδης, ἔτη ξγ′.
γ′ Ἀρίσταρχος, ἔτη λδ′.
δ′ Σπάνιος, ἔτη λς′.
ε′ καὶ ς′, βασιλέων δυοῖν ἀνεπιγράφων ἔτη οβ′.
ζ′ Ὠσιροπίς,[1] ἔτη κγ′.
η′ Σεσόγχωσις, ἔτη μθ′.
θ′ Ἀμενέμης, ἔτη κθ′.

Syncellus, p. 179.

ι′ Ἄμασις, ἔτη β′.
ια′ Ἀκεσέφθρης, ἔτη ιγ′.
ιβ′ Ἀγχορεύς, ἔτη θ′.
ιγ′ Ἀρμιϋσῆς, ἔτη δ′.

[1] Cod. B : ὁ Σάραπις Goar, Dindorf.

---

[1] The *Book of Sôthis* which Syncellus believed to be the genuine Manetho, but which in its original form was based upon Eusebius and Josephus, is dated by Gutschmid to the

APPENDIX IV.

The Book of Sôthis[1] or The Sôthic Cycle.

(*From Syncellus.*)

The years of the kings of Egypt, called Mestraea of old.

1. Mestraïm, also called Mênês, 35 years.
2. Kourôdês, 63 years.
3. Aristarchus, 34 years.
4. Spanius, 36 years.
5 and 6.   Two kings, unrecorded, 72 years.
7. Ôsiropis, 23 years.
8. Sesonchôsis, 49 years.
9. Amenemês, 29 years.
10. Amasis, 2 years.
11. Acesephthrês, 13.
12. Anchoreus, 9 years.
13. Armiÿsês, 4 years.

third century after Christ. It is not possible to divide the kings of this " Cycle " into dynasties, for their sequence is unchronological : *e.g.* 18-24 belong to Dynasties XIX. and XX., 26-29, 32 to the Hyksôs period, 33-48 to Dynasty XVIII., 49, 58 to Dynasty XIX., 50, 51 to Dynasty XXVI., 59-61 to Dynasty I., 63-67 to Dynasty XXI., 68-70 to Dynasty XXIII., 74 to Dynasty XXIV., 75-77 to Dynasty XXV., and 79-86 to Dynasty XXVI.

The *Book of Sôthis* includes names taken from another source than Manetho.

ιδ´ Χαμοῖς, ἔτη ιβ´·
ιε´ Μιαμούς, ἔτη ιδ´.
ισ´ Ἀμεσῆσις, ἔτη ξε´.
ιζ´ Οὔσης, ἔτη ν´.
ιη´ ῾Ραμεσής, ἔτη κθ´.

Syncellus, p. 189.

ιθ´ ῾Ραμεσομενής,[1] ἔτη ιε´.
κ´ Οὐσιμάρη,[2] ἔτη λα´.
κα´ ῾Ραμεσσήσεως, ἔτη κγ´.
κβ´ ῾Ραμεσσαμένω, ἔτη ιθ´.
        Οὗτος πρῶτος Φαραὼ ἐν τῇ θείᾳ γραφῇ
    μνημονεύεται.   ἐπὶ τούτου ὁ πατριάρχης
    Ἀβραὰμ κατῆλθεν εἰς Αἴγυπτον.
κγ´ ῾Ραμεσσῆ Ἰουβασσῆ, ἔτη λθ´.

Syncellus, p. 193.

κδ´ ῾Ραμεσσῆ Οὐάφρου, ἔτη κθ´.
κε´ Κόγχαρις, ἔτη ε´.
        Τούτῳ τῷ ε´ ἔτει τοῦ κε´ βασιλεύ-
    σαντος Κογχάρεως τῆς Αἰγύπτου ἐπὶ τῆς

---

[1] B : ῾Ραμεσσομενής A.   [2] B : Οὐσιμάρης A.

---

[1] The name Chamoïs is probably the Greek form of the name Khamuas: for Khamuas, the principal son of Ramessês II., see Griffith, *Stories of the High Priests*, p. 2 n. 2.

14. Chamoïs,[1] 12 years.
15. Miamûs, 14 years.
16. Amesêsis, 65 years.
17. Usês. 50 years.
18. Ramesês, 29 years.
19. Rames(s)omenês, 15 years.
20. Usimarê(s),[2] 31 years.
21. Ramessêseôs,[3] 23 years.
22. Ramessamenô, 19 years.

> He is the first Pharaoh mentioned in the Holy Scriptures. In his reign the patriarch Abraham went down into Egypt.[4]

23. Ramessê Iubassê, 39 years.
24. Ramessê, son of Uaphrês,[5] 29 years.
25. Concharis, 5 years.

> In this 5th year of Concharis, the 25th king of Egypt, during the Sixteenth

[2] The name Usimarê(s) is the first part of the *praenomen* of Ramessês II.: see p. 221 n. 4.

[3] It is tempting to see in this name the Egyptian *Ramesese-o*, "Ramessês the Great," although this term, so commonly used in modern times, is not found in Egyptian records (B.G.).

[4] On Abraham's descent into Egypt, see Peet, *Egypt and the Old Testament*, 1922, pp. 47 ff. (Abraham went down into Egypt in the First Intermediate Period, during Dynasties VII.–X., and left Egypt before 2081 B.C.) Sir L. Woolley, on the other hand, is satisfied with the traditional date of the birth of Abraham at Ur, *c.* 2000 B.C.; but he believes that the patriarch was not a single man, but a composite character (Abram, Abraham)—see *Abraham : Recent Discoveries and Hebrew Origins*, 1936.

[5] This description "son of Uaphrês" is a remarkable anachronism : a king of Dynasty XIX. or XX. is said to be the son of a king of Dynasty XXVI.

ιϛ´ δυναστείας τοῦ Κυνικοῦ λεγομένου κύκλου παρὰ τῷ Μανεθῷ, ἀπὸ
τοῦ πρώτου βασιλέως καὶ οἰκιστοῦ Μεσ-
τραϊμ τῆς Αἰγύπτου, πληροῦνται ἔτη ψ´,
βασιλέων κε´, τοῦτ᾽ ἔστιν ἀπὸ τοῦ καθολικοῦ κοσμικοῦ ͵βψοϛ´ ἔτους, καθ᾽ ὃν χρόνον
ἡ διασπορὰ γέγονεν, ἐν τῷ λδ´ ἔτει τῆς
ἡγεμονίας Ἀρφαξάδ, ε´ δὲ ἔτει τοῦ Φαλέκ.
καὶ διεδέξαντο Τανῖται βασιλεῖς δ´,
οἳ καὶ ἐβασίλευσαν Αἰγύπτου ἐπὶ τῆς ιζ´
δυναστείας ἔτη σνδ´,[1] ὡς ἑξῆς ἐστοιχείωται.

Syncellus, p. 195.

κϛ´ Σιλίτης, ἔτη ιθ´, πρῶτος τῶν ϛ´ τῆς ιζ´
δυναστείας παρὰ Μανεθῷ.

Syncellus, p. 204.

κζ´ Βαίων, ἔτη μδ´.
κη´ Ἀπαχνάς, ἔτη λϛ´.
κθ´ Ἄφωφις, ἔτη ξα´.
          Τοῦτον λέγουσί τινες πρῶτον κληθῆναι
Φαραώ, καὶ τῷ τετάρτῳ ἔτει τῆς βασιλείας
αὐτοῦ τὸν Ἰωσὴφ ἐλθεῖν εἰς Αἴγυπτον δοῦ-
λον. οὗτος κατέστησε τὸν Ἰωσὴφ κύριον
Αἰγύπτου καὶ πάσης τῆς βασιλείας αὐτοῦ
τῷ ιζ´ ἔτει τῆς ἀρχῆς αὐτοῦ, ἡνίκα καὶ τὴν
τῶν ὀνείρων διασάφησιν ἔμαθε παρ᾽ αὐτοῦ,
καὶ τῆς θείας συνέσεως αὐτοῦ διὰ πείρας

[1] σνθ´ corr. Müller.

238

Dynasty of the Sôthic Cycle as it is called in Manetho, the total of years from the first king and founder of Egypt, Mestraïm, is 700 belonging to 25 kings, *i.e.* from the general cosmic year 2776, in which the Dispersion took place in the 34th year of the rule of Arphaxad [1] and the 5th year of Phalec.[2] Next in the succession were 4 kings of Tanis, who ruled Egypt in the Seventeenth Dynasty for 254 [259] years, according to the following computation.

26. Silitês (the first of the 6 kings of the Seventeenth Dynasty in Manetho), 19 years.

27. Baiôn, 44 years.

28. Apachnas, 36 years.

29. Aphôphis, 61 years.

   Some say that this king was at first called Pharaoh, and that in the 4th year of his kingship Joseph came as a slave into Egypt.[3] He appointed Joseph lord of Egypt and all his kingdom in the 17th year of his rule, having learned from him the interpretation of the dreams and having thus proved his divine wisdom.

---

[1] Arphaxad, son of Shem: *O.T. Genesis* x. 22. See p. 26 n. 1.

[2] Phalec or Peleg (= division) : " for in his days was the earth divided " (*Genesis* x. 25). *Cf.* the name of the town Phaliga on the Euphrates,—not that the patriarch Peleg is to be connected directly with this town (W. F. Albright, *The Archaeology of Palestine and the Bible* [2], 1932-3, p. 210).

[3] For the Sojourn in Egypt during the Hyksôs period, see Peet, *Egypt and the Old Testament*, pp. 73 ff.; Albright, *The Archaeology of Palestine and the Bible* [2], pp. 143 f.; Garstang, *The Heritage of Solomon*, 1934, p. 147.

239

γέγονεν.   ἡ δὲ θεία γραφὴ καὶ τὸν ἐπὶ
τοῦ Ἀβραὰμ βασιλέα Αἰγύπτου Φαραὼ
καλεῖ.

Syncellus, p. 232.

λ΄ Σέθως, ἔτη ν΄.
λα΄ Κήρτως, ἔτη κθ΄, κατὰ Ἰώσηππον, κατὰ δὲ
    τὸν Μανεθῶ, ἔτη μδ΄.
λβ΄ Ἀσήθ, ἔτη κ΄.
    Οὗτος προσέθηκε τῶν ἐνιαυτῶν τὰς ε΄
    ἐπαγομένας, καὶ ἐπὶ αὐτοῦ, ὥς φασιν,
    ἐχρημάτισεν τξε΄ ἡμερῶν ὁ Αἰγυπτιακὸς
    ἐνιαυτός, τξ΄ μόνον ἡμερῶν πρὸ τούτου
    μετρούμενος. ἐπὶ αὐτοῦ ὁ μόσχος θεο-
    ποιηθεὶς Ἄπις ἐκλήθη.
λγ΄ Ἄμωσις ὁ καὶ Τέθμωσις, ἔτη κϛ΄.

Syncellus, p. 278.

λδ΄ Χεβρών, ἔτη ιγ΄.
λε΄ Ἀμεμφίς,[1] ἔτη ιε΄.
λϛ΄ Ἀμενσῆς, ἔτη ια΄.
λζ΄ Μισφραγμούθωσις, ἔτη ιϛ΄.
λη΄ Μισφρής, ἔτη κγ΄.
λθ΄ Τούθμωσις, ἔτη λθ΄.

Syncellus, p. 286.

μ΄ Ἀμενῶφθις, ἔτη λδ΄.
    Οὗτος ὁ Ἀμενῶφθίς ἐστιν ὁ Μέμνων
    εἶναι νομιζόμενος καὶ φθεγγόμενος λίθος·

240

The Holy Scriptures, however, give the name of Pharaoh also to the king of Egypt in the time of Abraham.

30. Sethôs, 50 years.
31. Cêrtôs, according to Josephus, 29 years; according to Manetho, 44 years.
32. Asêth, 20 years.

This king added the 5 intercalary days to the year : [1] in his reign, they say, the Egyptian year became a year of 365 days, being previously reckoned as 360 days only. In his time the bull-calf was deified and called Apis.

33. Amôsis, also called Tethmôsis, 26 years.
34. Chebrôn, 13 years.
35. Amemphis, 15 years.
36. Amensês, 11 years
37. Misphragmuthôsis, 16 years.
38. Misphrês, 23 years.
39. Tuthmôsis, 39 years.
40. Amenôphthis, 34 years.

This is the king who was reputed to be Memnôn and a speaking statue. Many

[1] See p. 99 n. 3.

---

[1] B : 'Αμεμφής A.

ὃν λίθον χρόνοις ὕστερον Καμβύσης ὁ
Περσῶν τέμνει, νομίζων εἶναι γοητείαν ἐν
αὐτῷ, ὡς Πολύαινος ὁ Ἀθηναῖος ἱστορεῖ.
    Αἰθίοπες ἀπὸ Ἰνδοῦ ποταμοῦ ἀναστάντες
πρὸς τῇ Αἰγύπτῳ ᾤκησαν.
μα' Ὧρος, ἔτη μη'.
μβ' Ἀχενχερής, ἔτη κε'.
μγ' Ἀθωρίς, ἔτη κθ'.
μδ' Χενχερής, ἔτη κϛ'.

                Syncellus, p. 293.
με' Ἀχερρής, ἔτη η' ἢ καὶ λ'.
μϛ' Ἀρμαῖος, ὁ καὶ Δαναός, ἔτη θ'.

    Ἀρμαῖος, ὁ καὶ Δαναός, φεύγων τὸν
ἀδελφὸν Ῥαμεσσῆν τὸν καὶ Αἴγυπτον[1]
ἐκπίπτει τῆς κατ' Αἴγυπτον βασιλείας
αὐτοῦ, εἰς Ἑλλάδα τε ἀφικνεῖται. Ῥαμεσσῆς δὲ, ὁ ἀδελφὸς αὐτοῦ, ὁ καὶ Αἴγυπτος καλούμενος, ἐβασίλευσεν Αἰγύπτου ἔτη
ξη', μετονομάσας τὴν χώραν Αἴγυπτον τῷ
ἰδίῳ ὀνόματι, ἥτις πρότερον Μεστραία,
παρ' Ἕλλησι δὲ Ἀερία ἐλέγετο. Δαναὸς
δὲ, ὁ καὶ Ἀρμαῖος, κρατήσας τοῦ Ἄργους
καὶ ἐκβαλὼν Σθένελον τὸν Κροτωποῦ Ἀργείων ἐβασίλευσε· καὶ οἱ ἀπόγονοι αὐτοῦ
μετ' αὐτὸν Δαναΐδαι καλούμενοι ἐπ' Εὐ-
ρυσθέα τὸν Σθενέλου τοῦ Περσέως· μεθ'
οὓς οἱ Πελοπίδαι ἀπὸ Πέλοπος παρα-
λαβόντες τὴν ἀρχήν, ὧν πρῶτος Ἀτρεύς.

---

[1] Αἰγύπτιον codd.: Αἴγυπτον Scaliger: καὶ add. Müller.

years later Cambysês, the Persian king, cut this statue in two, deeming that there was sorcery in it, as Polyaenus of Athens [1] relates.

The Ethiopians, removing from the River Indus, settled near Egypt.

41. Ôrus, 48 years.

42. Achencherês, 25 years.

43. Athôris, 29 years.

44. Chencherês, 26 years.

45. Acherrês, 8 or 30 years.

46. Armaeus, also called Danaus, 9 years.

> This king, fleeing from his brother Ramessês, also called Aegyptus, was driven from his kingdom of Egypt and came to Greece. Ramessês, his brother, whose other name was Aegyptus, ruled Egypt for 68 years, changing the name of his country to Egypt after his own name. Its previous name was Mestraea, and among the Greeks Aeria. Now Danaus or Armaeus took possession of Argos and, driving out Sthenelus the son of Crotôpus, ruled over the Argives. His descendants thereafter were called Danaïdae down to Eurystheus son of Sthenelus, the son of Perseus. Next to these, after Pelops the Pelopidae succeeded to the kingdom : the first of these was Atreus.

[1] Polyaenus of Athens (? of Sardis or of Macedonia), a writer of history, lived in the time of Gaius (Caligula).

Syncellus, p. 302.

μζ΄ Ῥαμεσσῆς, ὁ καὶ Αἴγυπτος, ἔτη ξη΄.
μη΄ Ἀμένωφις, ἔτη η΄.
μθ΄ Θούωρις, ἔτη ιζ΄.
 ν΄ Νεχεψώς, ἔτη ιθ΄.
να΄ Ψαμμουθίς, ἔτη ιγ΄.
νβ΄ —, ἔτη δ΄.
νγ΄ Κήρτως, ἔτη κ΄.[1]
νδ΄ Ῥάμψις, ἔτη με΄.
νε΄ Ἀμενσής, ὁ καὶ Ἀμμενέμης, ἔτη κϛ΄.

Syncellus, p. 319.

νϛ΄ Ὀχυράς, ἔτη ιδ΄.
νζ΄ Ἀμενδής, ἔτη κζ΄.
νη΄ Θούωρις, ἔτη ν΄.
        Οὗτός ἐστιν ὁ παρ’ Ὁμήρῳ Πόλυβος,
    Ἀλκάνδρας ἀνήρ, ἐν Ὀδυσσείᾳ φερόμενος,
    παρ’ ᾧ φησι τὸν Μενέλαον σὺν τῇ Ἑλένῃ
    μετὰ τὴν ἅλωσιν Τροίας κατῆχθαι πλανώ-
    μενον.
νθ΄ Ἄθωθις, ὁ καὶ Φουσανός, ἐφ’ οὗ σεισμοὶ
    κατὰ τὴν Αἴγυπτον ἐγένοντο, μηδέπω γε-
    γονότες ἐν αὐτῇ πρὸ τούτου, ἔτη κη΄.
 ξ΄ Κενκένης, ἔτη λθ΄.
ξα΄ Οὐέννεφις, ἔτη μβ΄.[2]

---

[1] Corr. Goar: ιϛ΄ codd.   [2] λβ΄ cod. B.

244

47. Ramessês, also called Aegyptus, 68 years.

48. Amenôphis, 8 years.

49. Thuôris, 17 years.

50. Nechepsôs,[1] 19 years.

51. Psammuthis, 13 years.

52. —, 4 years.

53. Cêrtôs,[2] 20 years.

54. Rampsis, 45 years.

55. Amensês, also called Ammenemês, 26 years.

56. Ochyras, 14 years.

57. Amendês, 27 years.

58. Thuôris, 50 years.

> This is the Polybus of Homer, who appears in the *Odyssey* as husband of Alcandra : the poet tells how Menelaus and Helen dwelt with him in their wanderings after the capture of Troy.

59. Athôthis, also called Phusanus,[3] 28 years.

> In his reign earthquakes occurred in Egypt, although previously unknown there.

60. Cencenês, 39 years.

61. Uennephis, 42 years.

---

[1] See p. 211 n. 2.   Nechepsôs appears again as Nechepsus, No. 80.

[2] 53-58 may be the 6 kings of Dynasty XIX., some of them repeated.   53 Cêrtôs may be Sethôs : 54 Rampsis = 47 Ramessês : 55 Amensês = Amenmesês : while Thuôris appears as 58 and 49.

[3] With Phusanus *cf.* Psusennês of Dynasty XXI.

Syncellus, p. 332.

ξβ′ Σουσακείμ, ἔτη λδ′.
    Σουσακείμ Λίβυας καὶ Αἰθίοπας καὶ
    Τρωγλοδύτας παρέλαβε πρὸ τῆς Ἱερου-
    σαλήμ.
ξγ′ Ψούενος, ἔτη κε′.
ξδ′ Ἀμμενῶφις, ἔτη θ′.
ξε′ Νεφεχέρης, ἔτη ϛ′.
ξϛ′ Σαΐτης, ἔτη ιε′.
ξζ′ Ψινάχης, ἔτη θ′.
ξη′ Πετουβάστης, ἔτη μδ′.
ξθ′ Ὀσώρθων, ἔτη θ′.
 ο′ Ψάμμος, ἔτη ι′.
οα′ Κόγχαρις, ἔτη κα′.

Syncellus, p. 347.

οβ′ Ὀσόρθων, ἔτη ιε′.
ογ′ Τακαλῶφις, ἔτη ιγ′.
οδ′ Βόκχωρις, ἔτη μδ′.
    Βόκχωρις Αἰγυπτίοις ἐνομοθέτει, ἐφ’ οὗ
    λόγος ἀρνίον φθέγξασθαι.
οε′ Σαβάκων Αἰθίοψ, ἔτη ιβ′.
    Οὗτος, τὸν Βόκχωριν αἰχμάλωτον λαβών,
    ζῶντα ἔκαυσεν.
οϛ′ Σεβήχων, ἔτη ιβ′.

246

62. Susakeim,[1] 34 years.

    This king brought up Libyans, Ethiopians, and Trôglodytes [2] before Jerusalem.

63. Psuenus, 25 years.

64. Ammenôphis, 9 years.

65. Nephecherês, 6 years.

66. Saïtês, 15 years.

67. Psinachês, 9 years.

68. Petubastês, 44 years.

69. Osôrthôn, 9 years.

70. Psammus, 10 years.

71. Concharis, 21 years.

72. Osŏrthôn, 15 years.

73. Tacalôphis, 13 years.

74. Bocchôris, 44 years.

    This king made laws for the Egyptians: in his time report has it that a lamb spoke.[3]

75. Sabacôn, an Ethiopian, 12 years.

    This king, taking Bocchôris captive, burned him alive.[4]

76. Sebêchôn, 12 years.

---

[1] Susakeim, apparently, is Shoshenk̦, or Sesonchôsis, the first king of Dynasty XXII. (Fr. 60, 1): Josephus, *Antiq.*, viii. § 210, has Susakos.

[2] In *O.T. 2 Chron.* xii. 3 it is said that Shishak brought up, along with the Ethiopians, the Lubims (Libyans) and the Sukkiims : in the LXX the last are the Trôglodytes, *i.e.* the "Cave-dwellers" along the west shore of the Red Sea (see Strabo, xvi. 4. 17). G. W. Murray, *Sons of Ishmael*, 1935, p. 18, suspects that the Ethiopians were negro troops or perhaps Beja nomads (*i.e.* Bedouin). "At any rate Shishak, like the great Mohammed Ali after him, realized the importance of Bedouin auxiliaries on a desert campaign."

[3] See p. 164 n. 2.   [4] See p. 166 n. 2.

Syncellus, p. 360.

οζ' Ταράκης, ἔτη κ'.
οη' Ἀμαῆς, ἔτη λη'.
οθ' Στεφινάθης, ἔτη κζ'.
π' Νεχεψός, ἔτη ιγ'.

Syncellus, p. 396.

πα' Νεχαώ, ἔτη η'.
πβ' Ψαμμήτιχος. ἔτη ιδ'.
πγ' Νεχαὼ β' Φαραώ, ἔτη θ'.
πδ' Ψαμουθὴς ἕτερος, ὁ καὶ Ψαμμήτιχος,
      ἔτη ιζ'.
πε' Οὔαφρις,¹ ἔτη λδ'.
πϛ' Ἄμωσις,² ἔτη ν'.

¹ Οὐαφρής codd.   ² Ἄμασις codd.

77. Taracês, 20 years.

78. Amaês,[1] 38 years.

79. Stephinathês, 27 years.

80. Nechepsus, 13 years.

81. Nechaô, 8 years.

82. Psammêtichus, 14 years.

83. Nechaô II. (Pharaoh), 9 years.

84. Psamuthês the Second, also called Psammêti-
      chus, 17 years.

85. Uaphris, 34 years.

86. Amôsis, 50 years.

[1] Amaês corresponds to Ammeris or Ameres the
Ethiopian, Fr. 69, 1, *i.e.* Tanutamûn, Dynasty XXVI.

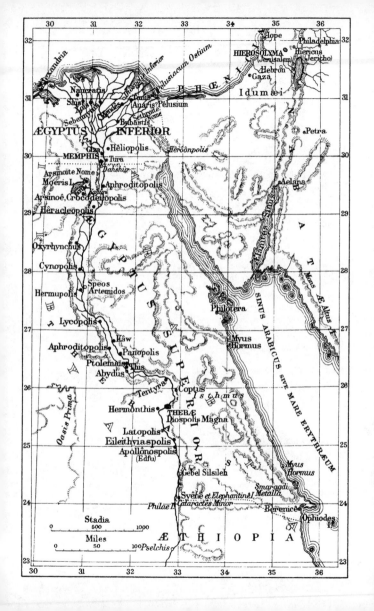

INDEX

251

INDEX

INDEX

INDEX

INDEX

255

INDEX

256